THE GOOD RED ROAD

The Good Red Road

Passages into Native America

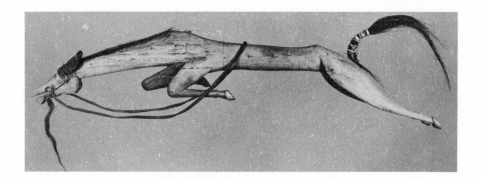

Kenneth Lincoln
with Al Logan Slagle

1817

Harper & Row, Publishers, San Francisco

Cambridge, Hagerstown, New York, Philadelphia, Washington
London, Mexico City, São Paulo, Singapore, Sydney

Earlier portions of this book were published in *Four Winds, The Greenfield Review, Parnassus, The South Dakota Review, The Southwest Review,* and *Native American Renaissance* (University of California Press, 1983).

970.1
Lin

FIRST EDITION

Library of Congress Cataloging-in-Publication Data

Lincoln, Kenneth.
  The good red road.

  1. Indians of North America—North Dakota.
2. Teton Indians. 3. Indians of North America—Social conditions. I. Slagle, Al Logan. II. Title.
E78.N75L56 1987   978.4'00497 . 86-45817
ISBN 0-06-250516-5

87 88 89 90 91 RRD 10 9 8 7 6 5 4 3 2 1

To Mark Monroe

and in memory of
Jenny and Felix Lone Wolf
Minnie and Bill Monroe
Emma Monroe
Terry Monroe
Candi Monroe
Lawrence Antoine
John (Fire) Lame Deer
Dawson No Horse

One-fourth of this book's proceeds goes to
the American Indian Council of Alliance, Nebraska.

JennyLoneWolf
6·17·75

Then when he had been still a little while to hear the birds sing, he spoke again: "Behold the earth!" So I looked down and saw it lying yonder like a hoop of peoples, and in the center bloomed the holy stick that was a tree, and where it stood there crossed two roads, a red one and a black. "From where the giant lives (the north) to where you always face (the south) the red road goes, the road of good," the Grandfather said, "and on it shall your nation walk. The black road goes from where the thunder beings live (the west) to where the sun continually shines (the east), a fearful road, a road of troubles and of war. On this also you shall walk, and from it you shall have the power to destroy a people's foes. In four ascents you shall walk the earth with power."

> JOHN NEIHARDT,
> *Black Elk Speaks*, 1932

Real soon, now, this is a turning point. The hoop, the sacred hoop was broken here at Wounded Knee, and it will come back again. The stake here that represents the tree of life, the tree will bloom, it will flower again, and all the people will rejoin and come back to the sacred road, the red road.

> WALLACE BLACK ELK,
> Wounded Knee, 1973

Contents

Foreword

The Good Red Road is a record of contemporary Americans, Indian and non-Indian, searching for a cultural heritage. Many have turned to Native American cultures, now for some four hundred years in fact, to meet challenges of the present and future with spiritual sustenance and inspiration. This narrative documents the difficulties as well as the rewards encountered by a passage into Native America; it is something of a contemporary vision quest for identity, guidance, grounding, and insight. The story in a very original way recognizes the power of Sioux holy men and elders today and gives equally revealing accounts of contemporary life on and near Indian reservations. Kenneth Lincoln is a rare individual who understands both peoples well; he has genuine concern for their respective points of view, and he represents both honestly, without prejudice, sentimentality, or favoritism. In his account he evokes the landscape of America in all its harshness and beauty through a complete cycle of seasons. The organization of the journey is masterful, presenting the travels of teacher, child, and students as a rite of passage marked by the seasons, changes in place, and the months of Native American lunar calendars.

The journey was begun at the time of the 1975 shootings at Wounded Knee, and it presents powerfully the despair and terror of life at Pine Ridge and in neighboring communities, as well as the older traditions and tribal bonds that gather these Indian peoples together still. The most important single value this work carries, to my mind, is documenting the aftermath of intense confrontation between two sets of American peoples: the Lakota-Dakota on the one hand, and their rural white neighbors on the other. It is a unique, richly informed, moving reportage of an odyssey into the heartland of the nation.

The seven years preceding the journey saw a period of great activism in precisely this area, beginning with the birth of the American Indian Movement (AIM) in 1968. There followed the occupation of Mount Rushmore by Indian activists, the Custer courthouse raid and 1972 sacking of the Bureau of Indian Affairs in Washington, the long occupation of the hamlet of Wounded Knee by the same angry activists in 1973, and the winding down to a tragic end with the shoot-out on the Pine Ridge Reservation between remnants of the AIM forces and the FBI. This was truly a period of historical significance; we will be realizing it more with the passage of years.

In a tradition of American travel narratives from Columbus through Kerouac, *The Good Red Road* appears like a refreshing breeze, coming as it does from a lifetime of empathy and understanding informed by twenty years of scholarly preparation and writing on contemporary Indian affairs. There is far more insight into the fears, meanings, and motivations of both sides of that era of confrontation than can be found in any recent publications. The narrative is one of a kind, though a fitting companion to such works as Richard Erdoes's *Lame Deer Seeker of Visions* or James Welch's *Winter in the Blood*. In the larger context of the American experience, William Least Heat Moon's *Blue Highways* or Robert Pirzig's *Zen and the Art of Motorcycle Maintenance* come to mind.

Lincoln and Slagle sustain a sensitivity to the most enduring subtleties of Native America, even through the frustrations, disappointments, and discomforts. The latter can serve to hone such sensitivities, but most travelers would give up the journey, not knowing the enduring rhythms of the land, seasons, and native peoples. The narrative style is outstanding, both spare and poetic, expressive of both the spoken word and the sacred, sometimes tragic history of the places visited. The "as-told-through" interviews with Indian healers, teachers, counselors, and tribal leaders allow the people to tell their own eloquent stories; and there are simply no such moving accounts of the Lakota healing sings and ceremonies. The final encounter with death sadly though fittingly closes the circle, completing the seasons of a passage into Native America.

All in all, *The Good Red Road* conveys the message that the old Indian ways are not static and set apart; rather there is a constant creative interaction between dynamic traditions and sometimes unsettling adaptations to the present—for all peoples. Lincoln, an Anglo professor bred in Nebraska, and Slagle, a Cherokee student originally from North Carolina, remain authentically open to their subjects through freshness of vision, a native sensitivity to differing perspectives, and fine observations on the character of America in all its diversity. The firmness of Indian tradition is always present as a horizon note, sometimes in things we do not normally consider parts of the equation, such as a stone, a place, a plant, or even a remembrance. These native things we must know and use in all their detailed significance as we concede that the old ways, for all people, have no final, closed meanings. They, too, pass with us along the good red road and the black.

The Good Red Road will find a ready and extensive readership, particularly among students of history, literature, anthropology, religion, ecology, and contemporary Indian affairs, to name just a few. It is a compelling narrative, a complete and extraordinary American document. Were it written by any authors less gifted and perceptive or any who did not have the trust of both peoples in contention, the book would not have worked. It does work because the voices are unusually penetrant, wisely unjudgmental. The narrative speaks justly, even poetically to both sides of a cultural gulf which shadows the complexity of life in America's native heartland.

Alfonso Ortiz (San Juan Tewa)
Professor of Anthropology,
University of New Mexico

Preface

The bush is sitting under the tree and singing.

OJIBWA

Such must be the future: penetrant and simple—
minus the scaffolding of the academic. . . .

WILLIAM CARLOS WILLIAMS

In the spring of 1975 I traveled the Dakotas with a band of UCLA students and my four-year-old daughter. The university let me teach an on-the-road seminar with a base at Jamestown College in Jamestown, North Dakota. We lived roughly equidistant from five reservations in North Dakota, between rural mid-America and the open plains, small towns and Indian tribal grounds. We talked with Native Americans, primarily Sioux, Chippewa, Mandan, Arikara, and Hidatsa, and with white farmers, ranchers, and merchants who lived near them. *The Good Red Road* is an ethnographic narrative taken from this field experience and from subsequent visits. The number of people present at gatherings and their names have been altered to tell the story.

The Good Red Road is autobiographical ethnography, an attempt to go home to the American heartland, seen through the informed "heart's eye" or Lakota *ċante ista*, as Native Americans once felt and still speak about our shared country. The narrative is presented as a literary document that invades no tribe's secrecy nor any person's privacy. "Dialogical" anthropology between Indians and whites, as Dennis Tedlock details most recently, requires letting "others" speak among themselves and with us in print (*The Spoken Word and the Work of Interpretation* 1983). Such dialogue, or intercultural talk, means, as well, letting ourselves respond significantly among Native Americans, indeed personally, to what happens around us "in the field." We must first dispel stereotypes, often the cultural baggage of out-dated or faulty ethnography. Romantic, primitive, or xenophobic glosses—those wild "noble savages"—project "native" images of distorted Indian "others" on peoples whose lives today are contemporary with our own, peoples who share this country with us, who view us as relative newcomers, if not invaders. In my experiences from childhood on, the Lakota (evolving among hundreds of tribes across the Americas) live "now day" cultures, as my adoptive Sioux brother says, even if their histories, languages, or epistemologies track back other directions from ours. Today we all live here, *native*, born or reborn in the United States of America.

Present-tense, intercultural understanding is thus a question of granting the *not*-other "other" a voice and place among us, to borrow from symbolic anthropology, recorded as illuminative "thick description"; that is, we can allow the distinctions between cultures to serve positively in our dialogues, and at the same time we can consciously *not* project the exotic "other" across the distances. We must also examine ourselves at a deeper level in all this. Dialogue implies negotiating the distances, respecting the differences, translating the variables, plumbing our own psyches.

So my students and I have gone among Western Indian peoples to find out about their lives and our own, interdependent today in America, some would say—and to take academic investigation and theory to its source in the daily particulars of current lives, both of the "others" and our own. *The Good Red Road* tries to fuse interdisciplinary scholarship, field studies, literary voice and narrative structure in a text addressed to specialists and general readers alike. The analytical thinking is embedded in the narrative, the scholarly research in daily observations, the social science in the human awareness of the story. It's good to ground our books and lessons occasionally in the real world.

"We are all descendents of Columbus," Tzvetan Todorov gives signs of a post-Columbian West in *The Conquest of America* (1985). Of the myriad colors and tongues and origins of Americans today, Clifford Geertz observes in *Local Knowledge* (1983): "We are all natives now."

American Indians have lived on this continent since as far back as forty thousand years or more, beyond the reach of record or memory. Once there were some five hundred cultures with as many indigenous languages north of the Rio Grande; over one hundred tribes called themselves, in various tongues, "the people." The five hundred and four officially counted tribes that remain today in all of the United States, plus over one hundred more extant tribes not federally acknowledged, may be grouped as some million and a half "Native" Americans, or "Indi'ns" as the Siouan peoples of the plains say. Native America is very much alive, and America can look to these original cultures for a sense of tradition, community, and natural history—native models to learn from. "Behold a good nation walking in a sacred manner in a good land!" Black Elk hears his grandfathers chant—a tribal family, tongue, earth, and ancestry.

The four narrative parts of the book—Wintering Home, Spring Tribe, Summer Visions, Fall Return—chart the seasons of the journey. I have borrowed Indian "winter count" names or "moons" to date our travels. With neither writing nor mechanized time, tribal historians once upon a time recorded the passing year through stories, sometimes imaged on animal skins. The months or moons were pictured and named according to lunar cycles; and the seasons patterned tribal life. Important events were remembered tribally, imagined artistically. Black Elk can speak of being born in the Moon-of-the-Popping Trees (December) on the Little Powder River in the Winter-When-the-Four-Crows-Were-Killed (1863). Or, according to Navajo legend of the Southwest, "In the winter, mother earth rests. The snow spirit covers her with a white blanket and all people should be quiet so as not to disturb her. This is called The Quiet Time and is a time for telling stories." These tribal examples are timeless variants on seasons of language, event, and human imaginings that make up what we call culture.

This story opens into a past rooted in the Great Plains, a journey up and back to personal origins in Native America, for I grew up among Sioux from the Rosebud and Pine Ridge Dakota reservations. The Monroe family of Alliance, Nebraska, adopted me into their extended family; the father, Mark Monroe, gave me his Lakota name, *Mato Yamni* or "Three Bears."

Al Logan Slagle, a Cherokee, was raised in North Carolina and the Southwest; he co-authors some of the latter portions of the story. In most of Chapter 9 and Chapters 18 through 32, the Rosebud sections, we have rewritten and included substantially all of his thesis, "Somebody Did Medicine," submitted for a Masters Degree in English, University of California at Los Angeles, 1978. We have tried to minimize academic scaffolding here, to root scholarship in living experience and dialogical interaction.

The Good Red Road reflects our collaboration on a journey into Native America. As brothers in the heart of the country, near its exact geographic center, we rediscovered America's origins: these included the people as tribal community, the plants and animals as a life-support system, the land as a living presence, the weather and seasons as natural spirits, and the sun, moon, and stars as daily gods in a "house made of dawn," to borrow a phrase many times borrowed from the Navajo. Certainly this is a catalogue of idealizations, but just as certainly it is real and necessary to us all—and no Native American culture does without such dreams of the ideal, or hopes for our human improvement. In our travels through Indian America it was continually the elders who asked, and sometimes charged us, to write this narrative. Our common understanding and respect is the book's intention, our children's heritage its vision.

Sha among the Lakota means interchangeably "red" or "good," and *sha-sha* signifies a good act. This narrative is offered in the good red spirit of all American "native" peoples. Deep-felt thanks to the many collaborators, from reservation to research library, who helped tell the story.

Mato hemakiye

Kenneth Lincoln
American Indian Studies
University of California at Los Angeles

"The Now Day Indi'ns"

The twists of history today place the majority of American Indians off the reservation. Only some thirty-eight percent of perhaps a million and a half Indians now live on tribal lands. This twice-displaced majority of Indians, removed to reservations a century ago and subsequently *re*located by the government (or *re*-relocated), is for the most part composed of mixed-blooded peoples, ranging from dark to light, who adapt to the American mainstream and exist biculturally, at no small cost and with sharp self-questioning. California, housing a migrant plurality from everywhere in the world, has the highest Indian population today, officially counted in the 1980 census at 201,311. Most of these transplanted peoples have been federally removed from other states, Navajos from Arizona, Pueblos from New Mexico, Lakota from the upper Great Plains, Apache from the lower. Oklahoma, or "red earth-people" land, ranks second with 169,000, originally the 1830s Indian Territory west of the Mississippi. Arizona is third in Indian population with 152,000, mostly Navajo and Hopi; New Mexico fourth with two Apache and nineteen Pueblo cultures totaling 101,000; and South Dakota fifth with Lakota, the second largest Indian nation.

Los Angeles alone quarters some 80,000 urban Indians. Oakland is pocketed with outriders of Lakota, Hopi, Pueblo, Navajo, and related Southwest cultures, among many others. Chicago, Minneapolis, Denver, Albuquerque, and Seattle support suburbs for off-reservation Indians, as well do countless small border towns around the 315 reservations in the United States. At least 150 Indian communities more are pressing for federal status clarification. This means that many Indians, earlier defined by geographies, histories, genetics, and cultures indigenous over centuries, have moved or been "removed" to

off-reservation villages, towns, and cities. They seek job opportunities, better standards of living, higher education, and medical facilities. They worry about trading older Indian ways and values for short-
term benefits in a modern world. Many try to escape the disadvan-
tages of being Indian—redneck prejudice, unemployment, malnutrition, and abject poverty, to cite a few. Some want to get away from
intolerable conditions on reservations, like the Lakota civil war smoldering on the Pine Ridge Reservation since the 1973 militant occupation of Wounded Knee.

So "being Indian" today, what my Lakota brother Mark Monroe
calls a "now day Indi'n," can mean living uneasily among white
people, in poorer sections of WASP-founded towns, south of the tracks,
or in city ghettos; holding a job, going to school, even to college;
staying sober enough to function like anyone else in white society,
where alcohol is the social anodyne; and mixing white ways with
Indian ways. George Lone Wolf remembers Jenny Lone Wolf, the
Oglala Sioux medicine woman from Pine Ridge Reservation and northwest Nebraska: "You take Mom, now, she was a good Catholic, an'
she had her Indi'n medicine, ya know, some of both." Indians can be
Roman Catholic or Episcopalian, Baptist or Mormon, yet still pray
with a Lakota medicine pipe in a Plains ceremony or take peyote to
see Christ in the Native American Church. They can ride the Manhat-
tan subway and go to an Iroquois sweat lodge for purification; run a
small business in Phoenix and attend an eight-and-a-half-day Navajo
Beautyway ceremony with medicine people, families and clans, sand
painting, chanting, and a spirit hogan on the desert. All this ceremony,
with or without credit cards in an Indian's wallet, is rich with dancing,
feasting, fasting, and praying. The ceremonies offer a healing suspen-
sion of ordinary time, out of the everyday sense of things. "We must
remember well that all things are the work of the Great Spirit," a
banner in the Holy Rosary Mission chapel quotes Black Elk, the healer,
who was both a Lakota *wicasa wakan* (medicine man) and a Catholic
catechist, christened "Nicholas" in 1904. Jesuit priests on Pine Ridge
Reservation today pray to the Great Mystery both with the medicine
pipe and the Catholic sacraments.

These new mixtures of being "now day Indi'n" (or American) are
no less "native" than changing conditions ever left people in North
America. Scandinavian farmers on the Great Plains, Greek steel mill
workers in East Chicago, black field hands in Louisiana, and Russian
Jewish shopkeepers in Los Angeles do not surrender ethnic definitions
over a few generations. Indians are even more ethnically self-contained

in many instances, since they have lived on separate and traditional
land bases, apart from the American mainstream, and they consider
themselves "Native" Americans, distinguished from all others.

There have been changes for centuries. The Navajo adapted with
newfound horses in the sixteenth century, as they moved into the
Southwest to trade with and plunder the Pueblos. The Lakota, somewhat earlier, migrated west from the Great Lakes woodlands out onto
the Great Plains. Renamed the "Sioux" or snake by French trappers
among the Ojibwa (also known as Chippewa), the Lakota emerged
from the forests as buffalo hunters with the horse, or "holy dog,"
replacing man's best friend 30,000 years native to North America. The
Mohawk of New York translate older codes of courage into high steel
work on construction sites, just as Indian firefighters are recruited
from reservations in many parts of the West. A Cherokee nowadays
uses Carnation milk cans as leg rattles in a stomp dance; he or she is
no less "Indi'n" than ancestors one hundred years ago, removed from
Appalachia to Oklahoma, who used turtle shells instead. There are
simply fewer turtles where the people live now.

Degree of Indianness is not measured, de facto, by any refusal to
adapt or by scarcity of organic materials for a ceremony, but is distinguished more by the spiritual significance of the ceremonies, as witnessed and infused among tribal peoples, performing the old ways
wherever they are, whatever their implements. If Cheyenne or Winnebago or Chickasaw or Papago relocate in Los Angeles, where five
thousand so-called "Gabrieleño" natives once camped, they bring their
Indianness with them into the city, redefining themselves. Good medicine is good medicine.

Being Indian, then, may mean adjusting the definition to the tribal
reality at hand, rather than living nostalgically in a mythic past. People
move from one place to another, or conversely, live in areas that change
as other cultures move in. Human time, place, and culture are carried
through cyclic evolutions that never stand still. For the September
Feast of San Esteban, an Acoma can climb 600-year-old cliff stairs 400
feet above a 7,000-foot New Mexico valley of squash, beans, and fruit
orchards. There in the Sky City, the Acomas traditionally dance Pueblo
rituals in ancient costume, pray for the balance of rain and sun and
crops, eat old-time bread from beehive ovens, and drink water at one
time carried on the heads of elder women in beautiful, old potteries.
Next day they can drive to the modernized Pueblo suburb of Acomita
in the valley below near Interstate Highway 70, where the people farm,
run markets, work livestock, or even commute into Albuquerque.

These Indians talk by telephone, as well as dance with rattles and drums; they drive cars and fly in airplanes, as well as ride horses; they hold jobs, vote, and pay taxes, as well as draw, paint, compose songs, tell stories, and make pottery in new applications of the old ways.

It is the threat of discontinuity that challenges Indianness today: how far the changes will go, how drastically they will alter Indian ways. "You can't relearn nothin' you never learned," says the Lakota Mark Monroe, who heads the Indian Center in Alliance, Nebraska. The young people, in large part, do not speak the Indian languages of their elders. Many of the ceremonies have gone underground or been abandoned. The medicine people are disputed. Sometimes the old people are ignored. The land has been mapped, allotted, subdivided, fenced, tracked with rail and road rights-of-way, and "developed" in non-Indian commercial ventures, as in South Dakota cattle leases or Four Corners coal mining or Southwest water rights. The wolves, buffalo, eagle, deer, migrating birds, bear, moose, elk, and antelope have been killed back or off, the forests cut down, the prairies plowed up, the rivers dammed and diverted. Indian people, along with all this, are pitied and shunted to out-of-the-way places as endangered species, left to their own demise and relieved of their natural resources. But the vanishing American just won't die off, Russell Means charges as a twentieth-century Sioux warrior in the American Indian Movement, though for white America the Indian "lives out of sight, out of mind."

For the majority of some million and a half variously defined Indians in America, being Indian involves not just the traditions or catastrophes served up on a buffalo chip of history, but a conscious set of choices. The central issue is what to fuse of the new and the old, improvisations and continuations from the past. In synchronous time, Indians shear sheep and drive the sick to Public Health Service hospitals, plant corn and collaborate on native language curricula, attend powwows and go to college, make native art and learn modern planning techniques for economic growth necessary to survival. These present-day people believe in themselves as Indians and act on that belief, within their own definitions. They realize themselves within a sense of Indian community. Their Indianness is not individually seized, but tribally granted and personally carried out, as the old ones personally carried tribal time down to where it is on their backs. In the older traditions, time is not passing around the people; we are time.

Being Indian, from Acoma to Pine Ridge, Tahlequah to Tacoma,

Wounded Knee to the Hopi mesas, upstate New York to down-home
Ohio, would seem, finally, to be *doing* something about seeing or being
or defining oneself Indian. It can be working with Headstart children
from farming communities to urban poverty areas. It can include
bringing goods and concern to the old ones, staying to listen to their
memories and wisdoms. Being Indian is as much behavior and attitude, life-style and mind-set, as a consequence of history or bloodline.
It may mean placing people above the possession of things. Such an
Indian life checks individual gain against the communal well-being,
not taking too much, not tolerating degradation, the energies of new
minds tempered with the tested patience and care of the old. Being a
"now day Indi'n" would seem, as with most positive human values,
more active than passive, although the inherited past obviously in-
forms tribalism through cultural continuity and a sense of common
heritage.

A Lakota healer told his people gathered in a ceremony the summer
of 1981 at Wakpamni Lake, Pine Ridge Reservation: "We're gonna
make it as we go along, generation to generation, addin' on an' addin'
on."

I

WINTERING HOME

Coming home was not easy anymore. . . . The distance I felt came not from country or people; it came from within me. I was as distant from myself as a hawk from the moon.

JAMES WELCH, *Winter in the Blood*, 1974

Candi Ompapi—*Oscar Howe*

BELOW ZERO

No one else exists when a cold high wind
Is blowing late at night in Nebraska.
Our buffalo grass house hugs the sod.
Ghosts of geese pass obliquely above

The pale street lights. You think the snow
Goes all the way to heaven, an iced terrace
For angels of some hoarfrost God slow
To wake on such a night. Storm-blasted

Glass windows shudder like brittle children
Who snap between their Father's whittled fingers.
All our animals retire to the basement
With spiders, eyeless mice and feverish gophers

Exhausted tunneling under the nightly winds.
Is His spirit kind, this God of barren
Prairies, mottled ponies, and cattle bones
Lost in the unfenced shortgrass? Where

Do the homeless find refuge tonight? Who
Will take us in? Here in our dead house
Clocks sleep like stones. The old man
No longer cares that two-fingered hours

Call like bronze flowers from a sand
Hills blow-out. A child closes his eyes
And prays loss of memory. Times
Come like this, unrequested, cold lies.

CHAPTER 1

Fugitive

Moon of the New Year (Quee'esh)

My battered white Volvo nosed through rush hour traffic on the San Diego freeway, a route once known to the early Spanish colonies as "The King's Highway." Beneath invading roadways lay the shards of an Indian trade route from the adjoining valley to the "Bay of Smokes," as Cabrillo named the hazy Los Angeles basin of some five thousand encamped natives in 1534. Even the Indian route had its predecessor in much traveled animal trails of a time beyond memory. Ravens still patrolled the traffic for carrion.

Under the pall of uncertain tenure, I was taking a leave of absence from UCLA to teach American Indian Studies somewhere in the Dakotas. Four students in two other cars were driving routes adjacent to mine through the Indian West. We would converge in the northern Plains for a traveling seminar. Jay, the son of a Beverly Hills doctor, was driving with Logan, my student of six years who cultivated a lifelong interest in alternative healing, specifically Indian medicine. Meghan, a restless English major from affluent Bel-Air canyons, rode with Kate, a salty single parent whose teenage daughter stayed behind.

My four-year-old daughter lay asleep on a backseat mattress: Rachel, child of light, my charge and companion—challenge to my patience, promise of life beyond a broken marriage, a translucent pebble I carried up the mountain. She saw the flight of birds in spattering rain and heard last year's robin, buried among the roses, singing in salmon petals. Her lyric child's voice lay under my city skin, now leathered "five thumbs thick," as the Iroquois put it.

"You don't know why you're going," my student Meghan said the day before, "but I see why you're not staying." She brushed back her dark hair as a blackbird riffles its feathers in the wind. "I want to go. Kate will drive with me."

I squinted into the freeway and for a time said nothing. My tenuous place in the city left me numb. A hitchhiker had scrawled on a chunk of cardboard at the LAX off-ramp, "ANYWHERE BUT HERE!" Taking this trip felt both like running away and turning to face the unknown.

"It's just a seminar on the road," I said, half to myself. "We'll be back with the tourists and summer smog. But you're welcome—" My throat tightened. Meghan got out and waved from the corner of Wilshire and Westwood, a long way from Jamestown, North Dakota.

Back from what? I wondered. Would we be just more white émigrés passing through Indian ancestral lands? What lay along this late winter road winding across the Southwest and up into the Great Plains?

I felt dislocated in this moebius strip of fast-lane America, the "City of Angels." Quick lunch stands came and went with inversion layers of smog; freeways flattened valleys and cemented river basins; twenty million motor vehicles jammed the superhighways. According to the Los Angeles Times, seventy percent of the city was paved parking and streets. "It's a city that would fill the Grand Canyon," a Navajo once told me.

Centerless, Los Angeles flared up in epicenters that drifted under a spell of urban insomnia: motion, no movement. I was afraid either of actually living it, or of turning it all into a cartoon. It seemed a Disneyworld Mecca that sucked in everything, a kind of surreal global magnet.

In my seventh year of California sun 'n surf, I was a homeless, single father. My daughter's mother had simply walked away, not looking back after our separation. She refused visitation or contact and swung a door shut on the past. The circumstances of our divorce were moot points by now; the reasons for Rachel's coming to live with me were never fully explained.

I was bunking in a communal bachelor house, when one morning I found myself hanging miniature chiffon, taffeta, and gingham dresses above a pile of old shoes in my closet. Their laces felt thin and soft, as finely patterned as snowflakes next to my old leather jacket and denim workshirts. It was another phase of my education.

This morning the Los Angeles Times printed a letter to the editor under the heading "Who's a Native?"

The term "Native American" used to refer to American Indians is a poisonous and unjust usage. When the government has taxed all non-Indians for hundreds of years to support the savages in idleness, the non-Indians have just as good or better claim to call themselves natives.

When you talk about Indian culture, you are talking about Stone Age barbarism, nomadism, perpetual war, and a tiny population. If the world goes back to that, any race that thinks it will be that tiny population could have a most unpleasant surprise.

WILL ENGLISH,
Tarzana

Tarzana, I thought, suburban wilderness of the celluloid frontier, shopping malls and all, White King of the Jungle. It was enough to drive a person down to the fossils in the La Brea tarpits. Judging by the finds there, coyotes had reached their present stage of evolution thirty thousand years ago. I glanced at a bumper sticker on a smoking VW, "The Moral Majority: NEITHER." In front of me a Winnebago RV with Delaware plates towed a Comanche toward the Mojave. Through the commuter smog I sourly imagined a four-wheel Battle of the Little Big Horn.

We headed east toward the rising sun which bobbed over San Bernardino like a muddy papaya. To prepare for the trip, I had been reading Bureau of American Ethnology reports from the beginning of the century. I drove along recalling from BAE reports that after ten days the Zuñi took a newborn from its bed of sand and presented the child to the rising sun. The grandmother sang this baptismal song:

> May your road be fulfilled.
> Reaching to the road of your sun father,
> When your road is fulfilled,
> In your thoughts may we live,
> May we be the ones whom your thoughts will embrace,
> For this, on this day
> To our sun father,
> We offer prayer meal.
> To this end:
> May you help us all to finish our roads.

The child's "road" or life was symbolized by spreading a trail of corn pollen, which imitated the sun's daily course—and this "road" was the spiritual score of the song. I cruised along with a million other Angelenos and wondered if my students, Rachel, and I would find our own "good red road."

Watergate, an economic recession, and the energy crisis cut across a generation of dreams in the wake of Vietnam; the denial of promise to a still young America seemed to calcify the present. The eggshell might never crack open.

My students had gathered for a mid-March "departy" at my home, joking in shirt sleeves and sandals about Dakota spring blizzards.

Kate put me on the spot. "Tell me, Professor, why are you taking us up there?"

"To trace the books back," I hesitated, "that is, to where these Native American writings come from—it was once my home." It sounded flat. Could I, or any other American these days, go home again? Meghan had worried through the winter on this. America had spilled southwest toward the Pacific. This trip back promised to be more than ordinary research or teaching. The "field" was the land of my ancestors, living and dead; the frontier was the "bloody loam" of Indian-White history, as the poet Williams put it, still for the Sioux an open wound. Some of the old-timers I knew had been alive at the time of the 1890 Wounded Knee Massacre, when my mother's father was born. My mother's family lines went back three hundred and fifty years to the third voyage of the Mayflower. Could "native" Americans ever come together?

Jay and Logan came to the door with a bundle of red wolfskin sewn around four fist-sized rocks. The stones were of strange though ordinary earth hues—chalk white, sallow, copper green, and charcoal.

"Take it," Logan offered skittishly, wrinkling his brow. The bundle gave off a sense of warm life; the furred stones felt responsive to my touch. It was as though the wolfskin covered the vertebrae of some animal.

"What is it?" I asked naively.

"A prayer," he mumbled, "a protector." His eyes shifted focus behind Coke-bottle lenses.

"From what?" I wanted to know.

"Not 'from' anything," he insisted, "*for* your well-being. Think of it as a guardian." He turned away to talk with Meghan.

Moon of the Snowblind (Lakota)

Across the Mojave Desert a mottled horizon seemed scooped from the earth. It left a concave lens of lava spills. The moon could have been plucked from Needles basin. Blotches of sage, yucca, and cholla lay singed by a sky bled of color. Waitresses in a roadside cafe wore holsters strapped to broad gunbelts. Long-nosed stage pistols slapped against their designer jeans—at least I hoped they were stage pistols.

I ordered coffee and a four-dollar cheeseburger, and we kept driving, Rachel munching fries on her mattress in the backseat.

A late winter storm gusted the car across the Southwest. North of Flagstaff the San Francisco peaks loomed snow-mantled through grey clouds. The *kachina* gods were said to winter in these mountains. My eyes strained over the empty desert, as we drove against the southwest spill into California. It seemed we were heading upstream into the country, doubling back on trails westward over the century. Rachel curled up to sleep. On the radio John Denver thanked God that he was a country boy, as a forty-mile-an-hour wind swept father, daughter, and pods of tumbleweeds across a horizon where the sunset stained crimson, then lilac over a Motel 6 billboard.

This was motion at last with movement. Emptying out, putting one hundred, two hundred, three hundred, soon a thousand miles, hours that stretched into days, between ourselves and a city of eight million.

People these days seemed frightened of what they might not get, hesitant to risk. Could I trust what little I knew on this journey? I feared the thickness and weight of my own ideas. Would we learn any more about Native America through this journey than by staying in Los Angeles and combing primary texts and rummaging the library? Would there be the hard, necessary insights?

"Make it new," the poets chanted, the quest in the questions, the draw in the unknown. Could we find a day to seek visions, a return pilgrimage on this road? Were the old medicines and healers and wise teachers still alive? Could I go back to Native America, home of "the people," as tribes once named themselves? They called themselves Arikara, "the people"; Cherokee, "real people"; Zuñi, "the flesh"; Pawnee, "men of men"; Biloxi, "first people"; Winnebago, "people of the real speech." It was worth trying to understand, one more time.

Red bluff foreheads jutted against the westering traffic. A feathering of spring snow laced the evergreen horizon, as we settled into the journey. I read during one of our many roadstops that Paiutes three generations ago sang this Ghost Dance song:

> The whirlwind! The whirlwind!
> The new earth comes into being
>   swiftly as snow.
> The new earth comes into being
>   quietly as snow.

Little Sandstorm Moon (Zuñi)

Navajos lined the highway east of the Grand Canyon, there to hawk turquoise, silver, rugs, and cedar "ghost" beads. The open-air sun shades of the lean-to markets rattled in the wind. Here Indians relaxed and socialized, but when tourists stopped, business was quick.

"Twelve dollars for these, ten dollars here, six dollars for these, these are five dollars." A young mother with her baby in a cradle board sat in the shade. At any small cry, she would place the baby on her knees to be rocked affectionately, keeping it quiet in the face of passing *Beligaana*, or White. Rachel padded right up to have a few words with a sheepdog snoozing in the shade.

Red iron oxides belted the desert around Tuba City, as we drove east to the Hopi mesas. "NOTICE" a posted sign warned. "You are entering the exclusive Hopi Reservation area. Your entrance constitutes consent to the jurisdiction of the Hopi Tribe and its courts. By order of the Hopi Tribal Council." Indian nations, by Supreme Court declaration, have been called "sovereign" for over a century and a half, "domestic dependent nations," according to Chief Justice Marshall in 1831. We were on their land.

Tassled corn clumps, bean rows, and squash mounds bunched along dustswept patches of the draws in any small place where soil and precious water might nurture life. The earth seemed to flow in shifting tones of grey, burnt sienna and brown, the terrain stretching far away, as severe and beautiful as another planet. The rocky ground could not be cultivated, but it remained vital to the eye and instinct, as from the beginnings of time.

A rectangular wooden sign blocked the dirt road into Old Oraibi, a village over eight hundred years *in situ*. "WARNING, WARNING," had been splashed brick-red on a white plyboard. "NO OUTSIDE WHITE VISITORS ALLOWED. BECAUSE OF YOUR FAILURE TO OBEY THE LAWS OF OUR TRIBE AS WELL AS THE LAWS OF YOUR OWN, THIS VILLAGE IS HEREBY CLOSED."

The Hopi cultural center appeared deserted, though two shops solicited Grand Canyon tourism. Unrepaired shop windows suggested an ambivalent attitude toward travelers through the mesas; still, the lamb and hominy stew with *piki* bread drew us indoors.

"Yuck, *blue* bread," Rachel said as she rejected the *piki*. I didn't tell her about the lamb in the stew.

We drove over to New Oraibi looking for Thomas Banyacya, the

Hopi prophet who was taking peace petitions to the United Nations. Just around the corner from the post office stretched a long adobe building with closed windows. It didn't exactly invite visitors. Several pickups, a Dasher with California plates, and farming equipment were parked in front, each vehicle with a ceremonial eagle feather hanging from the rearview mirror. We knocked at the front door and were shown in, after mentioning Los Angeles Indian friends who had forwarded introductions.

Thomas Banyacya was a short, sturdy man in his late fifties. His grey-streaked hair was tied back in a traditional *chongo*. Thomas wore sandals, white slacks with a dizzying black plaid, and a flower-print ribbon shirt of pink, violet, and green pastels. He perched on a piano bench like a polychrome wildflower and motioned us over to the couch, as he rubbed an afternoon nap from his eyes. His college-age son busied himself in the adjoining kitchen and soon waved us to the table covered with a red-on-white oilcloth. We were offered ice water from a juice pitcher.

"Do the old medicines still work for Indians?" I asked. Outside, all those eagle feathers dangled from rearview mirrors.

"Spiritual ways, yes, ceremonies, though some changed," Thomas thought aloud, his speech punctuated with glottal stops. "Every month we have ceremonies to keep our people balanced. We still live here in the center of the world. Not like those city 'powwows'—it's got to be spiritual, real serious, not just a place to get together and socialize. But this is a whole big problem of living in the right ways with the universe. Things changed. When money and jobs and drinking get in the way of the ceremonies, it don't work."

The younger, college-educated Thomas poured a glass of water, sat down, and broke in: "The Indian, you know, lives what the psychology books call a 'schizoid' life—Indian and white. He's got to walk that line between ceremony and getting along in the white man's world. It's real hard. He don't always keep it together. Then he starts to drinkin' to escape the problems."

Thomas rubbed his eyes again. "It's like those men coming back from war all these years, real messed up. They need old-time ceremonies to get them right again."

"Lots of Indians feel that the war is going on right here in America," his son added.

"You take this Big Mountain thing. The Hopis and the Navajos aren't fighting like they used to. It's the government stirring the pot—and the tribal council working for the Bureau of Indian Affairs! What they want are mineral rights, coal and uranium; they're gonna move Navajos off the land, prisoners of an economic war, just relocate them, like always with the Indians. Shoulda put us on wheels a long time ago—"

"Take the money and go," his son said with a straight face, "or go without the money." By now Rachel had lost interest in adult talk and was looking cautiously at some Mudhead *kachina* dolls on a corner shelf.

"We're talkin' about closing this reservation," Thomas warned. "Get the traditional people together, work with the Navajo too, who buffer us against the white world. Close off all the roads into the Hopi mesas. Twenty-four hours for a Snake Dance. It's been real dry this year. Corn ought to be way up here, bunching out now, but it's low, hardly anything. The bugs come everywhere from the desert to eat it. Even the coyotes and rabbits diggin' away the dirt, like this," he said, scratching at the floor, "to get down and eat what little there is.

"But we'll close our ceremonies to tell the white man we've had it. They come from all over the world to see Snake Dance—get here— stopped out of Winslow or Flagstaff by Navajo traditionals. We give 'em literature on why we have to do this, tell 'em to write Congress."

The older man's face glowed softly between my line of vision and the silvery blue light coming through the window. I noticed pots, pans, and ceramic and plastic tableware on a three-tiered shelf next to the stove and sink. *The Joy of Cooking* looked down on a box of Cheerios. The front room and kitchen were cluttered with the effects of a long life full of people: drawings and photos on the walls, spreads on the furniture, books and papers here and there, every space filled, orderly, humble.

"Back in 1948 the elders came and asked me to go out and represent them," Thomas explained. "They saw the whirling sticks—the swastika, you know—and the red sun change hands. They saw the gourd of ashes—the atomic bomb—and the war. These things are all set down in the prophesies, carved into stones in the mountains. We're gettin' together. Ceremonies all summer. Long about September, if the United Nations don't agree to hear us, we'll go down in the *kiva* and pray to the four directions for help. Then if that don't work, turn to the west, the man with a red star, millions like ants coming to change all this. Too much wrong done here. Tribal council just in there to protect their own pockets. We got to get back to the right ceremonies." He patted the oilcloth firmly for emphasis.

"The government of the people's got to change. We got to change it. It's in our old-time prophesies, carved into the rocks here.

"We'll do our ceremonies. We'll see then. Mebbe it all come crashes."

We left Oraibi driving east. The sunset cast the high desert in mantles of red-blush shadow. What was Thomas telling me to tell my people? It felt like some kind of spiritual tabloid with an ominous postscript. The whirling sticks? The gourd of ashes? Man with a red star? What would the *National Review* say about such Indian omens?

A hawk with tagging crows tilted in amber sunlight high above the mesa.

At Canyon de Chelly, inhabited for twenty-five hundred years, we made camp under cottonwoods spared by Kit Carson in 1864, when the cavalry scorched the Navajos from their peach tree canyon. Cotton fluffs drifted through a night of coyotes and crows, stars cracking overhead, the Spiritway splashing ancestors north to south through the dark. Here tonight I could see why the Hopi and Navajo didn't want whites messing around in their world with machines.

In the morning we drove southeast to Acoma, perched four hundred feet above the high, green desert in a slotted canyon. Adobe ten feet thick walled the people in this "sky city" on a mesa a mile and a half high. An old man in baggy jeans was painting white window frames under protruding log rafter *vegas*, as a group of ten Acomas, young to middle-aged, repaired a crumbling wall. Two children replaced broken stones in a walkway.

Old women came to sell their wares. Their hands were bony and dusty grey with glazing, thumbs bent back from winglike fingers, nails broad, wrists thick—these women had worked hard all their lives. Their eyes were deeply and quietly set behind bronzed, layered flesh. They were traditionally dressed in long velveteen skirts, dark blouses, and heavy black shoes; woven scarves wound around their pepper-flecked hair. Pablita Conchito was, indeed, pleased to trade with us, proud of her goods, and tickled to have in stock a strawberry soda for Rachel.

"There you are, honey. Now have a nice day with us." She meant it.

A dirt storm shouldered the car into Albuquerque, and from there we drove north to Santa Fe where Navajo and Pueblo women lined the governor's palace wall. They spread handwoven blankets and shawls daily to display turquoise, silver, and pottery.

A Navajo in sneakers told me a small turquoise stone sold for seven dollars "because of the grains." He added, "It's a sky stone—cures bad eyes."

"And the powder blue ones are most prized?"

"Now it all depends what mood you catch the white man in." He nodded, eyes bloodshot.

Further down the line an older woman was stringing beads.

"You can touch them," she said, and I did. They felt like small, milky eggs.

To the west nestled Los Alamos, a government city of seventeen thousand, made up of nuclear physicists' families. Again, new snow made the roads treacherous, as the car ascended a mountain pass to Valle Grande, the country's largest extinct volcano. Rumor had it that scientists were drilling thousands of feet down to tap heat in the earth's interior: force water down one pipe, it comes up steam in the other. The project could solve the energy crisis, eliminate those lines at the gas station. On the other hand, if this changed the earth's surface temperature, the white man would usher in another Ice Age and create a land bridge back to Asia. Then all of us could go back home, wherever that had been prehistorically. I began to think more about the Hopi warnings. There were many ways the world could "all come crashes."

With poor visibility and at best a sliding control of the car, we drove past the old Spanish mission on to Jemez Springs. Pueblo Indians over the Southwest rose against Catholic missions almost three hundred years ago in 1680; they drove out the priests and razed their missions. The black-robed fathers returned in less than twenty years, however, to try once again their monastic faith among wildlife and Indians; the church put them out to sparse pasture on the Great American Desert reserved for "vanishing" species. It seemed a little alcove of America's "elbow-room" expansion.

We stopped for lunch at Los Ojos, a cattleman's bar. Its walls were studded with deer heads and black bear hides. The horseshoe counter was draped with animal skins for knee warmers.

A stocky ranchhand shot straight pool. Another glint-eyed cowboy tended bar. Everyone kept his hat on. One young seed, sweat-soured Stetson low over his ears, hummed off key with the jukebox, "We don't smoke marijuana in Muskogee, an' we don't like the folks who do."

"Who ya lookin' for, Ace?" the pool shark snapped. I stood there a bit distracted, blinking, with Rachel on my arm staring into the bear's mouth.

"The Momaday house, uh, the Kiowa writer who grew up here."

"On down the road." He didn't crack a smile. "Hey, Charlie, ya got any more Budweiser?" He turned to his bank shot. "This here fella needs a drink bad." I didn't take it as an invitation to shoot pool.

South of Jemez Springs a box canyon arched magenta walls skyward. The river silted ocher from mountain snowmelt. I thumbed to the end of my dog-eared copy of N. Scott Momaday's *The Way to Rainy Mountain:* "Once in his life a man ought to concentrate his mind on the remembered earth, I believe. He ought to give himself up to a particular landscape in his experience, to look at it from as many angles as he can, to wonder about it, to dwell upon it. He ought to imagine the creatures there and all the faintest motions of the wind. He ought to recollect the glare of noon and all the colors of the dawn and dusk." There in the canyon's amber light, I understood how Momaday could look and listen so carefully to the land. The family house stood dark beside the road.

Further down, the Jemez adobe houses clustered on a flat valley floor where the canyon spilled southward onto the desert. Beehive ovens flanked earth-rounded houses; all rested quietly.

A green pickup began to follow us, so I stopped and stepped into the clay dust. A muscled Indian policeman smiled. "This reservation is closed to non-Indians," he said without apology or anger.

There was no hostility, simply statement of fact. A stillness settled between us.

"We are preparing for our spring ceremonies. You can come back at Easter, if you would like to visit." He gave the point time to register. "Do you know your way out?"

"Yes, I think so. Thank you." I meant that in the same spirit that Pablita Conchito had wished us a nice day.

CHAPTER 2

Alliance

Moon of the Crust on the Snow (Ojibwa)

The old Volvo crested a grass-pocked sandhill in northwest Nebraska. There against the glare of snow and sky clustered Alliance out in the open prairie. Seven thousand farmers, ranchers, and tradespeople were burrowed into the Nebraska Panhandle, not far from the Pine Ridge and Rosebud Sioux tribes, directly south of Wounded Knee, South Dakota. My people still lived here. Middle America's radio pundit, Paul Harvey, spoke out in every home.

The houses bunched to make up a town, much as the buffalo grass grew in clumps of tough ground cover. Though the people lived closely, they insisted and traded on their differences. Fences between houses were built lower, if a neighbor put up a fence; kids cut over lawns and empty lots on their way home from redbrick public schoolhouses. The townspeople gossiped in rival clans, just as the pioneers a century before or Indians long ago had banded together for mutual needs. The land required tribalism for all "leggeds," human and animal. Only the most lonely, desperate, or disillusioned chanced this environment alone.

I'd never seen Los Angeles as suddenly or distinctly as I now saw this Great Plains groundclump a few miles away on the rolling horizon. The LA motorist braked from stoplight to stoplight, freeway to off-ramp, among countless other motorists at any time of the day or night. Here on the prairie a road leaned vacantly into the horizon, the dark called for sleeping, and the wind blew hard from the northwest.

This was native America, timelessly, seasonally in change. Some said that Alliance was named for the union of two railroads, the Burlington and CB&Q, which merged to ship Texas cattle herded north to Omaha and Chicago. Eighteen coal trains a day now smoked through Alliance. Before this the Lakota lived here and called themselves "allies."

Gall and Spotted Tail and Red Cloud once hunted in the sandhills; Crazy Horse was bayoneted at Fort Robinson to the north. My ancestors' highways, the Oregon and Mormon trails, branched south along the Platte; Wyoming frontier stretched to the west; Indian territory was held off to the north; sandhill ranches sprawled to the east. And Buffalo Bill Cody had settled on the river.

Lewis and Clark first explored this rolling prairie known as the Great American Desert. In the 1870s the Deadwood stage drove gold shipments, camouflaged as buffalo bone wagons, through here to Fort Sidney. The Hole-in-the-Wall Gang wintered just over the Wyoming border. I'd heard all these stories and more in childhood from my great uncle Ted. One day, after cutting my hair on the back porch, he showed me the Colt .45 owned by his own uncle, a cattle rustler. My mother's grandfather had been a soldier at Fort Robinson.

Just south of Alliance, deep with riverbottom mud, lay "the Nile Valley of the West," the last green valley before the vast Wyoming prairies. Here my great-grandparents planted corn, beans, and potatoes, beside wheat, oats, rye, and sunflowers. The buffalo migrated by the hundreds of thousands along the valley bluffs, and settlers gave the bluffs the name "Good Streak" for the buffalo chips they gathered to heat sodhouses in winter. Indians here moved in time with the buffalo, at home in seasonal motion.

Gold rushers trailed the Platte River into Colorado, the Black Hills, Montana, and California as homesteaders rolled west. The Mormons, edging along the river's north side, trekked to Utah. With these migrant Americans came the cowboys, the drifters, the revivalists, the con men, and outlaws, the flotsam of a half-civilized America. The cattle drives from Texas ended at Sidney and Valentine in railroad stockyards; here my mother's father had worked as a train fireman. If fighting the climate and Indians weren't enough, these immigrants struggled with one another—sodbusters and cattle herders, reformists and revivalists, the law and the outlaw, the damned and the saved. My forebears were rock-hard men and gritty women.

After I had been home several days, my father came in from work
and fished two agate arrowheads from his dusty coveralls.

"Damn, if those Indians aren't still around!"

"You're lucky that your hairline recedes, Dad. No warrior would
touch that headpiece. Where'd you get these arrowheads?"

"Farmer brought 'em in a load of beans. They were harvested right
out of the ground, vines and all, and dumped into the cleaner bins.
The heads showed up in the cull bin with pebbles and low-grade
splits. Damndest thing, eh?" I felt the urge to twist his tail a bit.

"You know where beans come from, Dad?"

"Beats me—the ground."

"Indians. Fort Berthold Indians in North Dakota. Guy named Oscar H. Will, pioneer seedsman, got the first handful of white beans
there, back in the nineteenth century."

"So this is what you learn at school? Indian beans! Time for a cold
shower."

Feeling light-years distant from either urban coast this time home,
I read the morning paper: weather report, cold; local basketball scores,
low; letters to the editor, sour; classified ads, "Beefalo semen for sale!"
"Exotic breeds!" This was hybrid stock country. People tended to act
more instinctively—open-faced, rangy, direct, if slower. They dealt
less with the self-conscious mind, more with habit, prejudice, and
heritage. History stayed in the warp and grain of the moment, the
place, the people. It wasn't a town of international headlines, face
lifts, or business deals, and nobody "took a meeting" around here—
they just went to work.

My father now seemed restless with cabin fever, that depression of
a long winter waiting for spring. Two blizzards had smashed through
the Plains in six days; livestock losses were ten to fifteen percent.
Some vital forces deep down, and layered over by winter, now wanted
out, while the snows blew back in to smother spring. Temperatures
could fall seventy degrees in an April day, throwing the season's
promise backward in time. The wind always seemed relentless here,
creasing and aging the skin just as it eroded the land, the stones, the
twisted graceful elms.

The paper reported eighteen degrees below zero last night, the
coldest place in America. Two feet of snow packed the ground on
Easter Sunday. And how in God's name did the Sioux live here over
the centuries? Storms swept down out of Canada scouring the high
plains. People either withdrew and hibernated for a lifetime, or they
blew hard at the world, like the wind, not to be denied. With chafed

skin they blustered, embraced, choked, and bowled each other over. At least it was out in the open, plain-spoken.

"Are you going to see Mark today?" my father asked one morning over his second cup of coffee.

"That's where I'm headed." A man of few words and less appetite before work, my father had held mute sunrise rites over coffee and cigarettes as far back as I could remember. The cut in his voice echoed our differences on Indians.

"Well, come back with your scalp on," he chided. "On second thought," he said, pushing his chair away from the kitchen table, "you could use a hair cut. See you at lunch."

I had slept soundly through the night and woke to railroad cars thudding in the distance. Brisk northwesterly winds thrashed the elms and whipped the telephone wires so they whistled in thirds. I felt my lungs opening, my heart expanding, as the air blew in freely and the LA urban tensions dispersed. It was good to come home. But I knew the lows here as well—the tedium of slow, throwaway conversations, dulling habits of mind. My mother seemed stir-crazy winter-long, and my father, an intelligent and sensitive man, couldn't unwind after work without a shot of Old Crow. The place could leave an ache at the back of any brain. The winters drove every living thing underground but people; the summers bore down hot, stormy, and wind-baked. The Lakota winter counts in the old days gave only one "moon" each to spring and fall; the rest of the year was inscribed to frozen winters and hardpan summers. To survive, the people had to be as tough as the sod itself, once the very walls of their homes.

The old resentments between genders and generations ran deep on the Plains. Mari Sandoz, a local writer who fictionalized Crazy Horse, spoke of schisms where pioneer prerogatives gave men lawless rights over women, and loneliness was the rule of a land silencing the weak. Out of rootless desperation men would marry "anything that stepped off the train," her Swiss immigrant father Jules said; and his daughter went in fear of the old man until his death and burial in Alliance. When she received a national *Harper's* award in New York, Old Jules wrote the only letter his daughter ever received from him, one line: "You know that I think writers and artists to be the maggots of society." Mari's sister still cared for the family orchards to the east, in the sandhills where Mari lay buried.

Coming home for me meant returning to working parents, settled in the north end of town, and visiting my adopted Lakota family, who lived south of the tracks. I'd left Alliance swearing off a flatland where

the wind blew without mercy, the people tunneled tightly into themselves, and the community fixed its terms in knuckle-down drive
masked behind poker-faced instinct. And now I came back to gauge
my own growth from pioneer values, diluted as I was into the middle
class, and to ask what old ethics I still carried. What was my own
native America? Where had we come since my distant grandfather's
1607 winter in Jamestown, Virginia? How had the family lines of Giles
and Young and Bradford and Lincoln and Whitman and Johnston
trickled down to my times? My daughter's past and future lay here
too.

I drove east to Box Butte Avenue, a redbrick boulevard dividing the
town, then turned south past the grade school, the court house, and
two blocks of shops. In the cold, clear air everything seemed etched
into a landscape of obsidian shadows. Bare March elms rose brown-
laced against an azure sky. At the main intersection four businesses
squared off for local commerce: two rival banks, Montgomery Ward,
and Kings Korner Bar. Two blocks farther, a claybrick train depot dead-
ended the bottom of the main street.

I turned east into the morning sun along a highway bypass, and
then swung south again on Potash, a country road that trailed into
the sandhills. It was traveled mostly by farmers and truckers going
out of town.

The scenery changed: rusting machinery, empty boxcars, collapsed
shipping crates, blowing newspapers. Most times of day or night
someone, usually Indian, walked the graded road. Half the cars needed
work in this end of town. South Alliance dirt streets. Pale clapboard
houses several generations old. A tree-shaded park and the Burlington
baseball field. Along Indian Creek years ago I speared carp and swam
with dark-skinned kids who seemed somehow like me, yet different,
with clouds of questions behind their eyes.

The railroad underpass marked our dividing line, a narrow tunnel
of wooden pilings and trestles, always dark and dusty, fouled with
graffiti. On the other side of darkness, Indian Town. When our family
moved to Alliance, up from the Platte Valley, my grandfather drove us
down these dirt streets and pointed to Indians living in army surplus
tents. He made jokes about bucks, squaws, and puppy stew and
warned us to keep the dog tied up at home. I still feared this part of
town. I was a white outsider, a carrier of old injustices. Yet resistant
to the encrusted prejudices of my grandfather, I was drawn like a
curious and fearful child to these clay roads.

Throughout America more Indians now lived off reservation than on, more people now intermarried as "breeds" than traditional "bloods." The 1970 Nebraska census totaled 10,094 residents for Box Butte County: "Whites 9,669, Negros 36, Other 389." The county "Other" was a people indigenous to the land, Indians in uneasy residence, and statistics did not include the floating Lakota population which moved back and forth between rural towns and the reservations. These Native Americans counted neither as state residents nor highway fatalities. They had no official identity in the Dakotas, Wyoming, or Nebraska. A Lakota voter with no place to eat or sleep gave his residence as the Alliance city jail. He got drunk, arrested, and booked as a way of going home to bed and breakfast.

Williston Jones lived at Second and Sweetwater, in an alley shack just up from the old whorehouse. When I was a boy, a black pimp used to drive a white Cadillac down the dirt street called Sweetwater, where Indian girls drank whiskey in teacups with lonely men and disappeared along dimly lit halls. This forbidden part of Alliance was a place of mystery, shadowed by the railroad and Indian "tent city."

Williston or "Willis" went to public school with white kids like myself, here in Alliance eighty miles south of Wounded Knee. Willis was a mixed-breed Sioux Indian from Pine Ridge, just over the South Dakota state line. As kids we hung around ball fields and Indian Creek and the pool hall through the eighth grade—Alex Good Heart, Hank Little Pumpkin, the Wilson brothers, Tom Kosmiscki, Denny Garrett, Jerry Culp. Willis fought all the time. I still remember the rage in his face, an anger burning so deep that kids kept their distance. Even at Indian Creek, where we all swam and fished and smoked driftwood, everyone watched out for Willis. He'd turn on you for no reason. At thirteen I sharpened a metal shoe horn and carried it in my back pocket for protection down the alleys of South Alliance.

But as Willis grew older he got even meaner; he started drinking hard and ditching school. Then he quit Alliance. His anger burned him up. Every fight lodged in his stomach. He wanted to kill something, somebody. His mother died. His father died. His brothers and sisters scattered and died. He was dying, and cheap wine took the ache away at fourteen. Fourteen years old, an alcoholic. It still wasn't legal before 1954 for Indians to drink in public, so he had to steal for his addiction.

He was always fighting. "Lincoln, I'm gonna cut you up, white bastard," he menaced in the pool hall. He swung a belt studded with razor blades. Willis went to reform school, later the state penitentiary. Alcohol was his painkiller: symptom, escape, and finally the cause of his despair. Williston made a fist of that knot in his stomach and hid down there, all the while he was drowning.

So he went back to the reservation.

Twenty-five years later we met again, when I returned with Logan to the northern Plains consulting with alcohol abusers and Indian traditionalists on treatment. For Williston the reservation had been just as bad, or worse, than Alliance. There was less than nothing to do. Not low income, *no* income people, the saying went. Willis had been sleeping in junked cars and working odd jobs for a few dollars to buy white port and Schlitz beer. Summers he slept in the park. I last saw him hunkering on a street corner with T-Bone Wilson, his half-breed drinking buddy.

"I owe you guys something."

"Yeh, what for?" Willis asked.

"Talking, talking about your drinking. Giving reasons . . . Mebbe with your help we'll get a halfway house."

"Hell, that wasn't nothin'." T-Bone tossed his head. "We do what we have to. Halfway don't help anyway."

Willis looked up expectantly. A few dollars would help. He stared across the street at the Sandhillo Bar. A pickup pulled up with a full gun rack. The cowboy spat in the storm drain and went in for a beer. Willis looked straight at me with raw need, nothing but hunger in his eyes. I reached in my back pocket.

"Here's twenty bucks, ten apiece, for . . . services rendered. But promise me you'll eat something."

"You bet." Willis grinned and held out his hands. "A nice big burger at the Dairy Queen." They were up off the sidewalk.

"You guys take care, okay?" I had mixed feelings about giving Willis and T-Bone money to buy what was killing them, but they were starving. I knew that, too.

"Sure, we'll take whatever we can. So long, Lincoln."

Williston hobbled away with pinched-in steps. T-Bone lumbered after him. Williston's toes had frozen off when he was sleeping in wrecked cars several winters back and temperatures dropped far below zero for months. The scars on his leg were deep brown ruts where gangrene had set in a wound.

In 1968 Williston Jones listed the city jail as his home. Some of his friends had used their belts to hang themselves there—four I had known in 1968. Indian girls whispered hoarsely of being raped by cops in solitary cells.

Williston would drink and squat on Main Street near the railroad tracks. Every day the wine scraped his stomach bloody. His liver swelled out under his ribs. His eyes turned yellow and bloodshot. He seldom ate. Most days he drank hard and did nothing but hunker down and fester with rotgut. Some days between binges he laughed and dreamed of making a life, of the "old ways," of buffalo and Crazy Horse and the *Paha Sapa*, or Black Hills. His visions came lean. Most days just drifted by, one sickness to the next. He waited on a street corner for the cops to pick him up. It was the only way to go home.

"You'd make a good alcoholism counselor," I told him that last summer. "You've been around. You know what it's like being drunk, living on nothing. You talk straight."

"I got nothin' to hide," Willis said flatly.

In January temperatures dropped to forty below zero in northwest Nebraska. Indians on the "res" were huddling around wood-burning stoves. Citizens in Alliance stayed indoors. The schools closed. Williston was hungry and freezing. He went with Harley Poor Horse to scrounge for garbage behind the Safeway market. They found some old barbecued chicken and shared it. A few hours later Williston got sick and vomited. Harley called the city cops. Nurses at the hospital treated Williston for DTs and sent him home to the shack on Sweetwater alley.

The next day he went into a seizure. Williston died in an alley at the age of forty.

There was no autopsy. No inquiry into his death. No family. No mourners. No questions.

"He never did learn anything," my Lakota brother Mark would later say. "He lived in the white man's world, and the white man didn't want him in it.

"He was buried in a plain pine box. I always thought of him as my friend, even though he was down and out and no good. When he went to the hospital with convulsions, he'd call me up and say, 'Mark, will you bring me some cigarettes and candy?' I'd bundle my grandson up, and we'd take him what he wanted. Hell, I'd give him wine. Damn alcoholic's got to have it. I've been there." Mark paused.

"Well, he was the extreme of the Indian—an' he's dead."

Thoughts of Williston felt like old wounds as I drove up to a converted army barracks serving as the community Indian Center. Icicles splintered from sunlit eaves under roof patches of green asbestoes and tarpaper. A litter of mongrel pups yipped to announce the visitor, as I opened a wood-slat gate and knocked on the screen. A round child's face beamed through the sheet-plastic window.

"Uncle Ken!" Big-toothed smile, shy affection.

"Hi, Hope! How you've grown! I'm home again. Your Mom and Dad around?"

"Daaad-dy . . . it's Uncle Ken!" She padded barefoot into the kitchen, leaving the door ajar for me to follow. Mark came out of the adjoining room, grinning broadly, and held out his hand.

"Ken! It's good to see you, Brother. You been gone a long time. California finally drop in the ocean?"

"Not yet. I've been gone a year now. No big earthquakes. Just time to come home again." Little had changed. I'd stepped across a year, back over a thousand miles into the lives of people who did not forget.

"Hello Emma. Keeping Mark out of trouble?"

"Ken, you come back to be an Indian again?" Emma teased. "You got to eat dog stew this time."

Without any more fuss Hope turned to help her mother clear the breakfast dishes. I scanned the parchment yellow walls. The red dot on the gallon coffee pot traded blinks with Dirty Bird, the family parakeet, who perched on a curtain rod over the sink. A gilt-framed portrait of Jesus, dusky and long-haired, looked benignly down on the kitchen table.

Mark sat at the table. He was dressed in his usual brown slacks and a green shirt and wore his leather belt with MONROE tooled at the back. Mark carried himself with a compact fighter's determination. He was a man of temper and quick wit, a lively storyteller readily liked, dark-skinned and dark-eyed with a trickster's grin. His humor offset great pain; he'd "gone south" and back again, several times, as an alcoholic.

"Mark," I asked, "do you remember the ceremony when you made me your brother—the drumming and dancing, the old people praying and singing, everyone gathering down here. Something took hold of me then, not just the Lakota name, or the family adoption, or the people accepting me here . . . I've come back home to find out about my growing up, and where to go now. It's my way of finishing school." The questions were of real concern, Mark knew; we'd talked of such things for years. It wasn't Hollywood back here, and we weren't on camera; these talks were where my thinking began and my writing ended. "Tell me, are you still holding powwows?"

"Depends on how things are going with the people in South Alliance. We try to take care of our spiritual needs—but then you put up a sun shade for dancing, and first thing, here come people jus' to drink. Drinkin' and fightin'! We had to stop the dances; too many people got hurt." He shook his head and took a sip of coffee. "I'd maybe start drinkin' an' all, if we had those powwows again." There was a long pause. Emma and Hope washed the dishes.

"You see, Ken," he said more softly, "people die from that around here. We find a body over by the stockyards, or in a wrecked car." This shift in his talk startled me.

"Do the police do anything about causes?"

"No, not for Indians, not even an autopsy." His voice was dry as late winter leaves.

"Nobody asks questions?"

"No, they know the guy died from drinkin'."

Mark's voice hung flat in the room. His dark eyes searched my face. "Some get killed, too." He nodded toward his "deterrent," a .22 automatic rifle propped against a filing cabinet. A typewriter on a grey metal stand seemed to contest the rifle. Mark was a three-finger typist whose hand had been shot apart in Korea, and he chose now between words and bullets. There were still prisoners of war on the reservation; booze was their poison, painkiller, and disease. I took a deep breath and asked more questions.

"How long can a person drink like that, do you figure, and stay alive?"

"Hard to tell. Most die while their kids are young. Some go harder and faster than the rest." Mark shook his head and looked away, at a loss. "I don't know. Our food and medical programs in a way jus' make them live longer an' *look* better. Some of the girls sell themselves to white guys. God, God, *God!* What a horrible existence—"

I walked over to the coffee percolator and took my time finding a cup. We had spent many hours in the kitchen talking like this—it seemed our classroom, in a sense, as well as the place for family therapy and private counsel.

"Where do these dying people live?" I asked, turning back to the table.

"Guy's basement, or car, or hole in the ground, hell, any damn place." He took a long pensive draw on his cigarette.

"I remember a time at city council—councilman bitched he found a woman sleepin' in his car. He blamin' *me* for not gettin' *my* people a place to live! An' it was twenty-eight degrees below zero, colder'n hell!"

"People suffer less in the summer?" I wondered naively.

"If you can call sleepin' in the park not sufferin'. They get by anyway. Hell, you take ol' Willis. Neighbor came by to see about fixin' up his busted leg and found maggots eatin' in it!"

I took several slow breaths. Emma continued to wash dishes and said nothing. Her quietness accented the pauses.

"How do people sober up, Mark?"

"That's the roughest part for the Indian. White guy goes back to his community, his job, all his friends and family. They do everything to keep him dry. Indian guy's different, his people's different. He comes back from the detox center to a hard-drinking community like Alliance. Hell, that poor guy *can't* sober up." Mark lit another cigarette and leaned back thinking.

"I sent a guy to Hot Springs army hospital; he stayed there three days, and came back sober as a judge. Then his dad and brother got ahold of him. Forced liquor down his goddamn throat." Mark went through the contortions of shoving a bottle down a man's throat. "They make fun of him—laugh at him wanting to sober up! They think he's tryin' to be better than them. There's just no support there for an Indian alcoholic." He shook his head in dismay and tapped on the table with a plastic spoon. "Jus' no support . . . "

I didn't know what to say, so I kept asking.

"Did people drink harder when bars finally served alcohol to Indians?"

"You got to understand, Ken. Before 1954, when federal law gave Indians the right to drink, I used to watch the older guys. First, poor ol' guy would have to scrounge all over for a bootlegger. He'd give him the empty bottle, and maybe five dollars for a pint of whiskey. An' then he'd go out in an alley, or sneak it home and drink it all up, so nobody would catch him with it.

"You know we're just now gettin' educated *how* to drink. We never had the stuff in the old days." Mark thought some on this. "Drinkin'— I seen a lot of guys slug a pint of whiskey. Drink half of it, and hide it, drink the other half in an hour or so. In Alliance I've seen Indians take a quart of wine, drink it in one swallow clear down, without even stoppin' to take a breath."

Mark was back somewhere in his own past. I seemed to be looking over his shoulder. "See, a white man could sit around, drink with a cup"—he mimed drinking tea, little finger in the air—"go for maybe four to five hours. White man enjoys it and don't get quite as intoxicated. You give a quart to one of our guys, he drinks it up, chugs it down, jus' like he used to when it was illegal. Never learned *how* to drink." Mark seemed to close in on the problem.

"Even to this day, a wino'll take his quart outside, see there's nobody around, sneak it from inside his shirt, an' gulp his drink down. Never even taste it." He went through the furtive gestures of chugging from a bottle. "I couldn't go around a bar. Damn! White people drinkin' so slow it'd make me all nervous! I got to where I'd drink a case of beer a night workin' at the bakery. Go out to the park or somewhere, get drunk alone. Hell, if I'd gone on drinkin' like that, I'da been dead." He looked over at Emma imploringly.

"Sometimes I wouldn't even try to come home. I'd drink all day, twelve pints a wine in *one* day. Pitiful." Emma turned to the sink again and called Hope in to dry tableware.

"Jus' went as far as I could an' finally quit workin' at the bakery. Then 1968, I got committed to the veterans' hospital at Bear Butte. And I quit."

"How far down had you gone?"

Mark's voice dropped. "I couldn't eat, drink, do nothin'. I wanted to drink so damn bad I'd crawl down an' get it in the gutter."

He squashed out his cigarette. "Doctor saw me in the detox yard, 'Jesus Christ, man! You're in bad shape. Hundred and 'leven pounds! How come you're in worse shape now after two years of treatment?'

"An' I said, 'Hell, man, it don't do me no good.'

" 'If you don't quit drinking,' he said, 'you're gonna die.'

"They brought breakfast in. I couldn't eat. My liver puffed out like a damn big banana, you could *see* it!" Mark cupped his abdomen. "Two days later, an' I still couldn't eat. Doctor said, 'I'm gonna sit here until I see you eat that up.' " Mark's face was blank. " 'Okay, but I'm so damn shakin' I can't even cut it.' So he took the knife and cut it up. He held it and shoved it down my throat, then poked me in the chest, and I swallowed." He thumped on his chest, exaggerating a swallow. "Like a baby. *He* was a doctor!—an' he would do that, breakfast, dinner, and supper, for an *Indian!*" Mark was still incredulous.

"Next morning, I couldn't even chew, no control, like I was paralyzed. So I'd get the food in, roll it around in my mouth, he'd poke me on the chest, and I'd swallow.

"I cold turkey'd that out." Mark's jaw tightened. "Stayed isolated thirty-six days, and all of a sudden I remembered I was a human being. Started walking around on that ward. I had yellow jaundice, an' they thought I was gonna die! When I walked in the open ward, they all cleared out, 'cause they thought I still had hepatitis. Got that drinkin' out of bottles I found in trash cans." The story had drained him. We sat quiet for a minute.

"You think a guy's got to hit bottom *that* hard, before he's going to quit?"

"The only Indians I know, yes." Emma started rinsing the pans in the sink. I needed some sense of resolution. The story clung to me like sleet.

"How would you counsel Indians on drinking, Mark? What could anyone do?"

"I'd take pictures of Indian guys sweating beer, completely crazy. Show Indian alcoholics what will happen—they say it'll never get to them. Get right down there to the gut level, show 'em at home with the wife and kids, what the alcoholic goes through, epileptic seizures."

Mark looked up impishly. "We had an AA meeting up at your mother's church while I was still drinkin'. Bunch of alcoholism counselors showed us slides, you know, *white* people bein' drunk. All us *Indian* guys were sittin' there laughin'.

" 'That guy's havin' fun!' we'd say. 'He's got it comin', that sonofabitch!' There *we* are, sleepin' in the park an' crawlin' in people's cars, an' there's that white guy with his big car, wife, good home. You show an Indian goin' through withdrawal symptoms, layin' there in that alley, throwin' up that white wine. Drinkin' it and throwin' it up again; he'll eat his own puke for more wine.

"The Indian could say, 'That red guy looks like me. My God, it *is* me!' " His voice softened. "We're not like you, Ken. We're not *like* you. That white lawyer drinkin' his whiskey is not like the Indian gettin' drunk on wine, sleepin' out in cars, no matter if they're both humans. We figure we're never gonna be where that white man is— we're in a different position entirely."

CHAPTER 3

Mark

Moon of the Eagle (Cree)

In the "Rumblings" column of the *Alliance Daily Times* appeared a letter to the editor titled "Sioux Resident Tells Indian Plight in Alliance":

Would you please place this letter in your Rumblings Column, every word. There is much indifference in this town.

The worst indifference is total disregard for human sufferings.

I am referring to the recent deaths of Gene Black Horse and Joe No Leaf in the city jail.

Any Indian dying in the Police Chief's jail is bad business. Drunken Indians are his business. If the Indians stopped getting in jail, he would be out of a job.

The police would have the Indian believe he is picking him up out of the goodness of his heart; someone may run over him or something worse. There is some truth to that. I hear from too many white citizens that "the only good Indian is a dead Indian."

The reason people dislike an Indian is because he is a tax burden, a law breaker, and a poor worker. Other than that the white citizens like Indians, or so they say.

Not all white people share the common hatred for Indians. It is hard for them to help us if we do not help ourselves; in fact they are baffled by the attitude of the Indian. If I listed all the reasons why the Indian is what he is today, I could fill a book and each page would hang a white man.

To my people I say that now is the time for action, not speeches. I urge you to stop drinking and get off the streets. We should find a home for the homeless.

It is up to the elders to set an example. We have to get educated; no matter how we try we cannot win unless we are educated.

Our ancestors lived caring for each other and not drinking. Every day they lived, they lived to learn. Knowledge was a great asset to them. We are faced with a greater challenge; we are living in a world that is no longer ours, yet we must succeed, and we can if we try.

We should remember that Gene Black Horse and Joe No Leaf died in the white man's jail, whatever the reason. Never again must we let that happen to another Indian.

The white man loves to laugh at the Indian. They will probably laugh at this letter. They say we live to fight each other every day. We do not. We care for each other. That is why we back Mark Monroe. He is Indian and all Indians in the white man's world are pitiful.

Thank you,
Anastasia Black Feather
Sioux Indian

Mark was born in a log cabin on the Rosebud Reservation in 1930 and named for his mother's father, Mark Stone Arrow, an Oglala Sioux. His Cheyenne father's father, Sleeps Long Time, joined Buffalo Bill's Wild West Show around the turn of the century and took the name Monroe after the American president. When Mark was twelve, his father, Bill, moved the family off the reservation to find work during the war. "Buffalo Bill" hired out at the Alliance air base, a paratrooper training field, and the Monroes resettled here in Alliance south of the tracks. They lived, a family of seven, among five hundred relocated Sioux in World War I army tents heated by wood or kerosene stoves.

Mark quit school his freshman year. At twenty he enlisted to fight in the Korean War and was sent overseas as a first gunner. In an advance position near Ma-Jon, Thanksgiving Day 1950, enemy machine gun bullets riddled his left hand and leg. The army honorably discharged him with a Purple Heart and two clusters.

When Mark returned to Alliance, the Indian community welcomed him as a returning warrior. Sam Kills Crow Indian, a medicine man from Manderson, South Dakota, honored Mark at his homecoming with the warrior's name *Mato Yamni*, or "Three Bears." At the same time the rednecks in the local American Legion refused him bar service. Until the Civil Rights bill of 1954, Indians could not buy alcohol over the counter. They drank vanilla and lemon extract, hair oil, wood alcohol, varnish, or even antifreeze.

Mark and his brother Butch worked for a local bakery through the 1950s. As a teenager, I spent Friday nights in Bud's Pool Hall studying the art of bank shots, bragging, and hawking at murky spittoons. At midnight we teen pool sharks walked down the alley sniffing oven-fresh bread. We each carried a cube of margarine, a pocketknife, and ten cents to buy a hot loaf of bread, sold at the back screen by the baker's helper. This was how I first came to know Mark, whose boss drank himself to death. The head white baker, an exalted ruler in the Benevolent and Protective Order of Elks, bootlegged liquor to his Indian help. It was a hundred-year-old story in Alliance. In my great grandfather's time, Doc Holiday bootlegged pints of whiskey to Pine Ridge Indians inside plucked chickens. Not a lot had changed since the nineteenth century.

After ten years as an alcoholic, begging pocket change in the gutters, fighting bums in the alleys, sleeping in parked cars, and waking up in jail, Mark spent two years, off and on, drying out in a V.A. hospital. By now he could remind himself daily, "I'm an alcoholic, I've been sober for eight years. If I lay down and crawl the alleys again, then Indians will be sent back to 1941 when signs around Alliance said 'No dogs or Indians allowed.' "

In 1968 the local police denied Mark's family help after a white man assaulted his teenage daughter. No lawyer would hear the case. Only four years previously, the Civil Rights Act had declared, "No person in the United States shall, on the ground of race, color, handicap, or national origin, be excluded from participating in, be denied benefits of, or be otherwise subject to discrimination." Mark had read about civil rights. When he'd gone overseas in the war, he'd been introduced to Gandhi's ideas. So Mark incorporated a small group of Indians. Their charter stated: "We have organized an American Indian Council, a committee of nonviolence. We have no wish to violate the laws of the city or state. We have no ideas of revenge. We simply want to know our rights and what could be done when these rights are violated." For then, Mark and Emma could only try to comfort their sixteen-year-old daughter whose life had been changed by a white man.

To begin, Mark faced down three farmers on the board of a one-room country schoolhouse. A fourth grader, a German farmer's son, had called a younger Indian boy a "nigger"; for his backtalk the teacher had strapped the Indian. Mark threatened to file suit unless apologies were made and the teacher reprimanded. The school board, three Farmers in hipboots, said they'd look into the matter..

Mark then ran for city police magistrate. I worked beside him, and we became brothers, Mark sharing his warrior's name *Mato Yamni*. Those in better parts of town didn't see this as an honor. A longtime

Irish friend of the family, who bartended in the Elk's Club, turned his back New Year's Eve when I asked for a drink. Rumors were circulating of Communists in town. My long hair didn't help.

Mark's political platform went straight to the point. Since two-thirds of those jailed for drinking repeated their stays for the same reason, and ninety percent of these repeaters were Indians, the city needed an Indian magistrate. Mark reasoned that an Indian judge might try to get to the problems, rather than just jail the drunks. The treadmill *could* be halted, or at least decelerated. Some listened. The opposition pointed out that Mark had just completed high school by correspondence. Could such an Indian judge traffic violations and disorderly conduct?

As the first Indian to run for office in town, Mark received 612 votes, a good showing. He lost the election by a margin of two to one, but he opened a campaign for Indian rights. People began to talk and to take notice.

The American Indian Council moved into an abandoned barracks in South Alliance. For over seven years it sponsored an Alcoholics Anonymous program, GED test tutoring for high-school dropouts, medical screening and doctor referral, a boy scout troop, a team of Indian dancers, and a native arts club; it got a community garden going and vacant lots cleaned up; it built a softball diamond and a Lakota sun shade for powwows. These projects took shape out of much argument and discussion, as the Indian community saw their needs clarify. A red and white plaque on Mark's desk read: "Indians Scalp Their Enemies. Whites Skin Their Friends."

Mark contracted with government poverty programs for medical health care. The mean Indian lifespan was only two-thirds the national average. Such baseline diseases as tuberculosis, heart ailments, diabetes, alcoholism, and malnutrition riddled the people's lives. They weren't getting good medicine from either culture. With an income at half the poverty level and the highest unemployment in America, Indians couldn't absorb the cost of medical care, so Lakota in Alliance went without. White Alliance prided itself as a community of self-help ethics. Indians and local doctors eyed each other with mutual distrust. The government supplied vaccines, but doctors balked at treating Indians, unless they paid an office charge. Seven dollars was a good day's income for many Indians.

The Bureau of Indian Affairs hospital was located eighty miles north in Pine Ridge, South Dakota; here Indians could receive Public Health Service care. Mark thought he could set up a mobile lifeline, bussing people weekly with a blue Community Action van on loan from the Economic Opportunity Program, phased out in 1972 by Nixon. It had lumpy tires, no heat, and no health care equipment, but to the critically ill this battered old van served as a life travois.

Each week on Tuesday morning the bus left Alliance, drove north to Hemingford, northeast to Hay Springs, Gordon, and Rushville, then west to Chadron and Crawford, then north to Pine Ridge. It gathered the sick, indigent, pregnant, aged, and dying Indians of northwest Nebraska. These were roughly sixteen hundred displaced Native Americans, surviving in four cattle and farming counties, strung over two hundred and sixty miles of prairie blacktop roads that cross-hatched a grassland once roamed by buffalo, antelope, deer, and Lakota bands. Mark funded the program on a shoestring from churches and county agencies, ten dollars here, twenty there. After two years the old blue van with bloated tires and no heater presented a health hazard in itself.

The "Rumblings" column of the newspaper printed a letter in response to Anastasia Black Feather, this one under the heading "Letter on Indian Problem Answered":

Bravo Anastasia Black Feather! She must be very proud of herself to attack a fine decent man like our Chief of Police. I am sure that his job does not depend upon drunken people in "his jail." A town the size of Alliance will always have a Police force, and thank heaven for that!

How can she say an Indian in the white man's world is pitiful? I have seen and know many Indians who are not pitiful at all, and if they are, they want it that way.

If Mrs. Black Feather would like to see Indians who have established a great name for themselves, let her have a good look at the Shoshone Indians in Wyoming. They are noted for their excellent ranches and fine horses. Some of them live in beautiful homes. It is up to every healthy human being to take care of himself, except the old and disabled.

Mrs. Black Feather also says that the Indian people are not liked because they are tax burdens and lawbreakers. What does it matter if you are black, brown, white, or yellow? If you are a tax burden and lawbreaker you are not winning any popularity contests, I grant you that!

There are only two kinds of people: good and bad. Whichever group a person wants to belong to, that is up to them, but they will be treated accordingly.

Other countries and nationalities have gone through the same thing as the Indian people did, but they don't write books about it, where every page would hang their enemy.

Why doesn't Mrs. Black Feather practice some tolerance and take the white man as an individual?

Indians say that money is the warped god of white people's establishment.

It may be, but it is very necessary. Even the old Romans and Greeks used money. You just simply cannot go out to hunt your food, chew on the skin so it will be soft enough to make clothes, or chop down trees for housing. This is what all our ancestors did, but who wants to live in the past?

What else does the Indian want from the white man? Indian people can go to the finest schools for no money at all. They can obtain housing for very little money. I could name a lot of things that are just there for the asking. But who is asking?

To sum it all up: Every man, may he be black, white, brown, yellow or green for that matter, who makes a living for himself and/or his family, is a lawabiding citizen, a decent man, will be liked or respected by everyone.

This is the way society works. Yes, every society!

Melinda Kurtz
(Mrs. Elmer D.)

CHAPTER 4

Lone Wolf Coming Home

Edible Root Time (Nez Percé)

Mark's nutrition program, hot lunches at the Center for "anyone who declares a hunger," drew the town conservatives' scorn. Free meals smacked of handouts. Mark countered that the unemployed and underemployed brawled behind the local markets for morning garbage; his program fed human beings who otherwise prowled alleys for scraps. "Some of these guys have nothing," the paper quoted him. "And sometimes they can't get help at the welfare office because they have no permanent residence here even though they are permanent residents of Alliance." The table rules for "hunger" lunches: no AIM (American Indian Movement) members, no one drunk, no families where two or more adults were employed. In 1975 the program would feed 531 low-income people. An average of thirty meals a day were served, and over a thousand were taken to shut-ins. If someone showed up drunk, he ate outdoors under the shade elm.

On any given day, troops of people lined up, flocks of kids, five or six in a bunch, some accompanied by a shy adult, embarrassed but hungry. The kids would file to Mark's desk, screw up their mouths, and scrawl their names on the register, then with big smiles march over to the folding tables for hot dogs, macaroni, applesauce, two slices of bread, milk, and coffee.

The names spoke their living history: Norman Little Hoop, Hilda White Buffalo Chief, Isaac Pickitt Pin, Harold White Crane, Angie Flood, Moses Dawn, Barbara Kills Crow Indian, Ida Poor Bear, Loretta Whirlwind Horse, Inez War Bonnet. Said Wilson Crowe in a newspaper letter: "This is the issue: The confusion in our lives. We are

Indians, and we love the Indian ways. We are comfortable in the Indian ways. We do not want to lose out on being Indians."

A man in his late fifties staggered in, stewed to the gills, and scribbled "T-Bone Wilson" sideways on the register. Mark chewed him out for scaring the kids.

"What are you, T-Bone, white guy or Indi'n?" Mark challenged.

"I'm half and half."

"Which d'ya like best?"

"Neither."

T-Bone had large scabrous wounds on his hands. His grey and silver hair was greased back along the sides. Looming over Mark, he was potentially a handsome man, if he'd looked after himself; but T-Bone slept in the park, mooched booze, and clutched life desperately while destroying his body. This broken man was the half-breed of the West—rolled-over cowboy boots, denims with baggy seat, plaid shirt with snap buttons. As noted, he had been Williston's best friend. T-Bone joined the old-timers, Indian kids, mental patients on state care, other winos, and sheepish indigents who gathered up their paper plates, napkins, and milk cartons and filed down the hall, past the pop machine, to the kitchen. It was the end of another "hunger" lunch at the Center.

Mark walked over and tacked a pamphlet, "Indian and Proud," to the Center bulletin board: "If the Great spirit had desired me to be a white man, he would have made me so in the first place. He put in your heart certain wishes and plans, in my heart he put other and different desires. Each man is good in his sight. It is not necessary for eagles to be crows."

After lunch I crossed the dirt road to visit George Lone Wolf and his wife Myrtle, known as Lulu. The low-ceilinged Lone Wolf house was small, with a very old, lived-in feeling; a fix-it-up tone came from dark sheets of plywood paneling, old paintings, and curtained small windows. An oil stove, couch, TV, chairs, and fake fireplace more or less filled the front room under a black velvet wall hanging of a toreador and bull. An imposing portrait of Jesus hung to the left of the front door; a vase of plastic roses ornamented a table under the north window.

Lit by the sun streaming in the window, Felix Lone Wolf, George and Emma's blind father in his nineties, sat alone in the far bedroom. All day long he shifted from the bed to a chair, tapped his cane, talked to himself in Lakota, drummed on a wooden rattle, and smoked. A full-face photograph of Jenny Lone Wolf occupied a corner stand. She was at work in the kitchen.

I once saw a creased wallet photo of Jenny and Felix on their wedding day. Felix leaned forward dapper in a new suit and tie, felt hat tipped rakishly to the left; his spirited, alert face revealed penetrating eyes, decisive laugh lines, and thin lips with teeth partly showing through. Jenny, a dreamy country girl, sat demurely in a dark dress and wool coat; she had thick straight hair parted on the left, wide-set eyes, a long broad nose and pursed lips. On their sixty-first wedding anniversary a purblind, crippled Felix and a diabetic, arthritic Jenny celebrated with forty-two grandchildren and sixty-seven great-grandchildren. The Lakota word is *tiospaye* or family clan.

The photo on the stand showed Jenny or "Granny" quietly concentrated in her age, with a forehead hazel-creased, wispy grey hair, marked eyebrows arched over mahogany, moon-rich eyes that were deep-set, wide, and whorled with time.

And then she shuffled through the kitchen doorway to greet me. Her face glowed with kindness; her eyes were ablaze and translucent at the center, as though many years had opened infinite depth in the core of her vision. She was this town's medicine woman, advisor, gadfly, and communal mother. Her rounded chin and strong neck bore the cares of her tribal family.

"*Wakan, wakan,*" Jenny whispered over my gift of pink Black Hills quartz; the corners of the room seemed hushed to hear her speak. Her large-boned hands lapped over one another like silted pools of flesh and seemed to comfort an old wooden cane.

"Ah'm gonna pray for you," Jenny told me, almost talking to herself alone in the room. It was as though she let me overhear her prayer. "*Wakan,*" she whispered again, then closed her eyes, stroking the quartz in thanks. "You mus' go see *wicasa wakan . . . wicasa wakan.*" Her lower jaw moved wordlessly for a moment. "Talk to him, follow through your vision." She nodded her head with conviction. "Do ever'thing to act on yore dream. You mus' go . . . "

I knew then that the good red road had chosen me, not the reverse. Jenny had adopted strays all her life; her *tiospaye*, through Mark, had adopted me, no more Indian than any other mongrel immigrant. And now she was telling me to find a *wicasa wakan*, literally a "man holy," such as her distant cousin Black Elk or the recently buried Joe Chips. "You *mus'* go," she said. I had come home with many questions and she offered directions. She turned back to her work in the kitchen.

George and Lulu faced me side by side in old-fashioned parlor chairs like royalty. Lulu wore pin curlers and glasses, and her firm lower jaw had one tooth missing. Her voice rattled like moist gravel rolling through a barrel. George sat in a T-shirt with one sleeve rolled over a cigarette pack. He wore jeans and white socks and had a gold earring in his left ear. He, too, had glasses and was crippled by arthritis; the tips of two fingers on his left hand were gone.

George liked to joke, while Lulu rolled her words thoughtfully. They had been peyote Christians—members of the Native American Church—and both their voices sounded gravelly. George's interjections quivered up and down the scale, Lulu's stories seemed to echo from way down inside.

The Lone Wolfs had moved to Los Angeles twenty-two years ago, then back home this past year to be with family and to care for their parents. Lulu didn't want to buck the pace of LA, the congestion, the distance from Sioux land and people any more. But the reservation had become a troubled home, with too many conflicts, too much violence, and no opportunities. She was looking for someplace where Indians could be with other Indians—living both worlds free of stereotypes. At least she wanted a chance to make the best of both worlds, not to suffer the worst of each.

"Is there any place in the country," I asked, "where you could balance the Indian and white worlds?"

George shook his head. "Not this town, because of the prejudice . . . and the damn weather."

"Even so," Lulu added, "I'd say no matter where you lived, if there was a group of Indians there, you could have it. That way you could still live like the whites, but maintain your own culture."

"In other words, you're livin' half-an'-half," George tossed in.

"It's hard because . . . like with me," Lulu explained, "I'm trying to live like the whites and have the conveniences, you know, but still I'd like to keep what is actually, what *had* been mine. If I felt the need of a medicine man, I could bring him to my home, without any p'lice comin' around want'n to know if you're having a party or whatever."

"Some places you go through a lot of red tape . . . " George spliced in.

"Yeah, and ownin' your own home. Everybody says, 'Oh, you live in South Alliance.' It's a slum to them, but to me I like it because there's Indians around me."

George said quietly, "I think people can . . . get along with the white people . . . "

"Yeah, you could, 'cause we did it, for a long time. Like when we went to California." Lulu stared directly at me and rolled her lower jaw. How many hundreds of years of misunderstanding were summed up in the roll of her jaw, I wondered.

George agreed. "There's a hell of a lot of good people that I met in LA . . . "

"I walked up to a LA diner window," Lulu continued, "and applied for a job and the boss said, 'Alright, you start tonight.' I'm gonna work in the kitchen, I expected, have nothing to do with the public. I'd jus' better go back and tell him I'm Indian, so I called the manager back, 'Do you object to an Indian working for you?' And he said, 'No, should I?' And I said, 'Well, I just want you to know that I'm Sioux, that's all.'

"So I go to work and it's just him and me, and I'm back there mixing dough, and I seen a guy walk up to the window. I'm getting nervous because the guy just keeps looking. So finally I told the boss, 'You got a customer out there.' 'What do you mean *I* got a customer,' he said, 'what do you think I hired you for? Go find out what he wants.' And my knees were shaking so bad because the first thing that pops into my head—he knows that I'm Indian.

"And he asked, I'll never forget it, for an orange donut and a cup of black coffee. So I went and got them. He gave me the money, whatever, sixteen cents, but I was shaking so bad I spilt his coffee, I dropped his donut, and he said to my boss, 'Now Art, there's going to be the best help you ever had.' I put the money in the cash register, and I took my apron off. 'That's it. I'm finished. I'm goin' home.' And I did. I went home." Lulu's face was a wall of stone.

"But Art called me back, 'I don't know what it is with you, but you're going to get out there and wait on them people, because they're exactly like you.' But I had that Indian chip on my shoulder. I was there to pounce on anybody that even used the word Indian in any way, shape or form." She accented these words by shaking her head side-to-side.

"We lived twenty-two years in LA," Lulu said, shaking her head some more. "It took me a long time to get over feelin' Indian in a bad way, y' know? When I came back here, then I got to go the opposite way, be a dirty Indian again."

George groaned, "Aawwgh," and shook his head.

"I try to get that across to the Catholic priest, Father John, here one day. An' he told me, 'That's all in your head, Lulu. People aren't like that. I took Grandma Jenny and Grandma Mini and Grandma Pickitt Pin,' he said, 'all to church, and nothing was said.' So I said, 'For the simple reason that *you* took 'em there.'

"But if they hadda walked in there on their own an' sat down—the whites making some little gesture of moving away or pulling a shoulder or something—that uneasiness is there. An' I said to Father John, 'You don't feel it because you're not Indian.' Just little things, like you walk into a store and you sense that a person hated to wait on you, or they were watching to see if you were going to steal something, you know. Makes you *think* about stealin' somethin'."

People were coming in and going out of the house, children arriving home from school. A man worked outside on an old car. A tall Lakota in a blue nylon shirt, brown dress pants, tooled boots, and felt western hat walked back to visit Felix. His face glowed amber in the late sunlight. They smoked and talked Lakota and listened to the quiet; it was a distant chorus to our conversation in the front room.

"Well, the hard thing," I offered, "is that people like yourselves don't want to go back to the reservation. Things are too rough up there, and yet the cities are places *no*body wants to live. And a little town like this is still racist, even if things have gotten better over the years."

Lulu thought on this. "I'd love Alliance, as far as the town was concerned, *if* we had a place to go and do our own Indian thing. I've had a lot of people come to me and say, 'Well, I wish we had a place where we could start a sewing club.' Make quilts, or whatever, and sell them. Or make two of one kind, keep one for yourself and sell one, you know. If they felt like white dancing, fine, because the younger generation does, and still you have your older folks that likes the Indian doings."

"Well, a long time ago," George put in, "they used to have the white dance an' the Indian dance. They'd go half-an'-half."

"Just a place to gather and cut the monotony of day-to-day living."

"The box social, I used to like that," George reminisced, "because whoever takes a box, well you buy that, an' you have to eat it with them. When they had a ribbon dance going, goddarn, sometimes you couldn't even get a car started, but we used to ride horses, you know, or a board wagon. Put a bunch of hay in there and, hell, maybe fifteen people in the wagon."

Lulu butted back in, "Because even the birthdays we've attended, they cook the white man's food, fried chicken, potato salad, whatever. But then there's always that little piece 'a Indian, fried bread, *wojape* pudding, soup made 'a kidney linings. It's still there, so you're still mixing it together because it makes you feel good. It's just that one certain little something that lets you know still who you are and what you are and you still have it." Lulu had found her essential point. She rested her shoulders back in the armchair.

I thought of all the kids. "When you talk about teaching your children the Indian ways, what kinds of things are important to pass on?"

"Religion, above all, medicines, and . . . " Lulu paused, "—their own pride in what they are and who they are." George looked at his wife and listened. "The cooking and stuff, you know, comes later. Like even my boy, I've taught him baking potter bread. He's married to a white girl and, well, just the other day she called me up. She bought something for him, a cigarette lighter, and somebody liked it, and he gave it away. And she was mad at my boy for it, but I told her, 'You just don't understand our ways. We came into this world without anything and that's the way we're going to go out.' "

"Goddarn Indians don't value nothin'," George snorted and shook his head.

"We don't put a dollar sign on what we have or own. And if somebody likes it and is gonna enjoy it same as you did, fine—give it to him because it'll always come to you again."

"When you say religion," I pressed, "does that mean the songs and prayers and some of the old ways?" A long pause set in. Across the road a power lawn mower droned. I tried another tack. "How about naming? Anybody go through those old naming rites, where you go out and fast and chant, and try to find a name?"

"There's a lot that's lost now." Lulu's voice hushed. "There's groups of the younger generation that's wantin' to learn more about way back when . . . "

"You'd have to go powerful hard to find that," George insisted.

"How about Indian names themselves, in Lakota?" I adjusted the question, and Lulu broke in.

"Oh yeah, if you're gonna name somebody, you still have your doings, and your giveaway, and naming that person. If it happens to be someone else's name, then they get the permission to pass on the name. I went to one in the sandhills, and I mean it was the traditional, where you got up and went in a line, and they gave you a spoon of *wasna* and a drink of the chokecherry juice. It was beautiful. It made you feel good. But people forget . . . "

"Are there any books that help keep the old ways alive?"

"Well, there's Black Elk's two books, an' if you really want to learn something about now, read Lame Deer. He told it like it was, even up to his picking spuds and fighting with himself, trying to find out what he was to be, you know, his own conflict within himself."

"It seems that Indian religion now mixes Christianity with traditional things," I suggested. Lulu nodded.

"Even priests in St. Francis, where they were so dead-set against the peyote and the *yuwipi*, are learning about it. I've noticed in the Catholic church there's a lot of changes. It's none of that something-you-learn-from-years-down-and-just-keep-with-you. I think Dad and Mom are still the only ones who go by the Indian prayers that they were taught young." Felix now sat alone in his back room tapping a wooden rattle. He seemed of another age altogether, born in the nineteenth century and still dreaming the old ways.

George added, "He'd sit there and he'd pray Indian, just like a preacher. He's been at it for years and years."

"Emma wanted to come down here and record him, on Fridays when he's taking Holy Communion," Lulu went on. "She didn't realize that Dad, old as he is, would still remember them Lakota prayers that good. He'd just go through the whole Mass. So I told him about Emma's plan, an' he said, 'What the hell does she want to tape me for? Why doesn't she just go say her own prayers?' "

The phone rang and Lulu excused herself. George ran out of cigarettes and wanted a ride "up town," so we broke our talk for the day.

Outside, the sky hung misty grey with an expectancy of spring, the land anticipating new greens, a returning sun, leaf buds and tender grasses and breezes—all frustrated by a malingering, stubborn freeze. *The Farmers' Almanac* predicted the worst cold in a hundred years.

"It's been a hard winter," George said. "Thirty-two below zero on New Year's Eve, and it stayed right around ten or fifteen through the winter. Snowed the day after Thanksgiving and didn't thaw until Easter."

I dropped George off downtown and drove west at twilight, as the sun dipped under a rim of banked clouds flushing golden and bronze, and then melted into the plated horizon.

The wild geese came flying by night, low in the moonless, starry sky. Circling, they were attracted by the town lights; they honked to each other, dense white vectors forming wedges in the night. All migrated in a common direction, the rest of the arrow scattering around its leader. Orion was starshooting into the western horizon, as the Great Bear spilled liquid darkness over my sleeping home. The Spiritway trailed ancestral voices across a dense night sky.

CHAPTER 5

City Council

Moon When the Geese Return in Scattered Formations (Lakota)

Mark's temper was up with early spring. Since midwinter the city fathers had delayed roofing the Indian Center. They refused to support Mark's programs because the "law," their attorney argued, excluded funds for nonprofit organizations. The council covertly funded a Senior Citizens' Center. Mark threatened a class-action lawsuit. Pecking order in this town from the bottom up—Indians, indigents, old folks, kids.

Mark and I decided to visit a council meeting to press for a new roof. City Hall, a clay stone shoebox trimmed with Old Glory, hunkered across the street from the Carnegie Public Library. The council presided in the upstairs chambers. Photographs of city mayors groomed like respectable coroners—dark suit, darker tie, white shirt—stared intently from the walls, blurring into the past, the smalltown moguls of Middle America. Mark and I found seats near the back.

Mark's brother-in-law, Conrad Dacoteaux, sat along the north wall with six other Indian militants, all jealous of Mark's position in South Alliance. Conrad, an ex-Golden Gloves prize fighter, was feuding with Mark over their in-laws. "He hates my guts," Mark said. Conrad had worked for my father at the bean elevator, loading hundred-pound gunny sacks. I saw him once grip a twenty-pound sledge hammer at arm's length, tilt it back slowly, and touch his nose.

The city fathers trailed in, slapping frostbitten hands and stomping snow from their shoes, laughing about spring in Nebraska.

"And, whaddaya know, here's Mark!"

"Wants to buy the Indian Center from the city and roof it himself!"

"Road apples for shingles?"

"Who's that longhair with him?"

"Link's boy?"

"My Gawd, who'd think . . . "

Ike Leaguer, the town conservative, liked to champion the under-
dog, but . . . "Well, hell, Indian housing is going too far." This Great
Plains isolationist had been a slick man on skates, I remembered from
grade school nights at the roller rink. Ike with his policeman's whistle
benching the speed skaters. Ike waltzing on wooden wheels to recorded organ music, sliding backwards with crusty nonchalance. One
"ag'iner" roosted in every small town.

"Indian housing, d'ya say?" razzed the new plant manager from
Omaha. "Who owns that boarded up place at 101 Sweetwater?" He
winked, dusting his green and rust plaid sportcoat. "How about that
joint for some *low*-income housing?" The council grinned in unison.
The town brothel was closed two winters ago in a police raid. The city
fathers were said to look the other way at whiskey in teacups, Indian
whores who were high-school dropouts, and a black pimp at 101
Sweetwater. Locals condoned this moonlight dalliance until a get-
tough police chief came to town. The Old West hadn't aged much in
Alliance.

But housing was no joke to Indians. Today the railroad had phoned
Mark's seventy-five-year-old father, Bill, and served him notice: vacate
in thirty days. Strip-mine coal ignited a boom with the Burlington
Railroad, and another section of Indian Town had just been sold for a
switchyard. Old "Buffalo Bill" said he'd pitch a tent in the street
before he'd leave his home in South Alliance.

Kurt Podinsky, junior real estate partner, looked for the ringer in
Mark's proposed new roof. "What's the difference, Mark," he snapped,
owl-eyed in horn-rimmed glasses, "between *giving* you the building
to roof or renting it to you for a dollar a year?"

"A landlord who won't fix the roof," I muttered.

Dr. Gene Bowie, our family optometrist, hung back, trying to sort
out this mare's nest. "What do *they* want?" he asked me one day in
his office. A concerned man, Seventh Day Adventist, a liberal when
pressed, he'd *like* to help, but . . . "where do we start?" I suggested
a new roof.

"But will that help much?"

"It's a start."

The renewal of Mark's lease and new roof trailed on an endless
agenda. The mayor had a habit of commending citizens and making

speeches, so everyone settled in for the evening. Well-meaning, but hardly progressive, Mayor Lou was most concerned with golfers' rights tonight. A congenial man on and off the links, Lou had hired me as a boy to caddy for him. I felt again as though things hadn't changed much.

The council voted three to two for raising the golf course rates. Mayor Lou voted no, thinking the old rates already too high, and Councilman Ike voted no, thinking the new rates too low. The meeting droned on: a new parking lot, a statement of appreciation to the city snow removal crews, renovation of the tennis courts, a covering for the old swimming pool, bookmobile parking stalls, the zoning commission report, and community TV.

City Manager Rube Koznick took notes and kept his mouth shut, holding his own. New at the job, no-nonsense, a young man under zookeeper's pressures in a community of mixed persuasions: "I just keep the town in lights and water," he confided to me, "and when it snows, we shovel." Rube was a scratch golfer.

City Attorney Karl Fark sat and smiled. A very large man and a joking, noncommittal lawyer, guarded in his humor, he was light-years distant from Indian problems. "No problems here in Alliance—we *all* get along." Karl liked good scotch, the country club, prime rib, and the right friends.

Finally the Indian business. Mark and I still sat in the back of the chambers. The mayor stalled—he wanted more time to consider the proposed roof. Conrad stood up, mustering his AIM supporters, denounced Mark as a "self-serving Apple" and demanded that the council give *him* the Indian Center. "Mark Monroe doesn't speak for Indians in Alliance," he challenged. "*We* do—the Lakota Federation. And we want that building, goddamn it. The Indian people want Monroe *out* of there, *now!*" Conrad stomped out shouting expletives, and his protestors filed out with menacing looks. Attorney Fark blew cigar smoke at the ceiling.

Dr. Bowie moved (to clear the air) that the council put the Indian Center up for bid, then Mark could buy it at a fair market price. Nobody seconded the motion. The doctor said he would have voted against his motion anyway. Stymied again.

The realtor thought a dollar a year rent and a new roof smacked of creeping Communism. "Ya can't *give* away houses in this country!" No matter that the military barracks had been condemned and Mark had saved the city dismantling costs, unnested freeloading birds, and renovated the structure.

"I think we could tie this down by the next meeting, Mark," Mayor Lou said, deferring the issue. "You should check with the county commissioners, though. They're the ones to help you. Our hands are tied." Flushed face, apologetic smile, a politician's sidestep.

The Center had been promised action since the winter snows began. Now it was approaching spring. Conservatives and liberals alike remained politically ginger. They feared ramifications: Red Power, AIM, "hostiles" on the warpath.

In 1973 two sons of a wealthy rancher were tried in Alliance for the murder of Raymond Yellow Thunder, an off-reservation Lakota. The old man was kidnapped on a Saturday night spree, shoved pantless into an American Legion dance, then found dead from skull contusions in a locked car trunk. Local justice set about excusing the "boys," and AIM marched on Alliance with five hundred armed demonstrators. The militants demanded retribution and terrorized the city with an armed show of force, patrolling the streets in out-of-state cars. Our family minister, settled nicely in his parish, was forced at gunpoint to "give" twenty dollars to the cause.

At the other end of town Mark watched a medicine man cut thirty-six small pieces of flesh from an AIM leader praying for Yellow Thunder. It was a Lakota blood sacrifice related to "piercing" the flesh in a Sun Dance. Yet allegiances remained tangled: when the demonstrators began fighting among themselves, breaking doors, firing guns, and then flying the Indian Center's American flag upside down, Mark ordered them point-blank, "Take your men and get the hell out of my Center." Next day they commandeered City Hall. The city council couldn't forget.

Yellow Thunder's murderers were sentenced for second-degree manslaughter, the first such conviction in these parts. After two and a half years in prison, they would be paroled this spring. Only a few years before, a white migrant harvester had raped and killed an Indian woman and left her body toothmarked beside the road. He was driven to the stateline and told simply to "get out" of South Dakota.

Moon of the Wild Geese (Mandan)

The city council came to inspect the Indian Center roof: muddy dirt road, dripping eaves, no sidewalk, no gutter over the door, peeling tarpaper, a 1942 war barracks a hundred by twenty feet. The Bureau of Indian Affairs, I recalled, began under the 1824 Department of War.

Ants were crawling up through cracks in the concrete floor. "Don't step on your relatives," Mark joked with Emma as she scrunched a couple.

Respect, Mark and I agreed, was what we looked for.

The councilmen scraped their overshoes and paced deferentially through the barracks. "I strained my neck looking up," Mayor Lou said, surveying the exposed two-by-four beams. "Now I'd better look down for a while." He seemed embarrassed by the poor quarters.

"I wouldn't house my dog in one of these places," the real estate councilman said under his breath. South Alliance, south of the tracks, south of respectability, the old American story. The city fathers checked their wristwatches, mumbled apologies about getting back to work, thanked Mark for his courtesy, and departed. They'd see about the new roof, maybe this summer.

Standing to the side, Mark told me that Harold White Horse just sold his Pine Ridge land and moved in across the road. "Why not fix up your place, Harold, now you've got some money?" Mark had suggested. "Put a toilet in your house—"

"I'm an Indian," Harold rasped. "I don't shit in my house."

Harold bought a pickup, a new car, and two ponies.

CHAPTER 6

Wounded Knee

Moon of the Red Grass Appearing (Lakota)

On to North Dakota. Rachel and I drove toward Wounded Knee and stopped over the state line at the Crazy Horse memorial. No other cars were in sight. Kids trudged along the asphalt roads. The landscape lay bled of color.

Fog, drizzle, poor visibility—snow had drifted into the road cuts of an unmarked detour. Straw and amber grass lay leached under a sky without horizon. The blacktop road was scrawled into the grasslands.

Pine Ridge Reservation, Teton Sioux, "People of the Prairie." The sandhills were blurred through the car's pitted windshield. Junkers, bullet-pocked road signs, barbed wire, broken green glass, Indians walked Highway 18 toward Wounded Knee—the white clapboard chapel, foursquare belfry, red brick pedestals before the cemetery, a granite tombstone in memory of massacred Lakota. Survivors would not soon forget this execution of American prisoners of war: "HORN CLOUD, the peacemaker, died here innocent. COURAGE BEAR. CRAZY BEAR." Grey planks bordered the mass grave under a bannerless flagpole. A wooden cross tilted into a distant wire fence, stark white against the straw hills.

The church was gutted by fire last year, after the AIM takeover. The trader's market and museum were burned down. A corrugated steel roof warped flat against the frozen winter ground. Only the graveyard with its brick entrance pillars stood there on the hill behind church foundations where on December 29, 1890, cavalry Hotchkiss cannons fired two-pound exploding shells on surrendering Indian captives. The word "Battle" was smudged from a highway historical marker. Over it flared a spray-painted red "Massacre."

A mass grave for a hundred and fifty Lakota held vigil over the charred remains of the church. It emanated uneasy quiet. Indians said the place was haunted by murdered victims of American history. As a young man, Black Elk witnessed the 1890 massacre, an end to the Indian wars, and wept at his people's loss. John Neihardt wrote the story:

> And so it was all over.
>
> I did not know how much was ended. When I look back now from this high hill of my old age, I can still see the butchered women and children lying heaped and scattered all along the crooked gulch as plain as when I saw them with eyes still young. And I can see that something else died there in the bloody mud, and was buried in the blizzard. A people's dream died there. It was a beautiful dream.
>
> And I, to whom so great a vision was given to my youth—you see me now a pitiful old man who has done nothing, for the nation's hoop is broken and scattered. There is no center any longer, and the sacred tree is dead.

We drove on from Wounded Knee to the east, troubled, thinking to approach Batesland. Fog hung thick, visibility was almost zero. I feared the car was headed the wrong way toward Scenic, so we turned around, going back to the intersection. I stopped and asked a Sioux woman alongside the road for directions.

"Go back to Wounded Knee." She motioned west. I wanted to keep moving, not turn back. "That road ahead is pretty bad," she warned. Then she got in a battered Oldsmobile that drove east.

I followed, suspicious of her advice. About four miles in, where the map showed Batesland, the drifts crossed the dirt road, now bottomed with mud; ruts were a foot deep and worse in a slough of gumbo mud and melted snow. We made the first two all right, sliding and spinning a bit but continuing to move. As we drove on and on, mile after mile, the road got even worse. The featureless land seemed to question why anyone was there to journey into its agony. No sense to it. No animals or people or machines or houses in sight. The fence lines were shrouded charcoal fissures in snow drifts under a winter-dull sky.

"Can we go back to Alliance, Daddy?" Rachel whimpered.

The car slipped deeper into the winter-stunned land, descending two swales that stretched on like alluvial sky fans. We couldn't turn back. We careened through mud sloughs and bounced off snowdrifts.

Rachel grew more frightened. "Daddy, I don't like this. Let's go back to Grandma's."

I reassured her it was just like a sled ride and silently questioned what to do if we got stuck. No farms, no traffic. I would have to walk for help, with Rachel on my back. But where to? How far could we slog through the mud before nightfall? There had been forty-six unaccounted homicides at Pine Ridge since November.

Fifteen miles in, we came to a split in the road and a misplaced looking stop sign. I guessed at the map, started to go left, saw the impassable rise ahead, backed up, and went right. What was the right way out? We could be here for days, forever. The road narrowed and got still worse! Mud splattered and covered the windshield. I felt the road ruts, rather than saw them. Once the car spun to a full stop, wheels churning, no traction, hub-deep in the mud slough, sunk; then slowly, deliberately, it edged on out of the mess.

The car topped a hill. A plane sheared off-white parabolas into the snowbanks. It could be an improved road, firm ground, a way out. I stopped the car on the hill, got out, shook myself loose, and thanked *Wakan Tanka*, the "Great Spirit." We only had to negotiate a long hill. It wasn't easy, even downhill.

A small church came into view with three cars parked nearby. Blacktop! an improved, plowed road. A young Indian with long braids walked along the drifts. He wore denim and a white choker.

"Could you tell me where I am?"

"Wounded Knee."

"What do you mean? We started from Wounded Knee hours ago!" The young man looked blankly at me. I swallowed my disbelief.

"How do I get to Batesland?"

"Go back to Highway 18, the way you came in."

The young Lakota was curtly polite, yet distant as was this land arrested from spring. We had driven twenty-five miles of impassable country roads in a circle and come back to Wounded Knee, beginning in Porcupine, going east eight miles, south about ten, back west about seven. The detour made me shed a lifetime of Middle American ease. But I did *see* Wounded Knee country—in the fear of being lost out there. It was only a passing whisper of Big Foot's tragedy, murdered and frozen as he sought peace, but the fear would alert and stay with me. It was a lesson that could not be learned in the library.

Car mud-spattered. Engine caked. Lights dimmed out with dirt. The sky grew dark early.

Lunch in Martin, South Dakota. Sullen waitress, tasteless food, irritable customers. The day was just not sitting right.

Keep movin'.

Weather was the news on all the radio stations.

II

Spring Tribe

Artists are the Indians of the white world. They are called drea-
mers who live in the clouds, improvident people who can't hold
onto their money, people who don't want to face "reality." . . . We
aren't divided up into separate, neat little families—Pa, Ma, kids,
and to hell with everybody else. The whole damn tribe is one big
family; that's our kind of reality.

RICHARD ERDOES AND JOHN (FIRE) LAME DEER,
Lame Deer Seeker of Visions, 1972

Sunflower Figure—*Oscar Howe*

BACKROADS

Some days it doesn't rhyme,
doesn't even scan,
and the verse is much worse than free,
dumber than a hundred bars
of statuary—

Straight on, like driving
from Elko to Green River
one salt-flat night
a hundred years ago
when the river darkened to my right
and blinding walls of rock
slammed the other side
of a black-and-white highway.

On that all-night-long drive home
I thought we'd never see the light again.

And then
the highway ended
in a line across the land
and the sky descended
stony
on a Wyoming morning
as the river
churned green
and we kept on driving
into the nacreous
day
through a barren, unfenced, windmill
dawn.

CHAPTER 7

Jamestown

Moon in Which the Geese Lay Eggs (Lakota)

Rachel and I headed for Jamestown another four hundred miles north. We drove the old Volvo into North Dakota under tintype skies, tailed by our third blizzard in two weeks. I felt like a jackrabbit loping into a skeet shoot, and I was worried about my students arriving safely. They were, after all, California drivers, not exactly snowbirds. Dwarfed by a denuded winter prairie, I sucked in the cold wind and held Rachel by her armpits and knees, legs apart, red snowpants down to her ankles. She peed beside the car.

"This is it, kid. No gas station for miles around. If you've got to go, *go*." I stared at the puddling ocher on the frozen hardpan and held new respect for my scuffed harness boots.

The Jamestown American Legion stood guard across from a deserted train depot. Its brass and copper eagle in storefront relief was hammered flat as a highway sailcat. All his life my father had haunted such patriotic watering holes to shoot pool, play the punchboard for fishing gear, and lubricate his way home.

Opposite the state mental hospital towered sixty tons of cement bison, advertised by the Chamber of Commerce as "the world's largest buffalo." America's all but extinct totems materialized in Jamestown effigy—buffalo and golden eagle—and here we were to powwow with real Indians. The Plains Indian appeared in silhouette on state highway markers. Each spring, college students climbed the concrete Jamestown buffalo and painted its balls red. It was a far cry from Jamestown, Virginia in 1607 and my mother's ancestors. At least she would think so.

Logan and Jay had already arrived in Jamestown. They discovered in the Arizona desert that Jay's van was without heat, so they alternately drove, slept by the road, froze and hightailed it across the country for six days running.

"Logan spun a cocoon in his sleeping bag," Jay said, "just like a giant caterpillar. Man, the road ice *chewed* off our snow chains!" He thumped the tires. And now, wind blowing forty-five miles an hour, temperature fifteen above zero, we huddled together under new falling snow.

"Holy Moses, I never thought we'd make it!" Jay rubbed his ears muffed under a crimson stocking cap. "Logan drives like granny going to market eggs."

"We didn't crack any, did we?"

I remembered Logan, small and shy with dilated hazel eyes behind thick glasses, sketching a snow-blue King Lear in my freshman English class. His inquisitive intelligence hovered somewhere to the left of center; diseased retinas in childhood left him with miserable vision and the threat of early blindness. Logan made good use of his liabilities, though, as he seemed to catch sight of things from tilted angles. Now, six years later, he traveled with a first-aid kit, artist's tools, tape recorder, duffel bag of books, backpack, tube tent, and a wadded bedroll. A young man preparing for a life's journey, he was of middle stature and sported curly black hair and the alertness of a wild rabbit. He had a tic of wrinkling his nose over human oddities, which seemed to gather like iron filings to a magnet.

Jay vied for leadership. He was accustomed to taking control, and when threatened, he gripped down hard on things. From secularized Jewish stock, Jay had grown up a native of Los Angeles. Poised and quick in his motions, on occasion overly quick, he moved into situations with a strong sense of himself, often impatiently. Jay pressed for answers. He had an appetite for knowing; he was an explorer who put ideas into action. He talked convincingly, while underneath he seemed to search for his own spiritual focus. Handsome and deft, like a new pickaxe at the hardware store, he appeared more confident than the others, but was in need of their tempering. Among the "best and brightest" of a young America, Jay had some things to learn. I felt that he shadowed my waffling leadership, a younger if not flattering parody, and I admired his hunger to push down on things and to understand.

Jamestown College overlooked the river valley on a hill to the east. Its students greeted our troop hospitably. Locals with flaxen hair and powder-blue eyes milled around the California newcomers. They seemed genuinely curious of strangers heralding a long winter's end.

"You actually plough with a tractor in the summer?" Jay asked one sloe-eyed coed.

"What else is there to do in North Dakota?" she replied, ringlets bobbing, the farmer's daughter with a vixen twist. "Dad's getting me a Farmall cab with a stereo tape deck for my birthday."

"What do you do around here for fun?" Jay inquired.

"Toss buffalo chips on Fourth of July." She winked. "But that's only once a year." Jay wasn't sure whether she was putting him on. This wasn't exactly the beach crowd "hanging ten."

Presbyterian with liberal arts, a large nursing school, and a formidable track team—Jamestown College posed no giant step into higher education for those coming from North Dakota high schools. "The dean comes around early Sunday morning to count empties in the trash bins," Jay's flaxen friend swore. "The college thinks there's a campus drinking problem."

Our apartment suite—two plasterboard rooms and a kitchenette— was boxed into the corner of an empty dormitory. In Los Angeles I had replaced the backseat of my car with several hundred Indian books and topped them with Rachel's mattress; the books now fit into warm pine shelves lining the south wall. Our apartment windows faced east to a distant elm shelterbelt, where the spring sun would wake us earlier each morning. Jamestown was the hub of our wheel of travel in North Dakota.

Moon When the Youngest Wife Cracks Buffalo Bones for the Marrow (Lakota)

Storm-battered and road-weary, Meghan and Kate straggled in from Montana. They had trekked two thousand miles, enduring Kate's emergency appendectomy, car trouble, three blizzards, and a tight budget. The girls crawled out of a small blue VW stiff and spacey, but game for the Great Plains. They had ridden six days among duffel bags and books, laughing and bumping down potholed roads to the tunes of western radio stations and the Grateful Dead on tape.

Kate had been fasting since leaving LA, so she didn't mind the motoring hibernation—she was just a little frozen in the joints, that's all, and in awe of the Montana elements. California winter rains had given her no preparation for a return to the Ice Age. Eyes sparkling, her face lambent from the fast, Kate spoke in a high, almost childlike voice about putting on chains during a ground blizzard.

"This weather would turn a woman into a real man, eh boys?" She squinted at Logan and Jay.

Kate was a dishwater blond with a snappy kind of plainness—her complexion was fair but weathered. She had sharp eyebrow lines and hazelnut eyes. Talkative, fetching, with a sharp tongue and full-throated laugh, Kate decided to make the trip from California when she dreamed of carrying moccasins down a country road, first alone on a spring afternoon, then with other travelers. Her visions were salted with experience.

"I come from a long line of ballbusters," she snorted, thumb in her belt loop. She was a gutsy woman—earth in her voice and a bristling temper. Her upper lip curled slightly when she smiled, a challenge to all Marlboro men. "Watch out, mister." Jay raised an eyebrow, but said nothing. He wasn't that testy, not yet.

Kate liked to canvass auctions and horse shows, sketching cowboy hats, jawing with the locals, and sizing up horseflesh. Within her roughhewn hide flowed a marrow sweetness, a child's delight in being alive, a foster daughter's fear of being hurt.

Meghan was tall and had cascades of rich brown hair. She seemed graced with the form of a young antelope. Girlish and womanly at once, with searching chestnut eyes, Meghan followed her natural instincts. She was often a quiet presence who covered her angers and spoke through small gestures. She seemed a confused child of Los Angeles who sought a tribal family and a deeper identity of her own. A young woman with winter's resolve and spring's desires, Meghan grew into my daughter's confidante—coloring pictures, telling stories, exploring the woods. They laughed and chirped through late afternoons of winter half-light. Meghan was searching in both spiritual and worldly terms for her own adult self-image.

"Hey, old man, can ya spare a dime?" Kate called over a snowbank, as she moved gingerly with the stitches in her side.

"Well, we're all here," Meghan said as she clomped over the drifted snow in new hiking boots and eyed the redbrick dormitory. "What's for dinner, Doc?"

Inside the pre-fab dorm Kate staked her claim to the kitchen and catered a Navajo taco feast—puffy deepfat crusts wrapped around ground beef, onions, corn, cheese, tomatoes, and lettuce.

"Vittles! Chow time! Come an' get it!" ricocheted down the hall from the kitchenette. It was the beginning of our tribe. Food was no small matter.

During this band's gathering I mulled over the Hopi prophesies—
the whirling logs and gourd of ashes. As Thomas Banyacya had warned,
"Mebbe it all come crashes." What kind of medicine would we find, if
any?

CHAPTER 8

Thaw

Moon of the Breaking of Snowshoes (Ojibwa)

Mud-caked snow, locally dubbed "snirt," lay humped and wind-swept by fallow winter fields. Chuckholes a foot deep were flooded with runoff slush. The natural agonies of freezing and thawing put tremendous stresses on the land; the trees, the rocks, even the sky itself bore the weathered stretch marks of life coming and going. The people's faces, like eroded gullies, were creased with grains of age, the scored memories of countless births and deaths and seasons.

Jay and I drove to the National Indian Basketball Tournament in Bismarck, a town of grain silos cemented into the high, windy plains. With a nineteenth-century German leader's name, also the name for my favorite breakfast roll, Bismarck was the capitol of North Dakota. Its state bird, a character joked in Welch's *Winter in the Blood*, was the housefly.

Indian people in the audience seemed relaxed, friendly, some on parade in narrow-toed, shiny boots and ribboned western shirts and felt cowboy hats. Stylish in tribal dress, the women carried themselves with grace and strength. The older people sat with dignity at the centers of families. Rachel bobbed up and down the bleacher seats, making friends, as Jay and I sat quietly watching the game. We were the only whites in the auditorium.

"I'm a little nervous, Doc. This is the first time I've been a white minority," Jay whispered, looking down at his hands, "and basketball's always been my game."

"It's a long way from UCLA and the Bruin dynasty, for sure." I recalled the NCAA banners and beach complexions at Pauley Pavilion. "Maybe we'll see the game another way."

"It makes me feel like I have to watch myself," Jay said and shifted his weight on the plank bench. "Indians must feel that way all the time in white crowds."

It was hard to know how Indians felt in the white world, but UCLA was no center of Red Power, and the NCAA banners didn't quite stretch to Bismarck, North Dakota. The players here fought it out in a sandlot style of basketball—run, shoot, and the hotshot bagged the most points.

"These guys oughta learn to pass off," Jay said under his breath into a box of popcorn. A lantern-jawed Sioux in a western sportscoat turned around and nodded agreement. Helena, Montana lost the championship game for just that reason. The best shooter was a one-man show, fed by his teammates. They stopped giving him the ball in the second half, and the team stopped scoring.

"The other four seemed to agree on losing," Jay complained as we drove home under a spitting night sky. "How could they do that? Lose on purpose?"

"They were losing the other way, too," I guessed. "It wasn't a team, just Number One grabbing baskets." We drove back to Jamestown through a cold fog.

For the fourth time in three weeks, it snowed again, all through the night. The dormitory windows rattled in their frames.

"Daddy! There's bugs under my bed! Dark crawly ones!" Rachel piped.

"They won't hurt you, Rachel. They come inside to get out of the cold. Spring comes, they'll go back outside. Besides, they were here first, before us. We're camping in their home. Now go to sleep." I guessed that box elder bugs were the least of our worries.

Up reading, I began to hear a yipping outside, singly at first, a kind of lost calling, then more in chorus, what seemed twenty or so signaling voices. It wasn't Meghan and the others; they were rustling in the adjoining suite of rooms.

The image of Meghan wouldn't leave my mind. She had lounged in the doorway as I came in, hand on her hip in snug Levis. Ten years younger than me, she stood as tall, just under six feet, and her legs were lanky and firm. I was flushed from carrying Rachel in the cold, and I felt a quick warming as she said good night through the open door.

"Just a minute, Doc. I have a story to show you. Rachel had me

write it down today." She extended a red crayon paragraph on a child's
sketch pad:

FAIRY TALES

A fairy tale is a story for children. Here are some of the stories I like:
Sleeping Beauty, Beauty and the Beast, Cinderella, Lady and the Tramp, 101
Dalmations. The fairy-tale characters are troll, mermaid, princess, princes,
kings, queens. A fairy tale is sometimes a way for grown-ups to say something
to children. For instance, me—I don't have a mom; and dad tells me stories
about Cinderella and her mother.

I had nodded and been struck for a moment by how fragile everything was, from my two-person family to Great Plains history. I was
exhausted from the long day of driving through endless snow, so I
decided to tuck this conversation away for another time. "Thanks,
Meghan. We'll talk more when I can tell you the whole story. I need
to turn in now." I was drawn to her open honesty and warmth, but
at the same time shy of my own desires.

"Sleep well," she had called back, a smile playing at the corner of
her mouth. "Oh, one other thing. Did you ever hear of an invitation
stick?"

"No, it sounds extracurricular."

"Uh-huh. Today in the Bismarck museum I found a small carved
stick with red Sioux markings. You placed it by someone's tepee, if
you were interested in courting attentions."

"That so?"

"I wondered if you'd know about such things. Well, g'night now."

The yipping kept up outside, and I wanted my mind off Meghan
and Rachel. "Kids," I thought, "playing Indians." Then more skepti-
cally, "Students cutting up at night, maybe even mocking our stay
here." Then, no, impressionable after a long day, I imagined, "It
sounds like something from a century ago—the voices of Sitting Bull's
tribe, the Hunkpapa, fresh from Standing Rock!"

I got up to clear my fantasies, opened the window, jumped out
onto the grass, and looked into the half-moon sky fleeced with high
cirrus clouds. Canadian geese were migrating and calling to each other
over the street lamps, back to their northern homeland, a full-bodied
vector moving seasonally without loss of place or pivot. They carried
home with them, up and down the great flyway of the American
heartland.

I tried again to listen to these instincts, my own animal nature,
the skin part of me that felt and decoded the wind—not just how hard

or gently it blew, but the moisture in it, the smell, the taste even, the direction and what that direction might mean. I was listening, maybe even to hear my own breathing, my wind, singing the parabola of my own heartbeat. Homing. Wings and roots. Softer than a baby's eye-wink, Carl Sandburg said somewhere, dreaming the corn fairies of the Midwest. I climbed back in through the window and slept like a child.

Next morning the "snirt" still moped about, lying in unkempt piles, melting into vast lakes that drowned the flatlands. Spring wanted to blow on in, and occasionally we got sighs of a warm southwesterly, the near taste of green, promise of a higher sun, leaves, and infinite expanses beyond the clouds.

This land was primarily grazing acreage, real honest-to-goodness Roughrider Country, as the highway signs announced at the state line. The road markers were bordered with black Indian silhouettes. I looked for green meadows, hills, pothole lakes, an occasional tree row to accent the space, but little impeded the enormous flow of the terrain. The sky was so large that it would only be filled by storms that raged down out of Canada. There were countless species of clouds, and the weather dominated everything. The people looked right at you, like animals, even when you were just passing by. And the stares, for the most part, came without hostility, only open-faced curiosity.

There were no thaws during winter in North Dakota. The average January temperature held at eight degrees above zero and the ground froze three feet deep. In spring when about six inches of ground had warmed, the grasses down under turned green beneath the bleached stalks of the old year.

The meadowlarks sang out each morning in expectation of better days. Slowly, carefully, with rich yellow breasts and full throats, they tried to coax spring around in cascading triads.

CHAPTER 9

Turtle Mountain

Little Frogs Croak Moon (Oto)

Like some modern-day wagon train, our small band drove in tandem north to the Turtle Mountain Reservation, tucked along the Canadian border backwoods. Here was the most densely populated Indian land in the country—six by twelve miles of lakes and woods supported a tribe of ten thousand mixed Ojibwa, Cree, and Canadian French. The people declined to call themselves Indian and claimed to be French, speaking a patois called "Mitchef" or "Metis," meaning simply "mixed." These Metis cut French jigs during Ojibwa round dances. Their complexions were light-skinned and they referred to their darker cousins as "les sauvages."

We visited the BIA school on the reservation. "All my kids don't want to be Indian," an elementary teacher told Logan, her voice emotionless. She stared this fact into the floor. "A survey last year showed eight out of ten children claimed to be Indian by birth and the same number said they would prefer to be white. These kids shake their heads, 'No! No!' Their idea of Indian is what they see on television, the bad guys. Then you ask them questions about Indian culture, and they say 'Uh-uh, we aren't Indians. They murder, steal, rape. We don't want to be Indian.' "

Logan looked up at a poster taped to the school hallway where Jesse Greatwalker said to first-graders, despite statistics, "I like myself because I'm an Indian." Logan caught a flicker of his own childhood. Off-reservation Cherokee descendants in North Carolina were to be Indian in name only, since Andy Jackson's 1830s Removal of the "civilized" tribes west; but Logan's parents, shirttail cousins to each other, were each roughly a third Cherokee. His mother's great-grandmother, a "granny" woman in the hill traditions, still practiced the old ways up to her death, healing sicknesses and snakebites with prayers and "old people's tobacco," and hosting stomp dances at a mound in the hills near her home. Logan's aunt knew how to cook bear meat stew. It tasted a lot like gamey pork, he recalled.

Long ago, many Appalachian Indians—including the Eastern Band of Cherokees, Lumbees, Chowans, Haliwas, Saponis, Tuscaroras, and others—had hidden out in swamps, in hollows, and in the hardwood mountain hills of the Smokies, rather than be forced from their homes on the long march to Oklahoma. And North Carolina, let alone the federal government, wasn't eager to treat them as "Native Americans," regarded by most as unwanted casualties of a losing "removal." Unrecognized federally, many still had claims lodged against states and the U.S. government. An "Indian tribe" has been defined in North Carolina as a community of blooded relatives with at least quarter-blood descent, two hundred years' proven Indian ancestry, and ninety percent of the "tribe" proven to be legitimate "Indians." The need to remain Indian could account for the pattern of cousins intermarrying. To qualify as North Carolina "Indians," tribes now had to satisfy five of the following eight criteria: North Carolina Indian ancestral names still had to be current in the family; there must be kinship with other recognized "Indians"; they had to have birth certificates; or public records showing Indian ancestry; verifying letters from public officials; "proof" from anthropological or historical documents, or from presently recognized "tribes" and official organizations such as the National Congress of American Indians; any other "heritage" documents; the receiving of grants, government programs, or any similar projects designated for "Indians only." Some states have drawn up different criteria, and the federal government had its own way of counting tribes. Quarter-blood quantum was only one of over forty definitions of "Indians." The definition would eliminate "blood" Indians in a few generations.

World War II ushered in Indian "acculturation" with a Great White vengeance, and Indianness went underground across America. Logan's parents ran a truckers' roadhouse on old Highway 25/70 and melded into the mountain folk of the Smokies. They remained different in quiet but important ways in a time when segregation was still taken for granted. No one was refused service at Jack's Cafe, despite harassment and a dead skunk in the well. The outdoor performances of "Unto These Hills" still kept the myths around as pageantry. Behind closed doors families remained mixtures of "Indian" and American, tracing to colonial days and before. Roanoke Colony in 1587 was the first of many encounters and mysterious mixtures; when the newcomers vanished into the forest, they left one word, no more, carved into a post: "CROATOAN." No one has deciphered its meaning, or traced the colonists with certainty, but Lumbee historian Adolph Dial insists the Lumbees are descendants of Roanoke survivors who intermarried with Carolina Indians. Logan's cousins, who were geneaologists in North Carolina and Oklahoma, tracked their Cherokee, Chowan, and Catawba lineage back through two hundred years of American history, then found, incongruously, William and Mary Brewster and Patience Prence of Plymouth Colony snagged, like Charley Brown's kites, on the family tree.

So who is an Indian today? The BIA director in Sacramento testified before a 1954 Senate committee: "I just don't think there is any definition that you can give to an Indian. He is an Indian for some purposes and for other purposes he isn't an Indian. I am sorry, I cannot make a definition. We in the Indian Bureau are concerned with it also. We don't know how to define an Indian." According to current reservation lore, being Indian requires meeting two dozen anthropologists before you are twenty-one.

"You go on in and observe a class," the teacher prodded Logan and Meghan. "You'll see about these Mitchefs."

The two students entered the library. About thirty fourth- and fifth-graders clustered around their counselor, Moses Cedar, a Sioux in his mid-thirties who leaned back casually in an armchair against the wall. Feeling slightly intrusive, the visitors sat behind latecoming students without introduction.

"Ever seen a movie set?" Moses started the class.

"Yeah, yeah," several students chimed.

"The camera just sits there and things run by this way." He swept his hands to the right several times and made hand-signs to suggest a frame.

"I like to watch the lions," said one youngster. "I like *Land of the Lost*," piped in another, and several agreed. One offered subdued impressions of a pterodactyl cry, cawing softly.

Moses gently cleared his throat and looked toward Logan. "Could I ask you guys a question, your purpose in being here?"

Logan offered Meghan the floor, and the students turned to observe. "Well, uh, we're—we're here from California," Meghan stammered, "and we're st-studying Indian education. They know we're here in the office. We're just listening. Is that okay?" She was lobster-red from embarrassment.

"I guess it's all right," Moses consented. "Just made me wonder, you sitting there." He turned back to the children. "You guys are coming to a transitional stage, you know . . . talking about *Land of the Lost* and *Pink Panther*. You're not just little kids talking cartoons any-more, Mickey Mouse and Speed Racer and Popeye." Some snickered in the class. "Well, there are other things besides Yogi Bear and Huckleberry Hound."

"Or Shazaam."

"Or Sigmund the Sea Monster."

Moses got to the point: "I'd like to discuss the movie you saw after lunch. There are things that *you* have to look for, something like the *Ten Commandments* . . . "

"Oh," Meghan broke in, "what was this movie about?"

"It was about Indians," one student said.

Another, "The *American* Indians . . . "

"The American Indians—*before* the white man came . . . " said another.

Their counselor took over. "You guys watch a movie about Indians, and you say, 'Why, jeez, you know, well they came over from Alaska, across the ice, and they migrated into the Northwest, and the South-west, the Plains, and these guys hunted buffalo, did the Sun Dance, things like that.' But how many of you really know about the Indians *as* Indians, today?" No one spoke. "How many of you can go into a store and get on top of the counter and say, 'I'm an Indian'? A lot of you try to hide the part that's Indian. Everybody tries to be white."

Moses adjusted himself in his chair, tilted against the wall. "These people on TV get on the back-to-nature kick. Listen to Euell Gibbons, Bill Walton. Big Bill Walton, vegetarian . . . " A few giggled and glanced at one blushing student in a T-shirt and sneakers.

"That's *your* hero," Moses said toward the object of the giggling. "Yet how many of you practice really being Indian? People think I'm wrong socially when I walk into a room in front of my wife. It's because I was always taught that a man goes first. You go in a door and don't know what you're walking into. My forefathers did it that way, and I'll do it. If there's any kind of danger, I'll be the first to get it, not my wife, in front of her 'gentleman.'

"Well, how much do you really know about Indians?" Another long pause ensued. "Not a damn thing, huh? You girls know how to dance?" He directed the question toward a row of girls in front of

Meghan and Logan, who looked to either side and then simultaneously ducked their heads. "Typical Indians, right there. To be an
Indian—Damn!" He seemed lost for a moment, then came back: "*My*
season's coming up. I call it *my* season—rodeos and powwows. Just
watch the white people there walking around then, study them, note
how uncomfortable they look." He stared around as if watching people
go by. "See 'em walking around, looking all over everything, like they
never saw so many Indians in their life." He looked around the group,
then over their heads out the window, then back at his hands.

"It's really hard to be an Indian in North Dakota, you know. I
came to Mary College the first time and tried to cash a check. They
didn't even bother to find out *where* I was from, just looked at the
check, saw the 'Cedar' on it, an Indian name, and the first thing they
asked was, 'Do you go to school at United Tribes?'

"We . . . it's a continuous, ongoing struggle." The group had grown
pensive, a few students were fidgeting or bored. Moses' voice softened: "My brother just told me that Indians can't go into Chamber-
lain. I don't know, it's just, well, seven years ago, in a town off that
reservation, I can't remember his name, Donny . . . " Moses lost his
train of thought for a moment but continued vaguely. "It was an Indian
guy. He went into one of the bars and got drunk, and he drove into
this residential area. Ran over a little girl." With a long pause Moses
looked down at the floor in the middle of the circle. "It so happened
to be, you know," pausing, "a white girl." He stopped. "And then he
went back to the 'res'."

Moses looked at one of the Crow boys and said, "Remember that
White Horse guy? He got out of the service and got on a bus—his
family didn't have a phone. Nobody picked him up, so he left his
luggage and started walking home. Well, the white people were out
to avenge this little girl's death. Two carloads of teenagers started
abusing him on the road. They ended up killing him. Ran him down.
Then they started spinning out, running back and forth over his body,
hell—popping their clutches on the guy's brains. You know, they call
that a lot of fun."

Moses had gone beyond their tolerance level and he tried to salvage
a point. "It was just an ongoing struggle down there. From then on,
everybody that had a number '13' on a license plate, the 'res' number,
they were beating them up. Old men, old women, young kids, they
were getting their bones busted. That was just before the advent of
AIM."

"Being an Indian, I read in a newspaper, being Indian is AIM!"

He reflected a moment. "What do you guys think? Do you believe in AIM?" A few looked at him for a hint, quizzically. "No, no, I'm not on either side now. I want to see what you guys *think*." Moses stared at blank faces. Everyone sat still. "What's AIM?" he asked.

Someone mumbled something about "the Indian Movement."

"Hmmmmm?" Moses nudged them on.

"It's the Indian Movement," a Crow boy finally ventured. "The War of Indians Against Whites."

"A war, eh?"

The Crow boy, stammering painfully, tried to relate an instance of the War of Indians Against Whites, pausing frequently to rub his cheek. After about four sentences, the class sat with glazed eyes. The talk had gone far enough for today.

Moses dismissed them. "Let's take recess and play some basketball, eh?"

Logan and Meghan sat staring into their notebooks. There wasn't anything more to be said. They thanked Moses and left.

"Grade school was nothing like that in Bel-Air." Meghan blanched.

"They start early on the hard subjects here," Logan muttered and shuffled outdoors.

Bruno, the football coach, put us up at his place a block down the street from the family homestead. Bruno taught Indians social studies and football in the winter and farmed in the summer along the Red River Valley, some of the richest bottomland in America. He came from a generous and strong-willed German clan who believed that hard work and discipline were God's gifts to the free and chosen. The harder you work, the luckier you get, the saying went.

"Hey, look at this!" Jay pointed to a photograph of Bruno about to win a public high-school track sprint. The dog-eared photo froze the runners neck and neck at the finish, spectators agawk, Bruno straining into the tape held by two crewcut teenagers. Freckle-faced kids sported baseball caps, middle-aged fathers stood with rolled sleeves, and a pipe-smoking old-timer leaned with a stopwatch to his nose. String-bean girls clutched their pleated skirts, as a grandfather in coveralls waggled his cane.

"Isn't that somethin'?" Logan mused. "Right out of the *Saturday Evening Post*. But there aren't any Indians in the picture."

"Must be in a different track race," Jay observed. Apartheid was fairly de facto in this part of North Dakota.

We had come to talk with the Ojibwa, but the incessant rains kept everyone indoors. Turtle Mountain was shut in. Bruno's place stayed comfortable, but close. After reading and talking all afternoon, we began to joke about Bruno's self-installed shower and toilet that stood free-standing against a concrete basement wall.

"There aren't even any curtains on the cellar windows!" Meghan complained. "This communal thing goes just so far, you know, boys."

"We're supposed to be roughing it," Jay kidded, "cheek to jowl with nature."

"I'll keep my cheek to myself, thank you," Kate shot back.

I worried about our group's frustration with foul weather and staggered travel. We had been on the road almost a month. Aside from reading, cooking, working together, weathering storms, and visiting some reservation sites, the group remained stranded in the white mainstream of America. Blizzards had shifted into relentless rains, and still there were no buds on the trees. Was spring in North Dakota some kind of bad joke?

Watching "Skins" compete at basketball and teachers raise a level of red pride gave a window into the bicultural abrasions of Indian life; but we penetrated no further into Native America than what treaty-makers once called "the forest's edge." Were Indian cultures still active in traditional places we couldn't go? Would we whites be considered anything more than nosy tourists? Were the class readings—Black Elk Speaks, Land of the Spotted Eagle, The Sacred Pipe, My People the Sioux, Lame Deer—fabrications of a time past, or made up?

Logan was the only Indian among us, but his soft Cherokee features and amiable ways left him by no means an incarnation of the noble savage. As far as some hold-out Sioux cared, he was too light and too educated to be an Indian. Friend, pilgrim, healer, clown, teacher even, Logan in all his splendor just wasn't the dark and exotic stereotype America had fashioned of its aborigines. He reminded me more of Woody Allen or Bud Cort. In many respects—as a cultural composite in culinary arts, insight and breadth of reading, knowledge of plants and people—Logan was possibly our most "civilized" representative, but which civilization did he represent?

Our "tribelet" was composed of outsiders still, transient and amateur ethnologists, and I was author of their intrusions. I began to plumb my own alienation on the Plains. It was that "winter in the blood" natives feel, rejected by land and people, lost from a homing sense of self. This felt like the first and last American identity crisis.

"How about something to eat that doesn't remind us of mildew?"

Jay strolled across the room munching a saltine. The local restaurant, the Vendome, served as a gathering place, but at seven P.M. it was shut tight. Our ragtag tribe set out for the bowling alley cafeteria.

Along the main highway on this soggy Saturday night, bars in Rolla advertised with bloodshot neon the only other business besides bowling. Mud-plastered Buicks, Ford pickups, and rusting Chevrolets jammed around lights dim from long-ago holiday hangovers; no one outdoors, the close quarters of hard drinking indoors. The hamlet of Rolla was tipping close to stir-crazy from the flood of Dakota elements, snow, rain, mud, and doughbelly skies. Everything was heavy with winter sediment; living things seemed unnerved by the land's denuded stare. Farmers waited near panic for a break in the rains, impatient about spring seeding. They drank to bide time. The Metis drank to forget.

At the bowling alley we scuffed linoleum for fifty minutes waiting for cinderblock burgers, wolfed down the charred remains, and rallied to Saturday night in Rolla.

"It's enough to drive me to Southern Comfort or Bull Durham," Kate snapped.

Rachel and Meghan sidled toward a pinball machine, while I ordered a third cup of coffee laced with stainless steel. Logan and Jay squared off to bowl a couple of lines.

"If Mom could see me now," Jay chuckled, keeping score. Not one of them could imagine how people made it through the winters here. No TV, no rock radio, no movies, no beach, no Hollywood Boulevard. Jay picked up a corner-pin spare to edge Logan out in the last frame. "White man's burden," he said, defending the win. Giddy from the rain, we slogged back to Bruno's across misty vacant lots.

Meghan excused herself, "Some reading to catch up on."

Kate growled, "Ovaries in an uproar," and harumphed into the kitchen. Jay and Logan sparred about who would sleep on the floor and muttered their discontent at flies on the ceiling. Rachel chattered away about roller-skating.

Unrolling my sleeping bag, I found a small carved piece of cottonwood wrapped in sage. An invitation stick? Who was playing games now? I dreamed through the downpour of breaking curves into the ten-pin pocket. Splits all night long.

Sunday promised some relief, if only the Sabbath when nothing much could be done. The sun was nowhere near its weekly day. The rains puckered up for a while, then regathered to muffle any break in the weather.

Bruno's mother invited everyone down the block to a home-cooked breakfast. We lounged in overstuffed chairs talking sports, crops, climate, and local history with a neighbor in the propane trade. Bruno's mother served as the perfect country mom turning out the perfect country food and lots of it—highly seasoned German sausage, several dozen eggs, any style, cascades of toast with Ojibwa rhubarb jam, orange juice, hot coffee, and "if you're still hungry, boys, pancakes." They came dripping with butter and maple syrup.

Bruno encouraged us all by word and deed not to hold back. "You guys dig in now. Leftovers go to the critters."

"You don't know how good this goes down," Jay thanked "Mom" with a maple syrup smile.

"Makes us feel right t'home." Logan eased into a handmade rocker, as Pat and Meghan stretched out on the front room carpet.

Bruno suggested a muddy ride to the family cabin in the woods. We set out toward the reservation. The countryside glowed straw and amber near the wallows of the Turtle Mountains, thicketed with birch, box elder, ash, elm, cottonwood, red willow, and pussywillow. A red-winged blackbird keened by the road slough. "If yer passin' through, jus' pass me by," the car radio twanged.

Logan said it felt just like the Smokies in North Carolina—"real private 'n peaceful"—old mountains worn down into granddaddy hills. He showed Jay how to collect red willow bark for *kinnickinnick* tobacco by stripping the vermillion saplings down to an off-white second layer of bark. Dried and diced it could be smoked in a medicine pipe. A swatch of the bark, which was used long ago to make an aspirin tea, tasted nutty, almost sweet like pistachio.

The plants, trees, and grasses grew gentle here. They were water softened and protected in the boglands made up of reed marshes and honeycombed lakes. People lived back a ways off dirt roads, in small shacks surrounded by junked cars, each flanked by an outhouse with a slate-grey plank door swinging in the cold wind.

Gumbo sagged like cloudy molasses from the car tires. Along the way a gnarled, three-boled box elder, which Bruno called "the hangin' tree," spun our heads around, and we stopped at a deserted cemetery on a muddy country road. Graves with Scandinavian names dated back to 1834, a year in the Long March of the "Civilized Tribes."

Though freezing outside, our band was learning to warm itself inside. Meghan began a game of licking dewdrops from the willows, and soon we were all slurping water beads from the thickets, the amber droplets fresh and cleansing.

"Mmmm—honeysuckle rain," Meghan cooed. I noticed the budded tip of her tongue, her open smile and mouth, and thought for a moment how long I'd been single on the road. After two thousand miles, I stood in the rain and peered at Meghan's parted lips, not knowing whether it was winter or spring. She seemed intent on spring.

"You'll come around yet, Doc," she laughed at me. Around to what? I wondered. For several years I had been getting away—from an empty marriage, a blinkered academia, a polluted city. Meghan presented a new turn in the road.

Bruno's cabin and handhewn sauna stood secluded among the birches at Lake Upsalon. We chopped fresh wood and fired a small stove, then crowded in for a tribal sweatbath, chanting, drinking soda or beer, and then telling jokes. We sprinkled the white hot stones and fed birch into the flames, then ran down the slope to plunge into the ice-covered lake.

"Nobody knows you when you're down an' out," Logan sang, like an Appalachian tree toad. Tingling in the lake and elbow to an ice flow, I saw a four-inch perch swim across my left shoulder.

"Oh, Lord, won't ya buy me a color TV."

Two and a half hours we steamed, quick cooled, sweated, drank, and whooped for those who braved the ice: men and women in tune, even singing the blues as one, feeling heartbeats, yes, stomping life into our bodies. It was a secular rite of the sacred world.

The others were sweated out and ready to return. I wanted to walk through the woods around the lake, and Jay agreed to take everyone home in his van. I felt I could use the time alone, not to talk or think, just to move among the wooded hills at twilight. The rain had softened to a fine mist that crystallized like shattered quartz on the leafless branches. The opaque shafts of black-banded birch stood tall and gracile in the half-light. Silver webs of late sun filtered through the forest. Except for isolated blackbirds calling across the frozen lake, all lay quiet.

I circled the lake back to the pineboard sauna. The door hung slightly open. Moving to close it, I saw that the birch fire had died down to embers. I stepped inside to douse the glowing coals. The temperature had cooled, but there was a pungent smell of cedar, and the smoke lapped the small room where the light did not reach. Then I saw Meghan, lying still on the pine bench and wrapped in a plum-colored towel. Her thick hair hung loose over one shoulder.

"Meghan, I thought you'd gone back with the others."

"I told them I'd catch a ride with you. The quiet here drew me as the fire died down."

I turned to the coals' soft warmth and sniffed the penetrant odor of cedar.

"Where did you find cedar?"

"I carry chips in a bag of *kinnickinnick*. It's a dream wood, you know, a kind of Plains incense."

"And the sage, did you bring that too?"

"It's growing near the woodpile."

Meghan leaned toward me through the firelight, and the dark towel slid down her arms and legs. She moved tautly. Her cream body glided through the half-light.

"You need a woman to love," she said softly and touched me. "And in case you hadn't noticed—"

Meghan pressed against me, our mouths touching lightly. The pine walls softly reflected the steam and fireglow.

She turned to kiss me more fervently, and I traced her body lightly with my fingertips. The heavy sweet cedar smoked from the fire. We held each other closer, and I could feel the supple line of her hips, the rise and fall of her body, and my own passions. I had been on my own road long enough. I felt the walls of my body giving way to the darkness, collapsing inward, falling deeper into some hidden lake, down and back into soft forests, bathed in the quiet of night, as the birch flared and the cedar surrounded and swallowed us.

CHAPTER 10

Golden Valley

Moon in Which the Streams Are Again Navigable (Lakota)

Three California cars drove south down the western border of Fort Berthold Reservation, Highway 22 to Killdeer, Highway 220 east to Hazen, Zapp, and Center, then on down to Mandan and again to Jamestown along back country blacktop roads. Maybe ten cars passed us all afternoon. The radio reported that the Alaskan pipeline would *not* follow contours of the land, but dissect the terrain and erode the soil. I made a note to go with the earth's currents and grains, to move *with* thoughts and things out here.

Highway 22 trickled across the Little Missouri at the Lost Bridge, where for years the road had ended dead against a shallow but wide river drainage, underbellied with sluggish marshes and sloughs in still basins. The river was banked by eroded charcoal strata. Lewis and Clark bartered their way through here with peacemaking trinkets, eighty-seven silver medals in four sizes, traversing the Missouri breaks, and later came Catlin, Audubon, Maximillian, and the dauntless Custer with some forty hunting dogs in 1876.

The badlands opened around us, "common, wild, natural," as Lame Deer said of the Sioux. Stands of ash and poplar and elm bunched to pocket the darker scrub thickets. They stood fringed by gossamer saplings and traditional white birches banded with black rings. The slender birch rose absolutely straight, resilient and stiff at once. The trees appeared pliant, caressable, still disciplined, knowing where and how to cluster in these severe gullies: a morass of gulches, washouts, endless contusions of sandstone, limestone, clay, even catlinite veins, blood-red like arteries. The highway crews spread red clay and pipestone chunks on the muddy roads to glue a path over the gumbo.

I noticed red more these days—sienna earth, sunsets, sorrels, red-winged blackbirds, red willow, chokecherries, wild rose hips. Logan was carving a medicine pipe bowl out of a magenta red-brown stone he found on the prairie. The Lakota called the stones *Tunkáshila*, "grandfathers." Swirls of rock strata coruscated through the canyons, each stone caught up in the sweep of the earth—rich soft greys, sepias, straws, amber, mauve.

Now I could see the opening of *House Made of Dawn*: "There was a house made of dawn. It was made of pollen and rain, and the land was very old and everlasting. There were many colors on the hills, and the plain was bright with different-colored clays and sands. Red and blue and spotted horses grazed in the plain, and there was a dark wilderness on the mountains beyond. The land was still and strong. It was beautiful all around." The center of the earth could be everywhere in such a vision, Black Elk said.

Our cars turned off at Ilo wildlife preserve. We drove through a mile of muddy red ruts and were raced by a bay and an appaloosa in open-range pasture. The name "Ilo" welled up in my throat, curling my tongue, and I chanted softly, "Ilo, Ilo," lilting the long, open vowels. We stopped above the lake to hike down a packed clay road. Near the water I picked through a scattering of fish scales and bones and found the strong-wedged lower jaw of a walleye pike, notched and sharp.

Jay, chewing a blade of speargrass, turned into the wind rustling off the lake. "I've never known a place so absolutely without people. LA must be on another planet."

"Makes you want to sit down and just listen," Kate agreed.

The white-grey sky was flocked with blotches of cobalt over smoky red river currents. The flooded banks broke away and were lined with leafless grandfather cottonwoods, pale white against their contused settings; the ashen boles stood silently in muddy silt, waiting for sun and wind to curb the river again, to absorb the flood of a sky gone mad. Closer to the banks and up the draws clustered red willow saplings; they splashed ocher against the dull red waters and pallid sky. On the other side of the road, a hundred feet above the river, rose a mound topped by prairie grass and layered with sand and clay strata, quilted vertically in erosions: it seemed an earth sentinel.

Very still out here.

We drove east onto swells of open grassland, as Rachel marveled from the backseat, "The best badlands I ever saw." Yellow-breasted meadowlarks were trilling the sun back to life over the plains in clear cascades of thirds. Black Elk's "wings of the air" served as messengers to and from the gods, soaring, nesting, migrating, feeding on the marshes and newly seeded fields. The more contoured prairie grasslands were just flushing new green, still sepia, straw, and old winter-grey at the tips; they grew verdant down under where the spring rains soaked out the frost and winter kill.

The land opened out of the badlands to an aviary without perimeters: there were tufted ducks, grouse, canvasbacks, mallards, sandhill cranes, Canadian geese in flocks as large as a thousand, even an ivory tribe of pelicans, their sunflower-orange bills sagging with lake fish. Red-winged and yellow-headed blackbirds patrolled the marshes and perched atop last year's bushy cattails along the asphalt highway.

Overhead the sky was flocked with clouds and swatches of cerulean, as thunderheads piled billow upon billow, five separate clusters tumbling, sweeping, charging into the pools of serene blue sky. Plummeting lines of rain intersected diagonally with leaning rays of sunlight, reminding me of a Tewa song from the Southwest deserts:

> Then weave for us a garment of brightness.
> May the warp be the white light of morning,
> May the weft be the red light of evening,
> May the fringes be the falling rain,
> May the border be the standing rainbow,
> Thus weave for us a garment of brightness,
> That we may walk fittingly where birds sing,
> That we may walk fittingly where grass is green,
> O our Mother the Earth,
> O our Father the Sky.

But winter dies hard. Several swirls of snow brushed through the clouds, less vertical than the plunging rain streaks, rushing at the soft blues, refusing to give in to green spring. The struggle, at times a war, was carried on between old and new.

"What are we stoppin' here for?" Jay muttered, impatient to finish the long drive home. "Can't we just get this over with?"

"Dinnertime," I replied, holding back some, tracking a dirt road approach to a town that nestled in the green cup of a grassland valley. I felt something deeply, dimly remembered in the late afternoon glow. Jay squinted and fell silent.

The cars in caravan turned off Highway 200, marked with its

Indianhead silhouette, and we drove two graveled miles south to
Golden Valley, population two hundred and thirteen by North Dakota
map figures. I noticed from the map that we were a hundred crow-
flight miles from North America's geographic center. "Howdy Pardner,
Welcome to Golden Valley," read the handpainted roadsign.

"Chow time. Let's get somethin' to eat."

"Aw, come on, keep driving." Jay's resistance to food surprised
me. "No place in this town to eat, Chief."

We approached woodframe houses, built by homesteading immigrants from Russia, Scandinavia, and eastern Europe. They worked
the land, the animals, and their own bodies and spirits with a persistence matched only by the weather.

"There—'Cafe,' it says. See that lady in the window?" I swung
across the main street to park in front of a plain clapboard building.
"We'll stop here. I'll bet that woman can outcook your mother." Muffled grumble. "Beats dorm food, don't ya think?"

Gotta make time, the driving voice droned, and I braked to a stop,
partly because of my own cussedness, partly curiosity.

"Hooo, here you are again, Stanley," chortled Kate. "Look what
you drug us into! The place is closed. Come back tomorrow!"

There was nothing to distinguish the woodframe corner building
except the word "Cafe" painted in faded blue over the door. Things
don't always announce themselves in these parts, I reminded myself,
still hopeful. All the action's further down on the inside, behind the
noncommital surface. Everyone piled out, along with Rachel in her
snowpants, fire-engine pullover, and rain boots. Pint-sized Red Power.
The third car of companions pulled up, the two young people emerging stiffly, looking quizzical.

"Some of Mom's home cookin'," I encouraged with a wink.

"Is the place in business?" They were incredulous to a person.

I tried the door, opened it, stuck my head in. A firm, strong-armed
woman with tight lips met me directly inside the door, almost severely,
I thought, seeming to challenge my right to enter her place. "Are you
open for customers? Can we get supper?"

"What?"

"Can we eat here?" My God, I wondered, should I use sign
language?

"Yes." No smile. No welcome. Not even a nod.

I closed the door, waved the others forward. "Come on! Could be
a real feast," I muttered to myself. Some days you win, some you lose,
some you just hold your own. They all trundled across broken pave-
ment slabs where the three out-of-state cars parked in front of a place

called "Cafe." Whose "Cafe"? Whose forgotten part of the country? Golden Valley? The northwest end of North Dakota? No neon lights, no spangled invitations, no bargains or "genuine" claims. Not so much as a howdy. The windows were dark on the inside, dirty from snow and mud storms. Well, it was better than "EAT" signs on the more traveled, hard-surfaced roads.

No one in the place. There were three small tables around the room and a mess-hall table, where we six grouped like rabbits nervous for a hutch. A row of stools lined the soda counter. The vinyl on the stools was darkened from long winters. But wait now, a body could spin a bit, twirl some, on those stools. I poured myself the last cup of coffee from a turbid pot on a small table. The acrid bite cut down through the day and reached under the weeks of blizzard and wind and rain, the tiring frictions, long drives, meetings with Indian people at New Town, Minot, Turtle Mountain, United Tribes. Our own makeshift tribe struggled through the birth pangs of strangers learning to put up with each other. I looked around the room, as the others began to joke and mumble and unwind, wondering out loud why I'd dragged them into this godforsaken place and what mouldy fare they were fated to choke down. As a group they maintained a good resistance. McDonald's was a surer bet, Jay argued, than these roadside surprises. At least you knew what you were getting, plastic, cardboard, and all. "That's the problem," I contended stubbornly, "that's why we're in North Dakota, not Los Angeles."

A jukebox Johnny Cash sang "Don't Think Twice." A pinball machine labeled "Mibs" blinked "Prrinng," so I played a heartless game, scoring 2890, meaning neither win nor lose. There was just the playing, the testing of my exhaustion and reflexes, to see what was left, what could be salvaged to keep going. I didn't win any free games.

Behind a flat black register rose a candy counter flooded with sweets. Pink and skylark blue stacks of Double Bubble Gum reminded me of my Nebraska boyhood. Snickers, Butterfingers, Almond Joys, Mars Bars, Hershey Bars in piles. And Swisher Sweets in the corner, wine-soaked cigar crooks that stank like an outhouse. Copenhagen snuff, Red Man chewing tobacco, a pinch'll do ya in. My first smoke, at seven years old, was driftwood culled from the North Platte River; from there I graduated to tea leaves in a cob pipe, then I stole my father's Camels from the pickup glove compartment. I quit smoking five years ago in smog-belted southern California, after a retreat into the Sierras.

"Kraut Soup" topped the chalkboard menu; we read on down to "Roast Beef," "German Sausage," "Hamburger Steak," and "Veal

Cutlets." Everything was listed for under $2.50, the "Chicken Fried Steak" $1.65. My childhood took a swipe around an unseen candy corner.

"Daddy, can I have French fries?"

"Sure, sweetie, we'll splurge. Ice cream when we're all done."

An oblong Richard Nixon smirked like a doughty frog from the top of a poster tacked on the wall, "Presidents of the United States," Washington and Lincoln and the Great White Fathers marshaled below. Republican country, bedrock conservatives, I cautioned myself, mindful of my long hair and wire-rimmed glasses. George Washington signed the first treaty with the Indian peoples, three hundred and eighty-nine treaties and trails ago, as long as the grass should grow. "You can see that it is not the grass and the water that have forgotten," Black Elk once said. Then I looked closer at Tricky Dick, front-on, the glossed five o'clock shadow and shifty eyes, cigarette burn on the crook's nose. "Watergate" was penciled across the receding chin. The news crops up everywhere.

The students were ready to order from the proprietress, who stood in the middle of the room and let them come over to her, one by one. They wouldn't argue with this staunch woman, as they fussed in Turtle Mountain, when the waitress at the Vendome turned her back and walked away: no time and less tolerance for messing around with undecided city kids. Two cheeseburgers and fries, standard American youth fare. One German sausage. One Fleischkeuchel, a meat and onion pastry. Kate ordered a ribeye steak, cueing on my grandiose plans for a T-bone. "Hey, for real, grub, good eats," the students kidded. They were still unconvinced, but warming up to the possibility—vittles. The rule these days was what might be there, the unexpected. It was something of an old lesson, as the Ojibwa said, to feel the summer in the spring.

They nosed around, trading wit and stale breath. "Nixon." "Auction bill, you see that?" "Only one cook who's the waitress!" "Where are the customers?" "This could be terrible."

I took Rachel to the lavatory to wash up, and as I leaned over the porcelain with a pumice cake in hand, smelling the pine tar, I slowly took notice of the grainy texture of this greyish soap. There, in my own hands, where I would least expect, lay memory's key. Lava soap. Twenty years ago, my father's work at the elevator, dirt-caked hands, dust-shrouded coveralls, and Lava soap before eating. The fire in my flesh, my American earth being. This was it, the time warp. I'd driven several thousand miles, through three blizzards, twenty-five miles of gumbo at Wounded Knee, weeks of rain and hail and sleet, seventy-mile-an-hour winds, rummaged around North Dakota with a ramshackle tribe put together as a family, to step into my own place, one I never left in the privacy of memory, the small town, the grain fields, grasslands, hard-working, no-nonsense people, tight-lipped, stolid from winter, yet laughing somewhere deep down under, telling shaggy dog stories over coffee, jokes from farmers and ranchers and passing truckers and railroad men, even a polka or a waltz or a jig on Saturday night, before Sunday service and reverence, but today, now, on the job, all work. Dig in. Lava soap.

I led Rachel back into the cafe looking around. Her present was my past was this present, as our spiraling life lines overlapped, and time, for the moment, was a carousel. The proprietress unloaded her cabinets and refrigerator in military style: a battalion of pots, pans, tableware, glasses, knives, meat, vegetables, butter, bread, lettuce, tomatoes, potatoes all flying to their known places. Home is where the heart is, savoring.

A posted bill near the front door advertised an auction, May 2, 12 Noon CDT. Jim McCone Farm. "Machinery, Dairy Cattle and Dairy Equipment."

1971 No. 12 Massey Ferguson Baler
Easy-On Loader with Hay Basket and Grapple Fork
4-14 Cockshutt Plow
IHC Power Takeoff Manure Spreader
Choreboy Double 3 Herring Bone Milking Parlor
Syringes, Pipettes, and Insemination Equipment

The auction bill read like a country poem blooming in the weeds, strange and comic and familiar. The insemination equipment was advertised with country candor:

EXOTIC BREEDS:

2 Chinania Ampules
1 Beefalo Ampule
4 Simmental
3 Straws of Blonde

NOTE: Cows were Bred to Calve Throughout the Year. Therefore Some Will Be Milking Now, Others to Freshen Soon.
3 Guernsey Cows, 4 to 7 years old
2 Brown Swiss, 3 years old
9 Open Holstein Heifers, Bangs Vaccinated
2 Year Old Sorrel Gelding (Green Broke)

TERMS: Cash

Roughridge State Auction Co.

LUNCH WILL BE SERVED BY HENSLOW HOMEMAKERS.

The auction bill was addressed to "Herb Miller, Golden Valley, N. Dak. 58541. Please post."

So our hostess, working up a spring storm, blowing through her wares like an afternoon squall, was Mrs. Miller. Ma Miller, Hazel maybe? Or Ida, my great-grandmother's name? I wasn't brash enough to ask.

She brought on the soup and salad, French, Roquefort, and Thousand Island dressings so thick and rich you could dip them with a fork. The fare was looking up.

Logan's Fleischkeuchel arrived early. Thinly wrapped hamburger and onion roll, it was ritualistically devoured. Order another, "Ma'am, just like the first, please," ever so nicely. Rachel ate all her soup, some salad dressing, half her cheeseburger, and gave the rest to Jay.

"Not half bad, Doc," Jay gnawed away on a German sausage. Meghan tickled Rachel. Our tribe was coming alive again, talking, joking, eating, as the late sunlight fell mellow and lustrous in their eyes. "Anyone for McDonald's?"

The ribeye steak was served, then the T-bone, very hot, on metal steak trays, side orders of potatoes, a tomato slice, fresh baked bread, butter. Real butter. "Hell, Mom couldn't cook this good," Jay gave in.

The town policeman drove up in an unmarked white Chevy pickup with a red light bolted on the cab. Very big man, cowboy cop in a brown uniform. Without a word he strode behind the counter, poured a cup of coffee, took a candy bar, and then made a call on the house phone. He remained unspoken; an unstrapped .38 pistol dangled in his right-hand hip holster as he walked out. The left-handers in these parts were all outlaws, cattle rustlers, bootleggers, thieves, winos, Indian lovers. From the matinee movies I remembered the quick draw, a certain glint in the eye, cocked hat, pearl-handled Colt .45. People's reactions, their instincts, were quick out here, sometimes too quick.

Two locals strayed in as our band finished up, an older, portly, pale-cheeked farmer and a darker, horsey mechanic with "Lyle" sewn on his jacket, an "Airborne" insignia on the sleeve. Lookin' for some fun, as the song went.

Lyle spied Kate eating her ribeye. "Hey, Rufus, you oughta git some purple coveralls! You'd look good in 'em heh! Wow! Haw!"

Rufus took the trouble to grin, picked his teeth and said nothing.

Kate, wearing the purple coveralls, ate quietly. Uh-oh, the town wit and his country sidekick, gunsmoke grist. "No dogs or Indians allowed." I heard the sand in his laughter. California license plates borrowed trouble in these towns, not to mention "furrin" cars like the Volkswagen and Volvo. Yer ancestors, fellas, not foreign atall! Germans and Swedes—the old country.

"I *like* my coveralls," Kate called back finally.

"So do I," snorted Lyle. "Haw, haw, haw." Rufus grinned a second time. It wasn't exactly funny. All chuckled so as not to choke on the left-overs, scraped their plates, looked for one last morsel. What to do? Check yer spurs, pardner.

"Hey, you brickhead!" A crisp, clear child's voice cut across the room. Rachel, my own flesh-and-blood left-hander, was answering the guy, grinning, a trill in her four-year-old voice. She'd been picking up runs from the meadowlarks. The child called to him open-faced, un-intimidated: who are you, meatball, to challenge us?

Here we go. Fisticuffs, broken chairs, Rachel screaming, bodies scuffling, shattered glass, Dad flying through the window into the dirt street.

"Whut? Brickhead? Who's callin' me? Whut did ya call me, brickhead?"

"Brickhead," she insisted. Silence. I stared into my plate. Half-eaten tomato. The T-bone winked.

"Brickhead."

Then he laughed, deep down, tickled somewhere by her four-year-old pugnacity. Rufus actually laughed too. We all laughed and finished supper with fresh-baked lemon meringue pie.

We took a turn through the town as the sun set, past the Church of God of Prophesy, the outhouses all leaning south from the winter winds, seventy, some say eighty miles an hour, the rusty iron water-pumps unmoved in each yard turning green. An old Slav worked a chickenhouse with fat nesting hens and a strutting speckled rooster; he was shadowed by a black and white mouser. Meghan danced a jig in the road. "Come on, Rachel, let's skip!"

Jay played shutterbug with the Adventist churches, the pumps, the tree stands, the leaning outhouses mutely in agreement about the wind, and finally the local school rising four stories above the community, high as the water tower, topped with a liberty bell.

"Good place, eh?" I asked Logan, who was picking his teeth with a wooden kitchen match.

"In the immortal words of Clint Eastwood, 'swell.' "

"Beautiful, jus' beautiful," Jay seconded.

We drove north on a dirt road to the blacktop highway, the spring thaw giving way to revivings, the old again new.

CHAPTER 11

Chinook

Moon of the Black Bear (Carrier)

Our seminar on the road circled back to Jamestown, slipping from the red world into the white. The Jamestown axis served as Concord to our wilderness Walden, but it wasn't always the "good red" end of our road—the black asphalt had some chuckholes.

I still worried about the legitimacy of our forays into Indian lives and wondered if this expedition, like countless before, might be another diversionary backtrack. The wagon trails of Manifest Destiny cut old, eroding ruts into native America; would the story ever come clear?

Thoreau, America's herald of the wild, kept a dozen cryptic notebooks from which he expected to write the great book on natives. He died breathing "moose" and "Indians," but left no epic on Native Americans. Others since have tried—from Jaime de Angulo and Mary Austin, down to Peter Matthiessen and Gary Snyder—but are generally dismissed as eccentric, or worse. The white "highbrow," D. H. Lawrence warned, could write sentimentally of Indians "like the smell of bad eggs."

The wind howled all day long. This persistent voice disrupted the Plains silence, though it kept things moving, stirred up. The Lakota regarded *Taté*, the wind god, among the seven principle deities: sun, sky, earth, stone, moon, buffalo, and wind. "When a vision comes from the thunder beings of the west," Black Elk said, "it comes with terror like a thunder storm; but when the storm of vision has passed, the world is greener and happier; for wherever the truth of vision comes upon the world, it is like a rain." We were winter-logged. Black Elk's *heyoka*, or "sacredly comic," vision was overdue, as was spring in North Dakota. The intertribal word for warming spring winds, *chinook*, means "snoweater," and one could strip a foot of snow a day from the land. No weather here, the locals jawed over steaming coffee, just climate.

Our ragged tribe felt threadbare. I pressed myself, teaching my students and writing in snatches, trundling Rachel through snowdrifts and cloudbursts, while the others grew more and more irritable.

Meghan became my companion and Rachel's confidante, in the wake of Rachel's mother's exit. This far from the academic classroom, the lines between teacher and student had relaxed for the better, surely, but was I pressing my luck? Worry over academic propriety lingered like a cheap sherry hangover. I fell back on my favorite bumper sticker: "The Moral Majority: NEITHER." More deeply than this, I came to see that reconstructing my own family, friends, and home was a personal journey no less complex than the struggles to revive native America. I was learning to trust my own needs along with those of others; Meghan had her own designs which were her own business.

On other fronts, Kate, our testy matron, took to boxing Jay's ears. "Any guy shoveling down six oranges for breakfast," she snapped over a mug of reheated instant coffee, "lands on my shit list."

"What's so wrong with that?" Jay protested. "I *like* oranges." Logan tugged at the bill of his Farm Bureau cap and whistled the opening bars to *Dragnet*.

" 'Cause they're *my* oranges yer eating, buster." She glared stonily. "Did you ever think about the rest of us? Is this tribe stuff all talk?"

Jay's appetite was still there, but now a reprimand needled it. Not that he didn't deserve an occasional check, but Kate rode him hard.

Meghan had put herself on a starvation diet, paying dues on the quarts of vanilla ice cream that carried her through late winter doldrums. She was quick to be offended, testy about personal things, and her friendship with Kate frayed.

"C'mon, Meg," Jay goaded her, "let's pig out on orange peels."

"Stuff it where the sun don't shine, horseface." Meghan's teeth were set like rusted beartraps. Jay skated from the room in Kate's icy wake.

"What's this?" Logan dawdled over the remains of hash browns with a plastic fork.

"Damn the suck-egg luck," I groused. Enrolling a loose tribe in Los Angeles and keeping them tribal in the Dakotas were separate orders. The academic concepts appealed to everyone; life itself was a good deal harder to ride herd on day-to-day.

We tightened up and drew inside ourselves as the gender line split ranks. The men reacted defensively to the women who grew fractious.

"Time to dung out," Kate snorted in the hallway by the mailboxes.

"Come on, folks, listen to your own heartbeats," I counseled them somewhat hangdog, as I thumbed through the morning mail. The editor of *Salmagundi* saw fit to reject the opening chapter of my fledgling study of American Indian literatures: "I don't think this entirely delivers what it would need to do justice to its subject and answer the misgivings readers like me regularly express with respect to Indian literature." Why these misgivings so "regularly"? I wondered. Was this just a literary problem?

I thought back a few years to a 1969 *National Review* where Professor John Greenway published "Will the Indians Get Whitey?" This senior folklorist from the University of Colorado reviewed with "misgivings" revisionist history by Andrist, Josephy, Washburn, and other new historians:

> The lay reader should have a hardcore course in what the real Indian was like before exposing his raw conscience to books like these. He should know that the real Indian was ferocious, cruel, aggressive, stoic, violent, ultra-masculine, treacherous and warlike, though these are anemic adjectives to describe the extent of the Dionysiac extremism. As for Our Treatment of the Indians, never in the entire history of the inevitable displacement of hunting tribes by advanced agriculturists in the 39,000 generations of mankind has a native people been treated with more consideration, decency, and kindness.

God help us, "the real Indians"? Their "inevitable displacement"? Was this some bad academic joke? Most of the five hundred disparate tribes in this country alone were planters and food gatherers, not hunters. Whose "Indian" was the professor sketching?

About this time John Wayne was giving his opinions in a *Playboy* interview:

> Our so-called stealing of this country from them was just a matter of survival. There were great numbers of people who needed new land, and the Indians were selfishly trying to keep it for themselves.

So much for the wisdom of a hundred shoot-'em-up westerns. Professor Greenway capped the lesson:

> Without war and raiding and scalping and rape and pillage and slavetaking the Indian was as aimless as a chiropractor without a spine. There was nothing left in life for him but idleness, petty mischief, and booze.

This windy ignorance was not simple pedantry a step away from

Hollywood. I'd heard such claptrap from childhood on—not the least from my father, uncles, cousins, and in-laws. There were similar dismissals of artists in big-sky America. Writers were "the maggots of society," as Jules Sandoz told his daughter Mari. Lame Deer once said that artists were the Indians of the white world. Maybe this was so, given the artist's general condition of poverty, larger sense of displacement, questioning visions, and alternative work ethic in America. Even more disturbing, the suicides of Plath, Berryman, Crane, Sexton, Hemingway, and too many others documented a tragic analogy. "Each dead child coiled, a white serpent," Sylvia Plath wrote a week before she killed herself, abandoning two children. I truly did not know how to think about this, feelings aside, or about the Indian tragedies of history.

An American could turn to a tradition, at least, of the "word sender's" tribal centrality and dignity in Native American cultures, beyond the sad anachronisms of martyred artists and Indians. It had something to do with an old sense of home and hospitality, of vision and sense of place. Fifty years ago an Inuit woman, Takomaq, improvised a song while she prepared tea for her guest Knud Rasmussen on his twenty-thousand-mile dogsled trek across the North:

> *Ajaja—aja—jaja,*
> The lands around my dwelling
> Are more beautiful
> From the day
> When it is given me to see
> Faces I have never seen before.

CHAPTER 12

Standing Rock

Moon of Flowers and Blooms (Ojibwa)

Sunday dawned clear with light spring winds. Winter's crust was edging from the prairie. Sunflowers fanned in choral yellows and turned in unison to the sun; so did we, dozing and daydreaming outdoors on the grass by the redbrick dorm. We sensed the lotus breath of the Pacific after a long Canadian freeze.

"Let's go to the woods for a picnic!" Meghan spoke up, jabbing me in the ribs. "Any sport left in there, old man?" Wherever my sense of spring lay hidden, down under skin five thumbs thick, Meghan would tap it. She seemed streetwise about the need for play.

In less than an hour our bunch pulled into an old cottonwood grove, Troutman's Bend, by a stream muddy with spring snow run-off. Swallows keened above the current, darting in and out of willow thickets by the eddies.

Jay stumbled on a fallen prairie hawk, still warm, with its claws distended and eyes defying death. Logan placed chunks of cottonwood in the hawk's claws, then spread the wings and tail feathers, laying it to rest facing the sun. It was a late sign of the losses of winter.

Lying on my back, I gazed into a sky of nimbus clouds, the scattered tufts of light and cloud forming ideograms. Afternoon sunlight splashed through the cottonwood shadows. Smoky greens hung on the undersides of leaves, accenting the milky blues of the sky, a translucent azure repeated in the immigrant eyes of North Dakotans—eyes inherited from homesteaders who once peered through prisms of Scandinavian snowbanks at twilight. Spring greens faded into the

sky's receding blues. The Lakota word *tho*, I recalled, meant interchangeably "blue" and "green"—the continuities of prairie sky, still
waters, and open grasslands. There seemed fewer boundaries out
there, more gradations on these high plains.

There, in the brown stream's current, I saw the angle made by
migrating birds, and it came clear why wild things moved as they did:
a reed split the current into a wedge, and just inside this force, the
current broke into a slipstream. In such timeless patterns, geese and
ducks migrated thousands of miles a season through windy skies. The
shifting foremost point determined the rhythm of the flight for all.

Logan led me to a doe's body, frozen and desiccated in late spring
blizzards. He found a femur to carve into a spirit whistle. I took the
left foreleg, Logan the right one, giving thanks for agility and direction
in our travels. The deer would be a guide.

The stench of decomposing venison lingered on my knife and
hands long after we drove back into Jamestown—rancid sinews and
socket joints no longer in motion. It was a pungent, frightening smell,
like that of spent, stale sexual juices. This winter coat would not be
shed in spring, rotted internal organs would no longer feed the body,
but the deer in her decay startled my sense toward the living.

My deepest regret was the imperceptible slip of life into death.
Beings passed on irreversibly, each but once in the cycle of things. In
my weaker moments I wanted to clutch life, drag it like a horde of
possessions into my keeping. White Antelope, the Cheyenne, sang at
the 1864 Sand Creek Massacre as he died:

> Nothing lives long
> Nothing lives long
> Nothing lives long
> Except the sky and the mountains.

This was perhaps the oldest of wisdoms.

Logan, Jay, and I took the late afternoon to run above a thawed
reservoir north of Jamestown. As we blew out winter's stale air, the
fresh wind rushed in. A month ago we began jogging this country
road over snowdrifts, jackrabbiting from ice patch to crusted hardpan,
and now the road was corrugated into a spongy washboard. Chuckholes opened across the prairie where ground squirrels scuttled to
their burrows. Moonripe boulders, feathered with lichen, swelled under the dead, rustling grass. Ducks skittered in the coves.

"You've got to live the habits He gave you," Logan puffed, as we
trotted along.

"Whose 'He' do you mean?" Jay countered, punting a beer can down the dirt road.

"Figure it out—*Wakan Tanka*, Yahweh, Stone Boy, Adonai—take your pick." The point was not which faith, but *religion* itself, from the Latin root meaning "to bind." The world often seemed to unravel. The *yuwipi* healers—"they bind him"—were literally tied to the old Lakota ways of this sacred world. Did the medicine still work?

I sensed a spring pivot in our gatherings, a natural turn. "And many I cured with the power that came through me," Black Elk said. "Of course it was not I who cured. It was the power from the outer world, and the visions and ceremonies had only made me a hole through which the power could come to the two-leggeds."

I ran four miles of claypacked country roads back to our college apartment, thinking about the old man's humble acceptance of his role as a Lakota healer, literally a medium. It wasn't A.M.A. sanctioned, not by a long shot. Could a white man know anything of such power? Were such native traditions forever shrouded behind the Buckskin Curtain? Had we come any farther than Raleigh's Roanoke Colony?

When I walked in the doorway, Rachel lay curled up in a lounge chair, and she was sobbing.

"What's wrong here, Sweetheart?" She sounded like a wounded starling.

Rachel looked up, tears flooding her blue crescent eyes. "I can't stop thinking about my mommy."

"What caused this?" I asked and put my arms around her small frame.

"Apricots, whenever I think of apricot trees, or other kid's mothers, or painting," Rachel blurted out. Then she added more softly, "I wonder where my mommy is—will I see her again?"

"I don't know, Sweetie. That's her decision, not ours. Your mommy loves you, but she can't be here to explain things."

"Why?"

I knew no more than my child, and I knew as well that I couldn't make up stories, at least not the thin fabric of words that might tear eventually and disappoint her even more. There was no simple way to make it all better.

"She misses you deeply, too, Rachel. The pain of letting you go must have been too much for her to face. We'll make a life apart from her."

"Will she ever see me?"

"I honestly don't know. We have to give her more time. She has some growing up to do." Rachel sobbed more, in spasms like hidden rivers, and I could only hold her and help her talk.

"What do you remember about your mommy most, Honey?"

"Children, lots of children. She liked children, like Meghan does."

"Was she with children lots?"

"No, but I remember her that way."

"Was she with you often?"

"N-n-no," she sobbed.

I gathered all my courage together. "Rachel, you and I are together now," I told her, "and I'll help you grow up as best I can. Your mommy trusted me to raise you, even when she and I couldn't live together. You and I will make our lives work. Our friends will help; we have more family than most kids, you know. And the world has lots of mommies. These things hurt now, but we'll work them out." I hugged her then. With grief can come wisdom, perhaps; we ask for the grace of courage, Black Elk's vision beyond his suffering. Rachel was growing up with unusual resources and special adoptions—not easily, to be sure, but on a good road of her own. She would learn and tell her own life stories; mine were only part of her opening lines.

We walked through shelter belts of elm outside the dormitory and gathered sticks and rounded rocks. "Let's make a forest house in our apartment!" Rachel brightened up. We dragged leafless branches through the dormitory window, shaped them into a shelter on the rug, and decorated the indoor hut with butterflies, flowers, paper hats, and foil clouds hung with threads from the ceiling.

"This is our animal house, Daddy. We can live outside in here." Why not? I thought. The boundaries were sliding.

Moon When the Ponies Shed (Lakota)

We rambled for two hours west of Jamestown to the United Tribes Employment Training Center, south of Bismarck on the Missouri River. Indian families of all tribes enrolled here for fifty-two weeks of basic education with teachers from their own cultures. United Tribes integrated job skills with Indian traditions, personal health, and family support. Family was the tribal nucleus. The center housed, fed, educated, and skilled Indian people, including single men and women as extended kin of the tribal family. Mothers and fathers were individually trained for work, while the children attended Indian-staffed schools on the same grounds, once army officers' headquarters. They weren't far from Fort Abraham Lincoln—Custer's point of departure for the Little Big Horn just a hundred years ago.

Visitors were received as guests, though not particularly indulged; everyone was very busily at work. "The Indians here want desperately to learn," a mixed-blood counselor told me between classes on drug abuse and family planning. "They know that education means better lives for them, and they're disappointed when weekends interrupt their class time. There's no time to waste, no patience for poverty." I wondered if schooling had ever meant so much to my UCLA students. No fooling around, no lost motion, after so much had been lost. "We've got a hundred years of pain to heal," the counselor said. It wasn't a metaphor, but a statement of fact.

I browsed through the library rows of Indian books, tribal news-papers, and periodicals. The setting spoke of cultural pride, not red chip on the shoulder, but Native American confidence and dignity. Down the halls decorated with student art, I spotted the office of Hannah Stone, editor of the *United Tribes News*. Hannah directed public relations for United Tribes and hosted a weekly Indian television show out of Bismarck.

She rose to greet me. "Hello, I'm Hannah Stone. Nice to meet you. Sit down."

Gap-toothed, attractively middle-aged, hearty, and hard-living: Hannah was a woman with her thoughts in the open, and she made a point of meeting others head-on. Each week she counseled Indian convicts in the state penitentiary. Straight talk was her rule.

"Indians serve longer prison terms than whites because they don't understand the parole system," Hannah said. She was dressed in tan riding pants and a fire-engine red sweater. She knew her own mind and style and had a native western candor. "A white man will get out of the pen in three or four years on good behavior, where an Indian will stay locked up for his full twenty. The Indian thinks he's got to serve out the entire conviction. An' bein' locked up means sobriety, so he hits the bottle any time he's out of the slammer. You've got to have the right skin color to get outta prison and stay out in Indian country."

A toss of her raven hair sparked a flash of off-white beaded ear-rings. Married twice, the second time to a Montana Crow, Hannah had taken part in peyote rituals through the Native American Church. "You know somethin', I couldn't find my place once in a meeting," she said half to herself, "darndest thing." She looked out the window at the ashen skies and thought a minute, tapping long fingernails on a beaded Indian belt.

"Finally I left the meeting and went outside in the night, next to a big ol' cottonwood. I stood there under the moon and listened to the wind in the leaves." She toed the wastebasket pensively with her tooled boot. "I was lookin' for something and didn't know what it was. I stood there a long time, not even thinking. The moon just slid on down the sky. I didn't know what to do. I was lost." She stopped again, brushed one hand over the other, and continued.

"The stars were out. The leaves started talking to me, in a language I didn't exactly understand, a soft rustling like whispers or singing. But I still thought I knew what they were saying, from somewhere, even if it wasn't yet clear—like trusting someone who was speaking in a dream, when you can't hear the words right." Her face fell, then she looked up, apprehensive of whether I could understand. I was a white man.

"A lizard came 'round the cottonwood, out of nowhere in the night, and stuck out its tongue, then it scurried behind the tree again, quick. I went back inside, scared, more confused. It didn't seem right.

"I asked my friends for help. 'You'll have bad times, then good times,' the peyote road man said. That's all. 'Bad times, then good times.' "

Hannah's eyes grew very heavy, and her face dropped.

"I became an alcoholic, in the bars all the time. I had to have that drink or I'd go crazy, mean, fightin' mad. My marriage broke down, for the second time. I couldn't stop drinking. I started bleeding in my eyes, then hemorrhaging in my ears and nose and throat. I felt like I was blowing up inside.

"I went home and got ready to die. I saw myself a failure forever, no good, a damn wasted Indi'n." She drew her hand across the desk, as though clearing away dust. "I locked myself in my room and refused any food or water. I sat there on the floor dying, turning off each part of my body, one by one. My mother was locked outside crying."

Hannah stopped and lit a cigarette, inhaled deeply, tilted her head back, then kept going. All I could do was listen.

"My brother finally came home after a week and broke down the door. There I was on the floor, no food for days, hair matted, face bruised and streaked, filthy clothes. I couldn't even walk. My brother carried me like a baby." Her mouth flinched, and there were tears in her black eyes.

"I faced my own death." She leaned on the point and seemed to gather strength. "Now I consider myself reborn, a new Indian woman.

I've got a good job here. I'm working with Indians who need what I know and can do. You know, I feel at peace. My life makes a difference. I know who I am now."

Hannah and I talked for a couple hours, as the wind gusted fifty miles an hour in a heavy dust storm outside. The power lines blew down, and the electrical outage cast the room in a dusty grey twilight. Hannah's daughter called, worried about their horse corraled in the storm.

"Animals know how to protect themselves from dirt, Honey," Hannah reassured her. "We'll all be all right, don't you worry."

Our group left United Tribes and crossed the Missouri through flooding rain, then drove south over the Heart River to Standing Rock. Sitting Bull's homeland was eroded, unarable, almost as wild as the badlands. A flock of cranes caromed back and forth over the Cannonball River.

Descending the last incline into Fort Yates, I had strange premonitions of a car forcing us off the road. "What would I do right now?" I pondered, driving in something of a daydream. I absently judged the width of the road, whether the shoulder was packed, even the pitch of the barrow pit, wondering if the car would roll if we hit the ditch.

Three minutes later a tan Chevrolet drifted steadily across the yellow center line a hundred feet away, coming head-on. There were no other cars on the road. It seemed suicidal.

I edged toward the shoulder, veering as the oncoming car slipped closer in seconds, Indian driver slumped over the wheel. The car sheered by.

What could I do? The Chevy approached Kate driving behind me with Meghan and Rachel. It was coming in the wrong lane. Kate braked, hesitated, the battered Chevrolet persisted in its forbidden course, and Kate swerved into the other lane. The car slipped past her in the wrong lane.

I was watching all this in my rearview mirror, not daring to breathe or break the awful grace of the moment. Was he insane, forcing whites with out-of-state plates off the road? Drunk? Asleep at the wheel?

Jay's van came last in line. I watched in the rearview mirror, sucked in my breath, and chanted silently, *mitakuye oyasin*, "All My Relatives." Jay stayed in his lane; the errant Chevrolet glided back to the right. They passed within seconds, but they passed.

We stopped by the road and sat very still for several moments.

Meadowlarks were trilling on the prairie. Looking back, I could see the entire excursion—my four students and daughter, red road and black—all of us on the shoulder. Out here in the middle of nowhere, living hand to mouth, day to day, we had bonded somehow, and no one knew quite how. The danger that any one might not continue with us completed our sense of the whole: our tribe was not a luxury, but a necessity. Out here few made it alone.

"Close call back there, Boss." Kate had left her car and walked the gravel barrow pit to my window.

"Just leave the trick riding to Annie Oakley," I said.

"Sure, Doc."

We entered Fort Yates along an inlet blacktop road flanked by run-off Missouri sloughs. The flooded banks were strewn with reeds picketing the river. Leafless cottonwoods bleached in the draws, their boles reminiscent of old men's legs.

Then abruptly I saw it, almost too late, *"Tatanka Iyontanke,"* stenciled on a blistered brown roadsign. We turned off on a gravel approach to the burial site for Sitting Bull, legendary medicine man, warrior, song-poet, visionary, and martyr originally interred here, whose body was stolen back and forth by the Bullhead and Grand River clans at each end of the reservation. No one quite knew where it lay now.

Tatanka Iyontanke, literally "Buffalo Bull Sitting," was born on the Ree River at Many-Catches close by, in the "Moon of the Snowblind" or March, during the "Winter-When-Yellow-Eyes-Played-in-the-Snow" or 1831. A deliberate child, first given the name "Slow," he grew up with the persistence of the buffalo bull, which turns its head into winter storms and forages against Arctic winds.

His name came from a prairie vision. Slow's father, Returns-Again, went out hunting one day with three warriors when a lone buffalo bull came shagging across the plain. Returns-Again was gifted in the language of animals. He heard the names *Tatanka Iyontanke* or "Sitting Bull," *Tatanka Psica* or "Jumping Bull," *Tatanka Winyuha Najin* or "Bull-Stands-with-Cow," and *Tatanka Wanjila* or "Lone Bull"—mystic names for the Lakota four ages, from infancy, to youth, to adulthood, to old age. These were powerful signs.

The boy Slow developed into a young warrior. At fourteen he counted *coup* against a Crow, that is, he was the first of four warriors to touch or *coup* an enemy in battle, shout his name, and call, "I have overcome this one." Later the brave would narrate the deed with witnesses at the council fire. Touching death meant more than killing, hand-to-hand combat more than conquering. "White man's war is just shooting," the old warriors said.

When Slow first counted *coup*, his father bequeathed him the warrior name Sitting Bull, renamed himself Jumping Bull, and gave the remaining sacred names to nephews. These names were the highest honors for young men.

Sitting Bull rose to leadership in a society of warriors, the Midnight Strong Hearts, and he pledged to stake himself to his ground during battle with a scarlet sashed lance. The bandy-legged warrior was wounded in the left foot by a Crow bullet and limped most of his life. According to Stanley Vestal, "That old pagan loved his native soil with a love almost carnal, a love wholly mystical. Up before dawn always, he liked to bathe his bare feet, walking about in the morning dew. 'Healthy feet,' he used to say, 'can hear the very heart of Holy Earth.' "

All seven western bands of the Teton Sioux, "the prairie dwellers," acknowledged Sitting Bull their leader in 1876, as Crazy Horse and Gall and the Cheyenne Two Moon led warriors under him. The eve of the Little Big Horn, Sitting Bull sacrificed one hundred pieces of his flesh in a Sun Dance and had a vision of earless Bluecoats falling backwards into a fire. "Longhair" Custer, *Pahuska*, dubbed "Hardass" by his own men, could not hear well. Sitting Bull sang, "Ye tribes, behold me. / The chiefs of old are gone. / Myself, I shall take courage." Sitting Bull retreated into Canada rather than surrender to the reservation prisoner-of-war camp. "Let it be recorded that I was the last man of my people to lay down my gun." The reservations were fenced holding pens Indians could not leave without government passes; it was apartheid here at home.

There were constant disputes over the new acculturations required of Indians: Christianity, white man's dress, cattle, commodities, school, fences, roads, alcohol. In 1881, Sitting Bull was forced to return to Standing Rock, extradited from Canada to negotiate "peace." He traveled the country with Buffalo Bill's "Wild West" show in 1885 and was treated by crowds alternately as an ambassador and a blood-thirsty savage. "I have advised my people thus: when you find anything good in the white man's road, pick it up; but when you find something bad, or that turns out bad, drop it, leave it alone."

The year of the Dawes Allotment Act, when Sitting Bull failed to block the 1889 cession of Sioux lands and Indians took Christian patronyms, the great chief walked out.

"Indians! There are no Indians left but me!"

The desperate, apocalyptic visions of the Ghost Dance swept the Sioux reservations in 1890. Christ, the *wanikiya* or "make-live," was prophesied to return as a red man and restore all things Indian: whites would simply roll up and disappear, while the buffalo would return. Sitting Bull was skeptical. These were not the traditional visions of older medicine men, Sun Dreamer when he was a boy, or Black Moon when he was a great chief, but the frenzies of Kicking Bear kindled by a Paiute shaman in Nevada called Wovoka by some, Jack Wilson by others. The warring cultures fractured Indians among themselves—Indians split from their traditional cultures and very names.

Sitting Bull heard his oracle, a meadowlark, sing in the late fall of 1890, "The Sioux will kill you!" Bureaucrats wanted the fifty-nine-year-old chief out of the way. Jealous, frustrated kinsmen, including John Grass and Gall, were maneuvered into internecine rival corners against Sitting Bull.

At dawn on December 15, Sitting Bull's subordinate, Lieutenant Bullhead of the Indian police, ambushed the chief in his home; Sitting Bull and four Indian police were killed in the crossfire. Three hundred and thirty-three Sioux fled the reservation. The enraged Holy Medicine, a relative of a dead policeman, mutilated Sitting Bull's lifeless body with an ox neckyoke.

The Wounded Knee Massacre, the killing of women, children, the aged, and a few holdout hostiles led by Big Foot, took place two weeks later at Pine Ridge. Then the United States declared the Indian Wars ended and the frontier closed. The great chiefs were dead, the Plains fenced.

Abe Lincoln once defined a reservation as separate land where Indians lived surrounded by thieves. Vultures would be a more apt image. Sitting Bull's grave site, vandalized many times, was now imprisoned behind an eight-foot, barbed-wire fence, an old reminder of civilizing the West. A boulder streaked red and smoky grey was lodged on a concrete slab over the supposed grave: the Indian Bureau wanted to keep this chief buried, if indeed he did rest here. No one knew anymore. A pint bottle of California White Port lay shattered on an antpile. Beer bottles, wine bottles, pop bottles, and toilet paper were scattered wantonly around. It felt like a recently abandoned war zone. "The white man," Sitting Bull once warned his people, "knows how to make everything, but he does not know how to distribute it." The warning was lost among dark splinters of glass.

Despite the half-lighted drizzle, the discarded bottles, and the near accident on the highway, we felt Sitting Bull's power in the place. I first witnessed these mixed sufferings of loss and survival in East Berlin as a student, where a cinderblock wall and barbed wire divided "the people." A cold war still divided us from "them." The world was sorely in need of good medicine, healing ceremony, and a renewed red road. Indians were what a Tewa friend saw as the miners' canary of modern civilization—when the bird in the mine died, everyone was endangered. "Great Spirit, pity me. I want to live," Sun Dancers pray to the Great Spirit.

Logan unwrapped his newly carved pipe, packed it with red willow bark, offered it to the four directions, sky, and earth, and we smoked in homage to Sitting Bull—warrior, poet, holy man, chief of his people. Logan's red wolfskin, anchored with a stone, fluttered in the northwesterly wind. It recalled his "protector" when we began this road—not "from" harm, but "for" our well-being.

"*Tunkáshila*, grandfather spirit, be with our spirits," Logan sang in the chill wind; his was a kind of talk-singing, halfway between chant and prayer. We collected four hundred and five, the prescribed number, small white *yuwipi* or "binding" stones—translucent pebbles scattered over red anthills.

"I've heard people say ants carry these bits of crystal to us from ancestors buried in the earth," he said softly.

Our caravan circled the dirt streets of Fort Yates. Two Indian men in a green Volkswagen passed by several times, a shotgun barrel visible in the back window. They weren't hunting pheasants. Again a sense of fear clawed my stomach. The streets seemed watched by dark, empty windows. Tar papered vacant houses, weed lots, and liquor stores waited rain-soaked under funereal winter elms for something to happen.

"It is your own doing I am here," Sitting Bull told federal overseers. "You want me here and advised me to live as you do, and it is not right for me to live in poverty." Still, a century later, poverty decimated the Hunkpapa Sioux. The black road was deeply rutted.

CHAPTER 13

Tunkáshila

Deep-water Moon (Kutenai)

According to legend, the Hunkpapa Sioux once migrated and left behind a woman with her sick child. When the people returned, the mother had turned to stone, the child yet on her back. Standing Rock Woman still faced the turbulent Missouri, muddy grey in early spring.

At the Standing Rock community college Edna Stone Arrow talked to us, while Rachel entertained herself with crayons on the office floor. She was getting an education in sidewalk art, along with everything else.

"Are you a teacher here?" I asked.

"Yes," Edna said stolidly. "I teach my people's ways and history."

"Have you been to school?"

"No, not white man's school. I dropped out in grade school like most Indi'ns. Your ways are different from ours." Edna stood firm in her differences. With a mind of flint, Edna sparked little fires of words behind a toothless grin favoring the right corner of her mouth. She knew how to wield an older woman's authority, especially in the strong pauses between words. I was reminded that more than half of the North American tribes had "mother-right" cultures, as a Laguna friend once corrected my partriarchal leanings.

"We want to know our own history," Edna said squarely. "The holy men and women carry our ways in their dreams, you know. We older people remember these ways. We've been listening to elders a long time now. The teachings go back before what you call 'time' or history.

"Pretty soon now we're gonna publish the first tribal account of the Standing Rock Sioux. Our *own* people and past," she stressed, "Indian culture and history as we live it, as told by the people—our politics, religion, language, crafts, family and tribal knowledge. We don't forget, and we don't give up."

There was no pan-Indianism in the air here, as among some urban tribes; the focus was on the local people speaking and listening, even to the exclusion of other regions and bands. Edna Stone Arrow was decidedly Hunkpapa ethnocentric, in resistance to others glossing the "Indian" and threats of assimilation into white culture.

"Sitting Bull died, you know, 'cause he forgot the old ways. He took up the Ghost Dance, that Messiah craze. You know about that?" If the facts weren't straight, old disputes were. Tribal feuds lay embedded from the last century, and schisms were passed on to the younger people. Edna belonged to the Bullhead clan. The conflicts with white culture had incited Indians to kill one another, a sad old story of "hang-around-the-fort" friendlies and "savage" hostiles, "coffee-coolers" and renegades, those such as Red Cloud who signed treaties and negotiated peace, and those such as the legendary Crazy Horse who refused to the death. Today it was AIM versus Uncle Tomahawk and the Apples.

"I got work to do now," Edna told us. I thanked her and went to talk with Homer Burton, president of the community college. I asked questions, Jay jotted notes, and Rachel folded paper flowers, humming to herself. How much did this four-year-old hear and understand, playing at my feet by a long Indian road?

Homer, a wiry native Anglo with smoky green irises, liked living along the Big Muddy, and in turn was liked by Indians. "He's a little crazy," said a grinning Lakota student in a khaki parka. "He'd make a good Indi'n."

Homer seemed edgy as he stoked a briar pipe, billowed Amphora, then fussed at rolling a Bull Durham cigarette. His wasn't sacred tobacco.

"This college throws out the old academics, you know, abstract concepts of knowledge, theoretical skills. We're not 'preparing for life' here. We work directly with the reservation, get right to it. Use it, or lose it, Edna Stone Arrow says. Matter a fact, I'm gonna offer a course and just call it 'Indian'—teach what's happening on the reservation this minute, the people right *here*." He rapped his empty briar pipe on the oak desk. "There are a lotta things to be done as people learn, and no time to waste."

Cordial but busy, Homer was minding a keg of gunpowder on the rim of a political volcano. "You know there's a layer of strip-mine coal on this reservation eight feet thick in places. It's black gold to the power magnates, given the Middle East oil crisis." He sucked persistently on the briar and clouded the room with tobacco smoke. "It's not just the feds this time—the whole damn industrial world! This energy crisis makes Indian land *big* business. Forty mining companies are lined up around the Black Hills, just waiting like buzzards. We've got half the uranium and a third of the strip-mine coal in North America— all on Indian reservations. An' you can bet those politicians, no less than ever before, are looking for deals from Indians." Meghan's term project was about coal development in the West.

America came bargain-shopping again to Native America. The strange concept of "Salvage" dated back to the original Jamestown that first long winter of 1607, when my own hapless forefathers were rescued by Algonquin gifts of green corn. Telephone calls, emergency meetings, scribbled messages scrambled across Homer's smoky desk, as Indian leaders tried to head off this newest invasion of the *Wasicun*. "Fat-takers" was the translation of this epithet for Anglos; it devolved from a term meaning "white" or "snow" of the north, *Waziya*, once a color designating a vision of endurance from the northern, wintry grandfather.

In the Columbian beginning, some five hundred years ago, Europeans stole brazilwood for dyes from the Amazonian Tupinamba, labeling the latter "cannibals" after the words "canis" or dog-headed and "Carib," from which stems "Caribbean." They then robbed gold and silver from the Aztecs, accusing natives of heathen ways; it was God for gold. "New" Englanders imported European concepts of private property and economic competition, annexing land for tobacco and corn planting, and then asked Algonquins and Iroquois to share their native goods. And gold fever, the forerunner of Removal, soon spread through Georgia in the 1820s, to Colorado, then Montana, to California, then back to South Dakota in 1874, by telegraph from George Custer himself—there was gold in the *Paha Sapa* "from the grass roots down." The Cherokee, Ute, Crow, Yurok, and Sioux were persuaded with force to surrender this useless "yellow" stone.

Now, pocketed on reserves like starving, endangered animals, Indians gave up uranium in New Mexico, water in Arizona, game and fish in Washington, oil in Alaska, and coal-generated electricity in the Southwest Four Corners where the *Anasazi* or "old ones" lived a thousand years ago. Power magnates today demanded strip coal under half a dozen Great Plains states, as well as Black Hills uranium.

Not just Indians would be affected, but everyone: a Sagebrush Rebellion was in the making. Yet "Genuine Handmade Indian Turquoise" was powdered, reconstituted, and commercialized from New York to Los Angeles, along with the hippie fad for *heishi* jewelry, crystals in every bedroom, and pet rocks in the kitchen.

When Senator Dawes refused to acknowledge Sitting Bull's power in 1883 at Standing Rock, the Hunkpapa chief replied: "I am here by the will of the Great Spirit, and by his will I am a chief. My heart is red and sweet, and I know it is sweet, because whatever passes near me puts out its tongue to me; and yet you men have come here to talk with us, and you say you do not know who I am. I want to tell you that if the Great Spirit has chosen anyone to be the chief of this country it is myself" (Senate Report #283 of the 48th Congress).

We reentered the village of Standing Rock on the canal ingress road. I felt the tug of something along the river sloughs, spirits "gone south," as Indians said of the departed who traveled the Milky or "Spirit" Way. I stopped the car among the cottonwood trunks beached on the shoreline. Ducks swam in the murky marshes. My image of time shifted from a sequential roadway to the rippling surface of a bottomless dark pool.

I stepped from the car to walk down to the cottonwoods, feeling my way along through the sucking mud, not understanding exactly where I was going or what I was doing. "Be back shortly. Sit tight."

Jay didn't ask any questions for once. Rachel was absorbed at the moment in her crayon pictures.

I glimpsed a branch that seemed to beckon like a hand, but it changed shape back into a branch on my approach. A few yards farther, I came upon an uprooted tree trunk. In the viscera of the bole, bleached like bone, was nestled an antelope head formed from a root. The antelope was Meghan's totemic protector. I groped my way back through the fallen trees, trying not to conceptualize, but to trace the thread of instinct. It seemed an ancestral cemetery, the bone-white trees sacred in an earthly sense. If nothing more, this imagining was a release of conscious tension, impacted from the long winter traveling. I carried the root back to the car.

"Daddy, we got to water my willow!" Rachel piped up. I slid out the ashtray, carried it down to the river, and scooped water from under the oil film, picking up fingerfuls of mud. We planted my daughter's sprig in the ashtray.

"Fall back, spring forward," Jay said, glancing at his watch through this late wintery afternoon. Daylight Savings Time was just down the road.

We drove silently into Fort Yates and around the south side of town to a small graveled circle that overlooked the Missouri. It was near the "Standing Rock" of the abandoned woman and child where the river ran powerfully taciturn. Rounded clouds of waves rolled into the shore. I didn't know the color, shape, or location of what I sought, but felt I'd recognize a stone by this river; so like a blind man cupping his hands to the world, I looked for a *Tunkáshila* or grandfather stone. It seemed essential, for some reason here in Standing Rock, to my odyssey as Rachel's mothering Father.

After twenty minutes of lifting and overturning rounded granite, of smelling and listening to stones, partly hearing my own heartbeat and the wind off the water, at last I unearthed an oblong, heavy rock with a flat bottom. Its shape was solidly rounded, a *tunka* stone in the old Lakota language, implying special regard for the ancestral earth. I recalled that a common root bound the words *Tatanka*, "buffalo," *Wakan Tanka*, "Great Spirit," *Tunka*, "stone," and *Tunkáshila*, "grandfather" or "healing stone." The Omaha once sang a song like this:

> unmoved
> from time without
> end
> you rest
> there in the midst of paths
> in the midst of winds
> you rest
> covered with the droppings of birds
> grass growing from your feet
> your head decked with the down of birds
> you rest
> in the midst of the winds
> you wait
> Aged one

CHAPTER 14
───────

Summer in the Spring

Her name tells of how
it was with her.
. . .
The first winter this happened
we looked in her mouth to see
if something was frozen. Her tongue
maybe, or something else in there.

But after the thaw she spoke again
and told us it was fine for her that way.

So each spring we
looked forward to that.

"QUIET UNTIL THE THAW,"
Swampy Cree

Moon of the Carp (Carrier)

We moved to wrap up things in Jamestown and take to the open
road headed home. This migration came after eight weeks of spiraling
through North Dakota winters and reservations—Turtle Mountain,
Devil's Lake, Fort Berthold, Standing Rock—always coming back to
our center in the small college, whose founder thought the ground
sacred to Indians. Indian places spoke of earlier times alive to place-
naming, and moving waters got the most lively titles: Heart River,
White Earth River, Knife River, Tongue River, Little Muddy Creek. The
Cree said that to speak a place's name was to summon its history, its
"spirit," as with a person.

My students struggled to knock out papers, draw loose strands of
ideas together, write home, and pack gear for the eventual return to
the bay of brown skies, alleged "City of Angels." Jay was typing a
term paper on Indian alcohol halfway centers, and Kate was analyzing
soil samples for a UCLA geologist who had granted her some directed

research. Meghan was completing a tutorial with me on Shakespeare, of all things. Logan was out collecting and labeling native plants for a botanist. I pondered an imminent and ominous tenure decision from my UCLA colleagues. We all seemed uneasy, forgetting our ties, pulling back as though a diaspora were about to take place, though our trip was far from over. We now faced a month's travel through North and South Dakota, down into Nebraska, and home to California.

Meghan flirted with the college social wildlife, wading in beer swamps and descending into grass caves; this part of "advanced" education wasn't much different from LA. Kate made the rounds of rodeos, livestock auctions, and local saloons where the older animals romped. Jay was absent long hours counseling with a detoxed Lakota friend at the state mental hospital. Logan scurried about patching seams in the delicate fabric of our would-be tribe. I taught my classes with them and wrote and trundled Rachel from day-care to dorm, sensing frictions and being uncertain of solutions. I asked myself and the others for a makeshift summary by scotch-taping a set of questions, a sort of class final, to my door:

> Who are American Indians? What are tribal peoples? How do they
>   live traditional ways apart from mainstream America?
> What obligations come with a tribe? What freedoms?
> What particular place, this spring (?) in North Dakota, added to
>   your understanding of Native America?
> What is sacred to you here?
> What's the best joke you've heard?
> What is your personal relation to plant life,
>   to animals,
>   to the gods,
>   to an earth household?
> Do we live in a house made of dawn?
> If you had all the time in the world, what story would you tell?

We sat down the last evening to mesh plans. My apartment was littered with books, coffee cups, yellow scratch pad notes, loose typing paper, and dorm bills. It was a pan-academic setting. A cairn of unanswered letters cluttered the breakfast table.

Students wandered in singly. At first we talked of traveling in two groups back to California, boys out front, girls off to the side.

"This parallel route will never work," I worried.

Kate sniped something about "fast moving freight over the prairies."

"How 'bout an open forum to hash out our splits," Meghan suggested testily.

"Yeh, I'm ready for a fight," Jay teased, doubling his fists.

"Take *me* on," Kate poked back a little uncertainly.

The mood started out amiable, but edged. Each was of a different mind about traveling home. Meghan fussed that our cars could break down in out-of-the-way places. "Who would have a water pump for a beat-up Volvo in Gackle, North Dakota?"

"We need to stick together," Meg repeated. "The blind leading the blind, ya know?" She was still uneasy about camping outdoors.

"Just don't tangle me up with any rattlers," Jay teased her. Logan had counseled Meghan about her fear of rattlesnakes, drawing effigies and burning them, then marking her forehead with the ashes, but Meghan had a way to go with the wild things before becoming a clinician. She and Rachel shared a sisterly frenzy over box elder bugs.

"Okay, then, we'll video our last class tomorrow afternoon." I cleared my throat and played trail-boss teacher. "UCLA wants some document of this field work besides the usual term papers. Some deans aren't convinced we're on the academic square here in God's country. It's not legitimate learning, some might charge. What can we say to them?" There was shuffling of feet, and Meghan looked down at the floor glumly.

"We're just gonna rap on video?" Kate asked with splinters in her voice.

"We'll talk from the questions I've given you," I answered a little shakily. "Maybe begin with how we feel in this tribal experiment, eh, group therapy on tape?"

"Yeh," Jay raised his voice, "we need to work that out."

"On videotape?" Kate began to howl amid general snorts of laughter.

"As the world turns. . . . " Logan, too, was incredulous. Maybe my more conservative colleagues were right. This education-on-the-road might be a touch short on structure. No justified margins out here on the prairie, ragged edges all around. Three-by-five cards were out the window.

"Well," I continued, "people seem to be going their own ways this week. We pretend to pull together, but . . . " The bald accusation quickened Jay's face, always on the watch. "Ending the academic quarter is dragging us down. We've got differences of opinion everywhere. Should we stay together? Is it possible, even necessary to keep up this tribal idea? Why did we come up here?" The questions were mulled about the room. Kate frowned, and Jay tapped a pencil on his book cover.

"We're not Indians," Meghan started to say, "not a tribe in that sense, but we do look out for each other, and we've worked among

Indians for two months. I've never felt this close with peers or friends at UCLA. This next month on the road could pull everything together for us."

Logan muttered something that sounded like, "*We*, Kemo Sabe?" peered at me, and looked down.

"But just how much of a tribe can we be?" I pressed. "We pretend to carry around common goals. We study reservations, interview Indians and locals, try to live together, but we're only eating communally. Maybe it's just easier to cook and wash the dishes." Kate and Meghan leaned with their backs to the wall; Jay and Logan propped their chairs against the bookshelves.

Kate suddenly bristled, "Sometimes, Jay, I really feel like taking you on, boy, ripping you out for something like eating all our staples, but I want to remain . . . friends."

"What if *you're* not friends?" Jay replied hotly. "If we're not friends, let's fake it then? We'll be an academic tribe anyhow? Scholar-Indians in the library?"

"No," Logan winced, considering four years of law school. " 'Tribe' is a *political* term. We're *not* a tribe."

Jay turned back to Kate: "I have lots of things I want to dump when you piss me off, but I don't want to damage the group—and the group's damaged, tacitly and otherwise. Holding it back, then blowing it all up at the end—I don't know if . . . " His voice got softer and trailed off. There was a boy's face behind his urban bravado.

"We can't just have open aggression," Kate snapped, "kicking everybody in the balls all the time." She thought a few seconds, scrambling for a defense. "We don't have referees to officiate this kind of thing."

"But the false face or the slanted tone—there's no way to deal with hiding things," I argued, deciding to lay out my own gripes. "You avoid coming to terms with work up here. You've got no exams, no required papers, no imposed routines other than our class talks and daily journals. It's a different kind of learning than you're used to, but what *are* you learning?" A long heavy silence set in.

"Indian people have good cause to resent us here," I pressed on. "We drive through their lives and difficulties; we ask questions, nod, take notes, and what does it come to? Another summer vacation? Another grant? Another degree? Life is still desperate on the reservation, students slide home, professors vanish into the stacks, and America goes about its business, fantasizing, or pitying Indians . . . from a distance, from books and movies." I stopped. I'd reached a dead end.

"You know," Jay skirted my complaint, "I feel we've just got pocket friendships so far. And in class some always talk, some never. We should tell ourselves what we're up to."

"I talk when I have something to say, unlike some people," Meghan said. She was defensive about her quietness. "If I don't make noise, it doesn't mean I'm not listening."

"Some people are shy," Kate supported her.

"Nothing wrong with that," Jay continued, "but what if people need to open up?" His voice broke, and he looked down. "I dunno. How do we know if Meg has something to say—if she doesn't say it." Meghan laughed uneasily.

Logan drummed on a notebook with his fingers. "I've been reading people for the last couple weeks. Their tone says, 'Hello, how are you, please leave me alone'—down the line. We're being very deliberate in steering away."

"You hit it!" Jay was on Logan's signal. "Things have been very covert."

"What's that?" Meghan asked with sand in her voice.

"Under the skin. There's overt, and there's covert, which is under the covers," Jay grinned back, "like tepee creepin'."

"Don't make fun of me," Meghan pouted, "or I won't talk."

"I think we're genuinely concerned about each other," Jay continued. "That's where we're beginning as a tribe or family. An' we're learning twenty-four hours a day about Indian life *to*day—not stereotypes or sketches in books, but contemporary and complex people, like all of us." His voice dropped. "But frankly I'm not ready for this good red road business, vision quests and all. How far are we gonna go? Logan's cultural journey has something to do with a core in us; but *my* vision, as an American, is different from his, simply different. My spiritual needs are sacred, sure, but we can't all camp on the mountaintop like Moses. Some stay on level ground."

We talked for several more hours. Kate walked out of the room to cull her own angers and call her daughter in LA. Jay took over, trying to root out our problems, and Logan chimed in a distant angelus. I listened. Later, at night, I wrote my Lakota brother in Alliance.

Jamestown, N.D.

Dear Mark,

Greetings from the cold, windy north. We've been frozen in, hailed out, blasted with lightning, flooded, and snowed on through enough weather here to last us all summer in California. How do you do it?

We leave this Saturday for the Black Hills. Logan is going on *hanblechia*—the old rites alone on a mountain to fast, pray, chant, and dream. It's his Cherokee acculturation to the Plains—asking for some direction in his life, maybe even a name. Logan has been making some ceremonial things in preparation. . . .

After days of travel, thought, and talk we reached a point where things have worn threadbare, so the group had a long discussion tonight on the rights and responsibilities of a tribe. You've often said how hard it is for Indians today to pull together; it's no easier for *Wasicun*, maybe harder. At least I was warned.

We'll be back the first week in June. Could we all gather in the Center to tie some loose ends together? If powwow means "making medicine," as the books say, we need some.

Your brother, Ken

III

—

SUMMER VISIONS

When I looked behind me there were ghosts of people like a
trailing fog as far as I could see—grandfathers of grandfathers
and grandmothers of grandmothers without number. And over
these a great Voice—the Voice that was the South—lived, and I
could feel it silent. . . . Then I was standing on the highest mountain of them all, and round about beneath me was the whole hoop
of the world. And while I stood there I saw more than I can tell
and I understood more than I saw; for I was seeing in a sacred
manner the shapes of all things in the spirit, and the shape of all
shapes as they must live together like one being. And I saw that
the sacred hoop of my people was one of many hoops that made
one circle, wide as daylight and as starlight, and in the center
grew one mighty flowering tree to shelter all the children of one
mother and one father. And I saw that it was holy.

JOHN NEIHARDT, *Black Elk Speaks*, 1932

Dancer—*Oscar Howe*

STILL HUNT

Once an age ago
I hunted mudhens
with a single-shot
my father got from his old man
and came stumbling home
with a blood-warm jack
long ears trailing
the splat of its life.

We didn't keep that one
either.

Leading birds
three fingers
in flight
I tried to wing shoot
but could never quite
catch on.

Waist-deep
in the cold flat
river at dawn
pointing to the sky
with an old blue barrel
I often wondered
between black-outs
how we got
where I was going.

CHAPTER 15

Go to the Mountain

Planting Moon (Lakota)

Our three foreign-made cars left Jamestown and drove south along
hardpan country roads. Past speargrass meadows and greening winter wheat, we came to "White Rock Battlefield," scene of the 1863
slaughter. The state historical society again euphemized the butchery,
as at Wounded Knee, with the term "battle." This and other misnam-
ing, it seemed, went all the way back to the misplaced gloss "Indians,"
some thirty or forty million Native Americans a long way from the
Ganges and Oriental spices. Mistranslations—the wrong words for
peoples and places—were among the first misfirings against the original "Americans," named after a wandering Medici merchant four
hundred years ago.

Back a century, the Dakota Sioux were punished here for a Santee
uprising hundreds of miles east—another tribe, another place in Minnesota—but white homesteaders had angers to exorcise, and all "Indians" were interchangeable. A trader contemptuously remarked of
the Santee, starving in winter on a newly established and destitute
reservation, "Let them eat grass." Shortly after, the starving Santee
went on the warpath, killed the trader, and stuffed his mouth with
hay. So the day after Christmas that year, thirty-eight Santee captives
were hung publicly. Though President Lincoln commuted some hundred
sentences that day, two of the executed "hostiles" were not even
Santee.

A year later, the Santee insurgent Little Crow was well dead and
buried when Colonel Sibley, leading fourteen hundred infantry and
five hundred cavalry, pounded leather across the Red River at dawn

to surprise twelve hundred Dakota at White Rock. The soldiers massacred several hundred encamped families and took three hundred prisoners back to the new reservation. Today, on a sun-drenched spring morning, this prisoner-of-war history still stained the land.

On dusty plank shelves of the White Rock "museum," Logan found a "real Indian scalp," a donated war club, and the contributor's business card. Was there still a bounty-hunting trade? Tombstones commemorated slain white soldiers; none honored fallen Indian families. It was an old frontier story. I paced the so-called battlefield and flushed an irate bumblebee patrolling near a black pool of stone: a swallowtail fluttered from the clover and settled on Rachel's left hand. Each wing glistened iridescent with blue and yellow circles set in parallel rows of seven, the inner spheres flushing orange against black wings. Clinging to Rachel's hand in the car, the swallowtail seemed a sign of our own metamorphosis—crawling from the autumnal city, hanging in winter chrysalis, emerging in late spring, moving in summer flight.

We drove to the second of Sitting Bull's graves, near the Mobridge Cheyenne River Sioux, as the sun eased down over prairie waves of new sage and spring grass, and the group settled on a slope east of the grave. Everyone was a little uneasy preparing camp—Meghan was anxious about snakes, Jay impatient for a better campsite, Logan unnerved by dreams the night before, Kate hacking with a virus. Rachel fussed about going back "home," wherever that was. The local county police were out target shooting rats along the river. They slowly drove by in a moss-green pickup, but must have been hungry for dinner and so left us well enough alone.

The moon rose bulbous with spring pollens, as the molten sun spilled over the horizon. We were within a month of the solstice, and twilight lingered as an aureole against the night sky. The Beautyway shimmered across the Missouri—a reflected water path cast by the rising full moon. At eleven *hanhepi wi* or the "night-sun" began to eclipse; by one o'clock the copper-coin disc lay fully in the earth's umbra, and the silhouette was counterimaged in the campfire coals, ringed with stones that could burst sporadically like clay skeet pigeons. The night was strangely beautiful, shaded with fear, and questionably real.

I climbed a bluff above the Missouri, and the wind picked up erratically, changing directions from east to southwest. Sheet lightning flashed in the west, toward Sitting Bull's birthplace on the Grand River, only miles from his assassination. I sat alone on the top of the bluff. The night sky seemed filled with grassland emptiness. Something white winged by my right shoulder, and fear tapped me lightly, a ripple of the distant sheet lightning. I remembered a song that Owl woman sang to Ruth Underhill, southwest among the Papago:

> In the great night my heart will go out.
> Toward me the darkness comes rattling.
> In the great night my heart will go out.

Darkness closed around the sandhill. I stumbled down the bluff under eclipsed night, feeling my way through the sudden descent of shadows. The stars hung scintillant in the sky and sang their fear, "Tssik" and "Tssaa," as native bushmen hear so very far away. I looked to them for direction. Everyone by the campfire had gone to sleep. The wind was awake searching for the lost night moon.

Stillness settled around the dying coals; it was a classroom of a different sort, and I had no lecture notes. I got out my rattle bones, cleared my throat, and hoarsely chanted the moon's return through a song-poem from John Bierhorst's *In the Trail of the Wind:*

> The moon and the year
> travel and pass away:
> also the day, also the wind.
> Also the flesh passes away
> to the place of its quietness.

The Navajo speak of such singing as breathing out a guardian nimbus in times of need: "May it be peaceful all around me."

Translucently and with great care, the night-sun filled in its original shell, darkening from left to right, and then growing light like a copper fingernail. The earth's shadow slipped back into the night, lost among the vast frozen stars. *Aboriginal*, from the origin of things, I remembered, ancient miracles nascent in *čante ista*, the "heart's eye." The night—the loss of light—was teaching me to see.

Moon to Get Ready for Plowing and Planting (Oto)

Logan dreamed of himself driving through the Black Hills on a summer day. It wasn't a major augury, but nonetheless to be respected in the scheme of things. Near Firesteel he asked to drive the old Volvo, though he had little experience in handling a manual transmission. I consented with the trepidation of a surrogate father. There was a major hitch: Logan and machines, on the best of terms, struck an uneasy truce. I didn't mind being a guide, but what about my trusty mount?

The two-lane blacktop road, now state Highway 20, lolled innocently enough across South Dakota toward Isabel, then south to Du-
pree, west to Faith, then south again and west to White Owl. No
traffic to speak of, except an occasional tractor pulling a hay rake. I
braked the car into the dirt lot of a beekeeper's quonset. It seemed to
puzzle our intentions like a corrugated tin eye. Nothing to damage
here, I rationalized, not if all the tractors in South Dakota took to
Highway 20.

"Now, the trick is to *ease* out the clutch," I explained carefully and
patiently, as my father once instructed me how to shoot a gun—
squeeze the trigger, don't pull it. Some dank pubescent joke rummaged in the back of my mind, baggage from adolescence, and I
decided to leave it back there.

Logan sat pale as the gunmetal morning sky, overcast with spring
clouds. His jerking arms and legs appeared to have the muscle tone
of sunbaked rubber. He steadied himself, fisted the stick shift, stared
intensely at the dirt lot, and jumped the clutch.

The car lurched and shuddered to its very bones. I felt a pick run
up my spine. Logan's teeth rattled audibly, and Rachel startled from
her sleep in the backseat.

"CLUTCH!" I shouted. "CLUTCH! PUT IN THE CLUTCH!"

Logan had never heard me so point-blank. We tried again, more
slowly this time, and again my apprentice committed unwitting violence to the transmission, loosening windows and door handles. He
was shaken, but firm to his purpose.

We jerked around the dirt lot for fifteen minutes, Logan stiff as a
plank, me hollering, Rachel howling from the backseat, and finally
there was no avoiding it and no going back on Logan's vision. We
inched onto Highway 20, not a tractor in sight. Gingerly, tentatively,
Logan coaxed the ravished sedan along the asphalt and around the
banked curves. To slow and turn and shift into third gear kept all
three of us in suspense. No one said a word. Even Rachel remained
quiet on Logan's maiden drive.

We were late in joining Kate and Meghan, where they had pulled
off to survey a prairie dog village pocketed by the roadside. Sentinels
chirruped and fluttered their tails as we leaned against a fencepost.

"Logan just learned how to drive with a clutch!" I announced.

"Con*grat*ulations!" Kate snorted and clapped him on the back.
"Yore a real bronc buster now. Next thing you'll be racing tractors."

Logan wasn't talking.

We drove on to Bear Butte, *Mato Paha*, the vision seeker's mountain, rounded like a bear kneeling to the east. It rolled out of the shortgrass plain as a legendary Methuselah. The Cheyenne were said to have received a sacred arrow bundle on this mountain, not unlike Moses with the tablets on Mount Sinai.

Everyone finally regathered by sundown to camp in Spearfish Canyon, northern entrance to the Black Hills. Secreted among ridges, this box canyon once offered a winter retreat for the Sioux and Cheyenne, as well as a spiritual sanctuary and refuge to recuperate from battles. In 1877 the exiled Sitting Bull planned to return from Canada to this place then called "Water-Hole," where Cottonwood Creek flowed into the Spearfish; he got as far south as Standing Rock Reservation, where agents detained him.

The Lakota word for healing medicine, *wapiya*, has been translated "to make new by readjusting." It literally means going back to the right order, repairing an ill condition: *wapiya*, to mend up the sick, to "powwow" in the old Indian way. And a healing was taking effect among our small band, as we opened personal spheres to include each other. Meghan and I were helping untangle old family snarls about mothers and wives, fathers and daughters. It felt like several lifetimes sloughing off. Logan shuttled among us preparing for his time on the mountain. Kate had come off her high horse of riding Jay, who seemed less hair-trigger quick to force issues.

"Let's settle on a truce, Mister," she offered in camp.

"Thank you, Miss Kitty," he accepted. "Can we share some grub?"

As late sunlight filtered down the willow streambeds and shadows darkened the pines, I hiked to the canyon's south rim. The stones were striated with granite, quartz, and slate. There, shaded among birches, forty feet up the slope and angling diagonally across the pitch of the mountain, shuffled a pigeon-toed porcupine, feeding as he ambled toward me. Straw and tan bristles with a lambent green undertone layered his back. He could be seen as a lichen-encrusted boulder or an old man packing a forest sack. He was still dead set on me five feet away, so I edged out of his nearsighted path. The porcupine startled, turned his back and flared his quills.

"Who are you on *my* mountain?"

"A pilgrim, just looking."

"Hummph, well then, keep to yourself."

I remained still. Old Man Porcupine squinted over his shoulder, sniffed, and lowered his quills. He stared blankly through coal-button eyes and shagged off in another direction, munching birch bark with each wandering step.

I wrote late into the evening by campfire, then flashlight, insulated with long underwear, double socks, and lined gloves. The cold knifed through everything. Logan tried to cook spaghetti over a campfire, only to serve up thickets of starch with coagulated tomato sauce.

"I just *dare* anyone to complain," he said as he brandished a wooden spoon.

It was seventeen degrees by sunrise, and corn snow had fallen overnight. Ice laced the speargrass. The water bottle froze instantly when Jay pulled the cork. Kate was running a fever, Logan scraping pasta spoons in the creek, and Meghan on the nervous watch for bears.

I had awakened stiff from the cold. The canyon stretched blue-grey in frozen shadows. I shuffled around the dead campfire in coarse woolen socks and poked the thin crust of corn snow, then huddled on a rock near the stream to await the morning sun. What appeared comforting yesterday, by the end of a warm afternoon, now dawned stark and leafless. The needles on the pines arched against the morning sky, not so much blue as a colorless gun-barrel grey.

A dream had left me restless in the predawn cold. I saw myself falling through a vacant night, weightless with nowhere to land, and then grasping my ex-wife by the hand, momentarily suspended, only then to find Rachel between us, pulled in either direction by mother and father. I felt my own weight in her small hand and let go. Rachel vanished with her mother. I continued to fall endlessly. This stark sense of loss left me dazed, and I sat for a long time staring into the cold water.

"Meg, would you wake up Rachel, so we can get started with breakfast?"

"She's not in the tent. I thought she was with you."

"Well, where is she?"

"Don't ask me."

I startled myself off the creek boulder and came awake to Rachel's absence. The others dragged themselves from the rag ends of sleep and looked numbly around the canyon floor. There wasn't much to say. My four-year-old daughter in her red snowpants and parka had disappeared. I stood there stunned for the moment.

Jay took charge abruptly. "Call the park rangers. They can patrol before she gets too far away."

Kate fumbled for her car keys. "That takes too long. I'm going down the road myself. The kid must have heard those damn bikers last night and gone looking for the party."

"But which direction?" Meghan asked helplessly, choking back tears.

"What difference does it make? Let's get moving." Kate frowned as she belted her jacket against the cold.

"Wait," Logan stopped us. He walked deliberately over to me and stared hard through the thick lenses of his glasses. I could see his eyelids drawn back tightly, smoky irises distended. He motioned me to follow him. Kate pursued us, warily. Logan took something from his shirt and rubbed it with wild sage from along the streambed.

"Give me your hand," he told me directly, "the left one."

"Logan, we don't have time—" I started to say, irritated with this fussing, but I noticed that Logan was acting from intent, not panic. He seemed to know something the rest of us didn't. I held out my hand like a child, not knowing what to think. Logan drew his clenched fist across my hand. He knelt next to the creek and made a circular motion with his arm. Then he moved it from side to side and finally immersed his hand, all the while praying urgently but inaudibly.

I stood there startled, confused, partly in shock. I accidentally had seen Logan "go to water" before, but ritually, never in an emergency. It was just one of those things I granted him, not to be explained. He told me many years back that the ethnologist James Mooney tried to call eels in a North Carolina creek, chanting spells learned from old Cherokee conjurers. Snakes showed up from everywhere.

"Logan, stop it!" Kate snapped. "This is no time for gibberish. We've got to *move*."

"Move, then!" he said abruptly, clearly annoyed that Kate and the others had followed us.

"What?" she said, startled at what sounded like an affront.

"I can't go on if anybody else comes along, that's all. Okay?" he pleaded.

She held her stare, but softened. "This is for real, then," she said and turned away.

Meghan in tears followed Kate away from the stream. Jay paced around flustered, but then strode off through the woods, absently kicking things out of his way. I was caught between my own panic, which could send me running down the road, and indeterminate loyalty to Logan. I was the father here, the teacher, the leader, the trail boss. What should I do? I half-believed in the medicine rituals and defended their cultural purposes, but I had never used them myself. Did a white man have the adoptive right to live by these beliefs? Did mixed-breed Indians? Who did?

Now my own child hung in the balance, my lifeblood; I was terrified at her vulnerability. Rachel's innocence stripped me. I didn't know what to do, so I just stood there, fearful, hesitantly trusting Logan, paying attention. Did I have any choice? Another voice in me sided with Kate and Jay to take practical steps and call the authorities. Logan gave me a conspiratorial "thought they'd never leave" grimace, then squatted and began to splash water on himself.

"Now clear your mind out and look at the water. Think how clean it is." He continued to chant low consonants.

Each of us stood quietly. Logan looked down sharply into his cupped hand and spoke carefully, "Now, think, Ken, focus—look at Rachel. Where would she wander?" His instructions were simple and clear.

I glanced at his hand, and glimpsed something small and bright, then I gazed at the stream chattering by, eddies in the current. The first rays of sunlight sparked off pendant icicles strung under the banks. For just a moment I saw a flash of crystal flaming and dripping into the creek.

"I-ci-cles," I said, cutting each syllable as cleanly as with a scythe. "She would follow the streambed, trailing down the canyon where the water flows. She'd be picking icicles from the cutbanks. The kid plays with them like popsicles." I moved toward the creek. "My God, let's get to her before she falls in."

We paralleled the stream banks that ran east down the canyon's incline. The creek ducked in and out of willow thickets, around clay banks, past dark stands of Black Hills spruce, until about half a mile down it opened to a meadow. I thought only of crystals and icicles as we searched, and I felt myself moving through the brush without touching ground—led by the focus of clear, liquid stone. I could feel my heart pounding somewhere distant. My hysteria was checked by imaging the clarity of the ice by the stream, and I tried to see things as Rachel might see them. I felt for the child in myself, lost among confused adults. This approach made provisional sense, Logan had seen quickly, more so than running for a phone, or driving madly down the park road, or sitting paralyzed on a rock.

As the stream planed into a green crescent meadow burnished with Indian paintbrush, I caught sight of a fire-engine red flash in the banked sunlight. I ran down to a sandbar. There sat Rachel peacefully licking an icicle in the gathering morning light. She had been collecting rounded quartz pebbles from the streambed which were piled like opal marbles in the sand.

Moon When the Grass Is Sprouting (Quee'esh)

Our expedition pushed on to Lead, South Dakota, where the Homestake Mine still dredged the largest gold deposits in North America, discovered by Custer in 1874. Lead's sister city, Deadwood, proved to be frontier tawdry, as though Babylon with its money changers, hustlers, and sequined floorshows had invaded Lakota holy lands. These hills were, after all, the ancestral burial grounds of the Sioux. "Get rich quick," tinpan ghosts wheezed down sandstone alleys; storefront windows were trashed with "Genuine Indian Arti-Facts" (sic) and ceramic ashtrays. Mount Rushmore paperweights, beer-glass coasters with war-bonnetted warriors, and Black Hills gold-leaf were dumped in bins down the sidewalks. It made Tijuana look like a middle-class shopping mall.

"Would ya believe it, Ma?" Kate snuffed. "HANDMADE turquoise."

The Deadwood Historical Museum housed Indian relics, the usual: Sioux skull of a man named Many Tails, murdered in 1893 for his horses, and the crime glossed as a Ghost Dance uprising; 1889 photographs of Buffalo Bill Cody and the Indians parading the Champs Elysees; U.S. Army pictures of the 1890 Wounded Knee Massacre; and then a stuffed alligator in the basement, a two-headed stuffed calf splay-footed over a glass case of rattlesnake heads; war clubs and peace pipes looted from Indian burial grounds; Potato Creek Johnny's six-inch gold nugget, the largest such spoil gouged from the Black Hills, early gold incentive for bilking the Sioux of their holy grounds. Items of military dress were all lumped together behind one glass case in the basement: Prussian headgear, a World War I German helmet, and a Sioux warrior's parfleche. Indians were the only ethnic minority within the United States to bear the onus of war federally declared against them. Freaks, monstrosities, atrocities, war souvenirs—history here was not an ancestral tradition to be lived humanly, but a mutant form of tourism, a promotional trade in conquered indigenes, stolen gold, stuffed animals, prehistoric bones, and warrior skulls. I saw a nightmare Dakota Disneyland, festooned with the vengeance of the Wild West, though it was never so "wild" until the tourists arrived. The American imagination had gone berserk with frontier license, manifest destiny, precious metal speculation, and Gothic sightseeing. And some forty mining companies were lined up to dredge uranium from the Black Hills.

Wandering and frustrated by the motley elements in this part of our pilgrimage, we came to Sylvan Lake, now overrun with campers.

Here beneath the snow-capped Harney Peak, a holy mountain, Sitting Bull once envisioned an eagle in the shape of a man. It was a mythic vision consonant with classical Greece, an Icarus of the northern Plains. Hang gliders today seemed a sorry substitute.

Kate absolutely refused to camp in a snowbank, "No sir-ee, thank you, no."

"You know, Kate," I twitted her, "in the long winter of 1864, Fanny Kelley was taken a white captive of Sitting Bull and adopted as Brings-Plenty's wife, 'Real Woman'."

"The hell ya say," Kate growled. "If bunking with Sitting Bull in a snowbank makes me a real woman, I'll go back to Hollyweird."

Jay also insisted we find a more suitable campground, so we turned the wagons toward Center Lake. Feeling old and bushed, for once I listened and followed. We settled down at the lake's west end, boiled up the remaining tangle of day-old spaghetti, and Logan inaugurated the chosen ground by baking plum cobbler from scratch in a frypan.

"This Cherokee chef's a genius, no question about it," Kate crowed as she chewed down dessert.

"Pasta always tastes better the second day," Logan smiled, "with plum sauce."

Center Lake was quiet, wooded, a peaceful pool with bullfrogs and tree toads echoing in double chorus. Few people, fewer fish, many rocks and pines. Stone cliffs jutted reflections of ancient warriors in the still lake waters. The inlet stream flowed by the camp, and to the left rose two lookout mounds of soft, weathered granite. *Tunkáshila*, I thought, the stone grandfather spirits. The search for a vision would continue here. Logan decided it was now or never.

"We'll put some wood on the fire for you down here," I told him, an arm around his shoulder.

He blinked like a barn owl, shrugged, and said: "Just don't worry. It's hard to do this without the formalities, but my time's come. Things will take their own course. They always do."

"We're here when you come back." Kate hugged him and let go. "Don't be gone long, y'hear?"

So Logan left in the late afternoon. A patchwork visionary, he was not at all worried about appearing the fool, but rather liked the idea—sacred and foolish, however seen, touched by the gods. Logan's spot would be to the north, on top of the ridge, between two lightning-scarred Jeffrey pines. There in the middle of quartzite, lichened rocks, and pine needles, where the brittle pine sap tasted of honey and cloves, he waited for his vision. It remained to be seen if time, circumstance, and fate would favor him; some came back empty-handed.

We gathered in camp among late afternoon shadows. Clouds drifted in from the west, puff-white against a pellucid sky. The sunset cast a red shawl over these meditative hills, gentle pines, and lakes still as morning dew. "My grandfather used to say," Lame Deer told Erdoes, " 'The earth is red, blood is red, the sun is red as it sets and rises, and our bodies are red. And we should be walking the Red Road, the good north-south road, which is the path of life.' "

The earth smelled moss-damp from afternoon showers. We sat around a smoldering hundred-year-old tree stump to talk, click bones, shake rattles, and chant vision songs. *Tunkáshila, onshimala ye, wani kte.* Sawn logs for stools pressed the mandalas of ages into our rumps. Ocher, gold, and bronze embers crackled, lapping the air currents, as charred ashes flaked away like winter skins.

I sat quietly staring into the coals, and Meghan said, almost under her breath, "I'm going up in the morning."

"Up? Up where?"

"On the mountain."

"What do you mean?"

"I'm going up on the mountain—alone." She gave each word quiet emphasis.

"But why?" Her announcement caught me off guard. "You're not Indian, you're not a man, you're. . . . "

"It's not an Indian quest; and you know better than most I'm not a man." She let that sink in, then continued resolutely. "I'm going for my own needs—a time to be alone, to go down into myself. I want a deeper connection with who I am, and this will help."

Did I have any say in this? I felt stymied, less so the great white father. I was not as firmly opposed as she was decided, but I scrambled for deterrents. "Have you thought very long about this?"

"Long enough. It's something I have to do, a dream, you could say, that I want to follow through. Logan has counseled me." Her firm jawline did half the talking. "Think of it as a retreat, an Irish Catholic on a pilgrimage, repectful of the Great Spirit, or whatever one calls God."

I found myself edging toward her position; my objections were groundless. "Indians here used to pray to 'the Spirit that Moves-moves' or *Taku Skanskan*. It was their sense of 'gods' in things." This was the best I could muster, given the moment.

"Fine," she returned, "that spirit moves me too. I want to live my own good life in America. I know how to fast, and pray, and wait— my Catholic religion taught that. It's a cleansing, a woman's spiritual privacy. Anything more I'll just take as it comes." Meghan was open, yet adamant. It wasn't my right to play professor, father, or protector at a time like this. She had her own mind about things.

Meghan traveled light at sunrise toward a western peak above the road. I gave her a blood agate. Each of the others in turn dropped something into her hand.

"You'll be seasoned by these mountains," Kate told her companion, smiling against the tears. I recalled an old Papago woman's vision song:

> No talking, no talking.
> The snow is falling.
> And the wind seems to be blowing backward.

CHAPTER 16

Cry for a Vision

Moon When the Tree Leaves Are Green (Lakota)

I was torn by Meghan's leaving camp. She was fully capable of surviving in the wilds, no less than Logan, but I hadn't anticipated her going off alone. I'd never asked her position on such matters. What if she had wanted to go all along? She wasn't Indian, granted, but she tendered her own reasons, legitimate enough, for going on a retreat, recognized in hundreds of religions. She wasn't a man, or a warrior, but those exclusions wouldn't hold up these days, least of all among Indians from cultures where women exercised considerable power. Meghan had caught me on my blind side, doubly so; I wore the blinkers of cultural bias to indulge a closet chauvinism. The professor was forced to reassess our passage down a common good road.

Logan had a family heritage and tribal history to draw on in these matters and, most importantly, a life's commitment. He wasn't Sioux, though; he certainly hadn't grown up in the old Plains ways or even on the reservation. He was hardly a full-blood or "traditional' in the strict sense. Could a non-Indian woman, from Los Angeles of all places, step into this setting? Was California "non-native" by definition, in spite of being the state with the largest population of Indians in America? What did it mean that Los Angeles housed the largest urban Indian concentration? How "native" could a given American be? The word simply meant "born" in this land. My worst fear was that we were still playing Indian. Yet it finally seemed a question of the right intention, tested against deep self-examination. And how "Indian" were Indians today? Was it strictly an issue of blood quantum?

I decided to swim the lake; the early morning water was a murky bottomless green. The cold assaulted my stomach from below; it felt as though I were clutched by a fist of ice. Halfway across, my arms and legs turned numb. In just a matter of seconds I was in trouble, as the icy mountain lake made me cramp. I told myself to swim with the least effort, accepting the jade cold, the effort, the exhaustion as a passage of renewal. Don't think, don't react, just swim. Most of all, don't break stride, don't panic. Each pull was like tunneling through a mountain. I pushed on through the belly fear, sidestroked to the bank, and crawled onto the shore. I felt light-headed and foolhardy gasping in the morning sun, and my thoughts veered to Logan and Meghan on their mountains.

Don't fuss it, I thought. Let them do what they need to do. There seemed no arbiters outside one's chosen culture, no better judge of things than one's conscience and experience within a given tradition. This was perhaps the most native way in any culture: ceremonies making the old ways accessible to the people. It was not Indian against non-Indian here, but a relative balance of all people and things: "the people," most simply, found themselves "at home" with one another in a common land. That vision was rooted in necessity and circumstance for all of us, Center Lake to LA. Such a vision could bond the world itself, paying attention to the Hopi warning that it might "all come crashes."

I went back to rouse the sleeping camp for a drive to Thunderhead Mountain. North of Custer, west of Mount Rushmore, Korczak Ziolkowski had hewn 741 steps up 600 vertical feet of mountain granite and backpacked power tools up the sheer face for twenty-five years. He had dedicated his life to a dream of an *in situ* sculpture of Crazy Horse. "Praxiteles always wanted to carve a statue of Alexander the Great out of a mountain of Pentelic marble," Korczak bragged. "Michelangelo wanted to carve an equestrian out of a mountain of Carrara. I am doing this out of a granite mountain."

Henry Standing Bear seeded the vision in 1939: "We want the white man to know the Indian had heroes, too." Korczak traded the National Park service 360 acres of grazing land for Thunderhead Mountain, and after thirty years of blasting away six and a half million tons of granite, he now envisioned an Indian museum, hospital, and university honoring Crazy Horse. The top of the mountain was beginning to look like a profile. All this was a few miles north of Custer's namesake, this centennial of the Little Big Horn and bicentennial of America's independence. Korczak recalled when he began sculpting the mountain at the close of World War II: "Custer had one motel and

14 sawmills. They thought I was crazy carving an Indian. They despise Indians. Now Custer has one sawmill and 34 motels—for all the tourists. They still think I'm crazy but I don't care."

In a meadow near Game Lodge fed eleven shaggy brown, russet, and black bison. They stood shoulder-high to a tall man, were twice that in length, and weighed up to two thousand pounds. Massive heads thrust a third of the body over the forelegs; small, almost dainty hips followed. Once there were some fifteen million buffalo from the Rockies to the East Coast. By 1900 there were but a few hundred left, and Indians north of the Rio Grande had been reduced by a proportion of twelve to one, from about three million to a quarter million. This century, Indians have grown by a multiple of six. The buffalo now number perhaps three million.

After a dinner of rainbow trout over an open fire, compliments of Ranger Dave, our outdoor host, Rachel was allowed to stay up for campfire talk with the grown-ups.

"Would you tell me a story, Daddy?" she yawned.

"What kind of a story, Pumpkin?"

" 'Bout a horse maybe." I remembered the Lakota for horse, *sunka wakan* or "holy dog." Plains tribes had no mounts until the eighteenth century when Spanish runaways were traded north.

"Do you know what a unicorn is?"

"A horse with a horn?" She perked up. "I saw it in a book once."

"Yes, it's a very old horse, back before counting time by years, when people just dreamed their way through the days. Do you see where the moon is now? That copper-colored moon was the eye of a unicorn made of stars, who hobbled across the sky each night on three legs. He'll come right over us tonight, if you keep looking up." Rachel lay back and tried to keep her eyes open. I felt her small spine round in my arms.

"Well, the moon used to drift along on a cloud, really a young woman with her hair floating like moss underwater. Cloud Woman would laugh at that stumbling old unicorn. 'Leave your crooked legs behind,' she called in a voice of a hundred stars singing real soft and high. 'Float through the skies, take your light from the sun, and change each night!'

"But that unicorn wanted things his way. He wouldn't go without his legs, even when they were so awkward."

"So what did he do then?" Her voice was barely audible.

"Well, he had a friend, a buffalo with a serpent tail. There he is now—those seven stars just ahead of the moon. Serpent Buffalo had *two* horns to show off. He swam through the deep waters of the night with his body coiled, and he mocked the poor unicorn for falling behind. Serpent Buffalo told him to give up his silly horn and stiff legs and swim the night sky."

"So what did he do?" She nuzzled under my cotton-fleeced jacket for warmth.

"That little unicorn loved his legs too much. He said no, *no*." I felt the pull of sleep into the Dakota night and hesitated. Thank God we had no television.

"Is that all, Daddy?" Rachel yawned again.

"Well, there was a funny coyote who had wings like a bird, those six stars just above the unicorn there. Coyote Bird flapped around the sky. He thought maybe the unicorn should break off his horn."

"What for?"

"Use it as another leg, Coyote Bird thought. Dumb, huh?"

"Yeah, that wouldn't work," she caught on. "Then he couldn't be a unicorn any more, just a horse."

"Yep. So the unicorn limped through the dark on three legs, just like always, and sometimes he cried getting left behind. Lightning began to flash where his hooves stumbled against chunks of stars. And thunder followed him all along the Milky Way, what the Indians called the Spiritway. Then far below on the earth, right here in the Black Hills, when people began counting months by winter moons, there grew a little pine tree, just about your size. She chanted a song for rain tears and it went like this:

> Wa-kon'da,
> here needy she stands,
> and I am she.

And under the new falling rain, the little pine tree grew so tall that she touched the unicorn's shoulder. She rose into the sky and became his foreleg." Rachel was breathing evenly, perhaps asleep.

"Now, just before they go to sleep, all the pines on this lake look up to the sky and hear the unicorn singing with the night wind:

> Before me peaceful
> Behind me peaceful
> Above me peaceful
> Below me peaceful
> All around me peaceful
> In peace it is finished."

In her cardinal pants and coat Rachel lay dreaming in my lap. She had made up and danced her own "Firebird" in the forest today and had delighted to see a "robin redbreast" as a sign of spring.

The timing here in our lives was most essential, I felt, the pacing that carried one foot over to the next, one person to another, one generation to its children. It was the rise and fall of seasons, of sun and moon, of stars and wind; we periodically touch the earth again, then rise and move on.

Moon of Moulting (Loucheux)

Logan returned to camp unexpectedly at sunrise and crouched over the smouldering fire with hair disheveled and his clothing matted. There was a strange buoyancy in his movements, almost a feral presence, as though an animal looked out through the human casing. I thought of the Cree reference to animals as "other-than-human persons."

"Mornin'," Logan greeted me. When he stood up, he seemed taller, older possibly. Logan scuffed around in a state of distraction, like a man who had just walked away from an accident.

"I had this dream that I was lost looking for a man's house by the sea," he explained, "searching around for people who would agree to having a meeting there. I came up to people and begged them to gather to do this important thing, and they just looked away or dissolved. People have to realize the need for unity, or there will be none. Look at us, here. I couldn't remember my own name."

He seemed helpless for a moment, more in his dream than standing there. It dazed me.

"Then I woke up, I think. All I could see was thin sunlight that filtered through a white fog. Something pale and soft stuck to my hands. I looked down to see this white floss." His hands were smudged with pitch and down as though he had been plucking sticky chickens. "Then I looked around and found this on the ground." He handed me a bleached twig, notched at the top, split at one end. It was nubbed with tiny burls that seemed to be the eyes of a crow.

"I had to come back. I couldn't stay any longer. It was enough. See, something came to me a little while ago. I guess I've been thinking about how I was named for my grandfather because I was born two weeks after he died. It's really not *my* name, is it? I mean, it doesn't really describe *me*. How can you live by the names you get on a birth certificate? Your birth name is what they remember you by when you're dead. But your *life* names, your *living* name, is what you *do*, what happens to you. Now I can say why I feel uncomfortable about given names—they're not earned, just a kind of shield, even a deceit, aren't they?" He looked for some affirmation.

"I tried to remember my name, and when I gave up, because I'd done my best, what I saw was a crow's wing, clear like crystal, at sunrise."

Logan's fasting, isolation, and dreams left him almost incoherent, certainly disoriented. He had gone into his own dream time, stunned out of the ordinary world we think to know. He could only repeat softly in a startled voice, "White . . . Day . . . Crow." He added as a seeming afterthought, "But you know what? I bet they'd never put *that* on my grave marker. If I die, don't call me 'Logan.' Please don't." His dream of a crow at sunrise seemed, as yet, an emerging icon, a still-clarifying vision, perhaps the first draft of a sacred name.

Meghan returned to camp later in approaching darkness. I could sense her presence before actually sighting the telltale flicker of white on her coat sleeves. The tormenting cold wind and rain had given her, inversely, a clarity of mind and renewed sense of the strength that comes from going without.

"Well, I made it back. No snakes, no bugs, no bears. I've fasted alone on the mountain. It's hard work." Her voice was softly staccato, as she looked down into her folded hands. Rather than having her nerves stretched thin, Meghan seemed purged of incidental worries, gently subdued, even peaceful.

"I had some dreams—not visions, and not especially Indian. I heard these four older women haggling in a pawn shop; they were trying to set a price on a child ballerina dancing around an antique clock. It was me. I was there watching and listening, but they didn't know, as though I was both audience and author of the scene. Then I looked up a long flight of stairs, and a teacher walked through a large oak door, and I was left alone, with some typing sounds in an empty schoolroom. Nobody was there. Finally I heard a woman crying. I woke to my own tears." She turned away and knelt by the fire. I let her be and gathered dry pine. She had done this for herself, not out of idle curiosity, but the personal need for definition—to clarify her own "road" into womanhood.

Kate feasted this homecoming with fresh buffalo and corn stew, naturally seasoned with new sage the bison had been grazing in the spring-green hills. We weren't sure what to make of the passages on the mountain. Perhaps it was best just to accept them back—keep quiet out of respect for deeper voices, echoes of what Black Elk heard as "the Great Voice silent." The talking would come in due time. We all came, at best, as American cultural breeds, and success or failure of "visions" wasn't an issue. I thought of the Papago who journeyed four days across Southwest deserts to collect salt from the Gulf of California yearly. After four pilgrimages carrying no food, little water, and casting a prayer stick into the ocean, the Papago initiate returned "ripe" to the tribe. How ripe would we return to the City of Angels?

Moon of the Sea (Loucheux)

I woke at sunrise. It was a day to climb Harney Peak, then drive on south to Pine Ridge, Rosebud, and Alliance—the last leg of the journey. I wondered how this ancestral mountain, the center of the *Paha Sapa*, might move us. It had been half a century since Black Elk offered the pipe up there with Neihardt. I remembered a 1931 photograph of the holy man standing on this mountain. Dressed in flannel long underwear, ceremonial moccasins, and eagle feathers, he held the sacred pipe to the west and chanted:

> In sorrow I am sending a feeble voice,
> O six powers of the world.
> Hear me in my sorrow,
> For I may never call again.
> O make my people live!

He seemed an aged eagle invoking the winds that had carried him through a lifetime. Each year the Black Hills were more infested with tourism as America commercialized its cemeteries, à la Forest Lawn. Trickster would defile his own nest, the legends warned, till he suffocated in his own excrement.

We burned the stump mandala stools, as two hours of rain pelted Center Lake. It was the spitting kind that drives chill into the bones. There was some resistance to breaking camp under these conditions. Everyone moved with effort, as though underwater. Kate snapped a plastic tube tent down, and Meghan stared disconsolately at the fire ashes. Jay was restless with my organic sense of leadership—loose, he complained, not much direction at all. I argued self-determination, an old American tradition, but this was no way to go tramping up a mountain. Logan, impatient with the hassling, went off by himself. Rachel pestered me for a Big Mac. And the rain kept falling.

We drove to Stockade Lake. Custer camped here on French Creek in 1874, with his braided wagon train of gold seekers, and openly violated the 1868 Red Cloud Treaty. Black Elk said his people lost the Black Hills like "a handful of snow." The canvas wagon tops must have resembled wandering fungi to Indian scouts on the ridges. Now the place was overrun with weekend campers, mobile homes, and tourist facilities. A hot shower was the closest we could come to a sweat bath, and I rubbed down with sage.

Several hours behind schedule, we departed again for the mountain in a rain squall, negotiated a tortuous highway, and edged through a one-lane tunnel behind a lumbering Winnebago, up and back to the vision mountain. No turning around.

"This is a helluva way to get on the mountain," I growled.

"Get *up* there," Logan insisted, "*then* we can bitch about it."

To our astonishment, hail, then snow and sleet showered Sylvan Lake. We shouldered packs and started the cold five-mile walk up the mountain, wet and miserable. I lugged a plastic water tank and Rachel on my back. Logan was still sifting the details of his mountain vigil, especially the strangeness of the name White Day Crow. Meghan had reached her own deeper reference points, not in terms of visions so much as of personal understandings, openings. Kate was processing her own journey, more vitalist than visionary, and Jay was tempering. I felt part trail boss, part pilgrim. And now, together, we headed up the grandfather peak, *Tunkáshila*. Rachel's red boots clopped against my sides. The clouds flossed sunlight between squalls of mixed rain and snow. "In carrying water and chopping wood lie the Tao," I had read somewhere at a rest stop—another "way" or road for all natives.

The old stones towered in the distance, and moss trailed from shaggy Black Hills spruce. The smaller rocks scattered in scree collages—ferrous red and pink, sandstone tan, cinder grey and black. Broken shards of quartz freckled the trails. To the south the "Pinnacles" thrust up in vertical spires, and below them tumbled ancient, lichened mounds of granite.

"Go to a mountaintop and cry for a vision," old voices chanted.

Jay forged ahead, Kate paced herself, and Meghan lagged back, fatigued with smoker's lungs. Logan mustered the stragglers, including myself. I was tiring as the water sloshed side to side and Rachel shifted her weight to my shoulders.

When we crested the mountain, the others decided to stay the night in an abandoned ranger's cabin. It was domesticated after a fashion, with wire bedsprings and mountain rats scuttling through the woodpile. Alone I climbed on to the domed top of the granite peak and found an indentation on the western rim. It faced south on a ledge, about three feet deep, four feet across, and east to west the length of two men. A low cedar shrub grew at the east end. Some dead branches, too wet to burn, littered this cupped rim to the world. They took on partly recognizable shapes—a thunderbird, a ghostly trunk, a moose, a triple cross, a hand, a brace of antlers, and a charred fan. Everything seemed an image of portent on this mountaintop. Black Elk called this "seeing in a sacred manner." It wasn't part of the regular curriculum.

Rounded peaks stretched out below in wooded softness. A long-engrained wisdom rested in these old mountains where Black Elk, Crazy Horse, Red Shirt, or Red Cloud came to "lament" for visions. Encrusted boulders ancient as the sea surrounded me, "older than men can ever be, old like hills, like stars," Black Elk said in 1931 of the *Tunkáshila* or grandfathers on this mountaintop.

Too cold to write. I slept with stone visions and dreamed old songs:

> *On top of Paha Sapa*
> *predawn light*
> > *Heyoka hey hoka hey!*
> > *Heyoka hey hoka hey!*
> > *Heyoka hey hoka hey!*
> > *Heyoka hey hoka hey!*
> *Free freezing on top of dream mountain*
> *the highest point*
> > > *on the sunrise side*
> > > > *of turtle island*
> *Blowing mists*
> *clouded rocks*
> > *shape changing*
> > > *wispy stone*
> *Moths feeding*
> > *fluttering*
> *touch my forehead*
> > *in early dawn*
> *Mitakuye oyasin.*

Sleet laced my face in the early hours, and frost speckled the rocks. My feet got so cold I made socks of my gloves, buried my hands in my armpits, and slept in a fetal position, head sloping eastward toward the cedar and daybreak star.

I caught a brief but lasting image of Crazy Horse, while I was chanting and offering the pipe at sunset, and the image reappeared in a dream: a swarthy man in buckskins, fiercely concentrated, eyes not to be denied. He challenged my presence on the mountain, his single purpose riveting my quest. "Crazy Horse dreamed and went into the world where there is nothing but the spirits of all things," Black Elk once said to another white man. "That is the real world that is behind this one, and everything we see here is something like a shadow from that world." I hung for a moment, no more, between shadow and spirit, then awoke.

Jupiter passed fiery through the night; Ursa Major wheeled through the stars; a sunrise moon hung crescent in the sky. At first no colors flared in the sunrise, no shadows, as mist blanketed the mountain. Suddenly light broke under the clouds, as though the world tipped open. Morning colors fired in that instant—golden, peach, coral, rose—edging shadows west of all objects. Spring greens billowed beneath their stone mantle in the canyons below.

For two hours the sun burned through cloud banks. Mica and quartz reflected the morning light from every angle, just as the bowls of rainwater and snowmelt had caught the dying sun and held it at dusk.

I washed in a freezing pool, rubbed myself with cedar, then tasted a red rosehip. Soon I was climbing down through a ravine and picking my way back to the ranger's cabin. A large open-hearth fireplace beckoned inside where everyone still slept. It had been a night of rat invasions, and they woke with varmit jokes.

On the trail down the evergreens stood accented against meadows, and wisps of moss whiskered the spruce. Only a jagged horizon of stone spires, the Pinnacles, resisted the peace of *Paha Sapa*, where the mountains had lain down in soft pine mounds after ages of weather, sun, and night. Mica dust sparkled in the trail like miniature windows that caught the flecked morning light. I wondered what spirits in the earth might be watching.

CHAPTER 17

Pine Ridge

Moon of the Breaking Up of the Ice (Loucheux)

Five pilgrims and a child drove down out of the *Paha Sapa* and onto the plain, tuned to Paul Harvey's crackerbarrel radio news.

"You have to stay up past midnight to catch this dingdong in LA," Kate snipped. "Or drive to Bakersfield."

In Rapid City we stopped at the Lakota Indian Museum. Tribal paintings hung on the walls, among them a modern collage entitled "Yellow Thunder's Murder." A man's silhouette stood against a sky of flattened stars that were jaggedly scintillant. The painting was awash with angry reds, violent ochers, and churning blues. His skull was made of wadded newspaper print.

A young Sioux artist watched as I studied the canvas, then introduced himself. "That's my work."

"I know the story," I nodded. "The Yellow Thunder trial was held in my home town."

"I was ready to kill a white man, any white," he said. His voice was hushed. "I bought a hunting rifle when I heard of Yellow Thunder's murder. Too many whites walk away clean from their dirt." Then, even more quietly, he added, "This painting cleared my mind. We don't need more deaths to change things."

We pushed on toward Pine Ridge, through the Badlands and Buffalo Gap. The blacktop followed an old trail from *Paha Sapa* to the prairie among stretches of Plains meadow, lost creeks, washouts, and white clay buttes. There were no other cars on the road. A sorrel flaring its mane cantered down the asphalt road near Manderson, where Black Elk first talked with John Neihardt, and we continued on south. Since the 1973 Wounded Knee take-over at Pine Ridge, this reservation of broken promises had been ravaged with crime. I drove along reflecting on the land's emptiness. Suddenly I was forced to stop at a misplaced crossroad.

"We should be in Pine Ridge by now," I muttered to Meghan. "I don't remember any other road through here." Nothing there but an impassive stop sign and horizons of prairie. I looked to the left: the hill, arched brick pillars, church foundation, no church. We had been here before—we were back in Wounded Knee.

The radio reported among grain and livestock prices, "Six people were injured in a Pine Ridge gun battle two nights ago. An Oglala man was shot and killed in a bar." The Pine Ridge newspaper later featured an editorial on the "Nation's Hotspot":

Confrontation and terror increase here by the day. Indians confront Indians in a life and death struggle for power and survival, and the United States government has shown an incompetency that stands starkly against the Bicentennial celebration.

When Joseph Bedall Stuntz, Coeur d'Alene Indian, and two FBI agents were killed in a shootout at Oglala, it was only the tip of the iceberg. Reportedly, about 16 persons were in a house in Oglala, and the agents believed their prisoners were in that house. The two agents were found dead about five miles southeast of the reservation community of Oglala, close to the village of Wounded Knee, site of the infamous assassination of Indians nearly 80 years ago and the occupation by Indians for 71 days in 1973.

Although the state officials and the FBI now claim the hunt has been discontinued, Pine Ridge Reservation was besieged with hundreds of FBI men, sheriffs, as well as persons sent by the BIA and the Department of Justice, to 'investigate' the violence. It is alarming that every incident of shooting, harassment, and violence appears to be clouded. Anyone who goes to Pine Ridge in an attempt to get the truth is taking his life in his hands.

A dust-caked green Dodge prowled the cemetery hill. It seemed to keep watch on our California cars driving up to the knoll. A red scarf was tied on the fence behind the grave of one hundred and fifty massacred Sioux, mostly women and children. Another strip of red fluttered from a barren elm. Black Elk remembered Wounded Knee in December of 1890:

Then suddenly nobody knew what was happening, except that the soldiers were all shooting and the wagon-guns began going off right in among the people. Many were shot down right there. The women and children ran into the gulch and up west, dropping all the time, for the soldiers shot them as they ran. . . .

It was a good winter day when all this happened. The sun was shining. But after the soldiers marched away from their dirty work, a heavy snow began to fall. The wind came up in the night. There was a big blizzard, and it grew very cold. The snow drifted deep in the crooked gulch, and it was one long grave of butchered women and children and babies, who had never done any harm and were only trying to run away.

A fresh grave had been dug for "Phillip Black Elk" this spring day eighty-five years later.

We left Wounded Knee, not saying much, and headed east to Batesland, but mistakenly careened north to Porcupine. We missed the road to Winner. I fumbled with a map for directions, a familiar highway number at least, but the travel atlas showed no roads into or out of Wounded Knee. We passed Rattlesnake Butte and turned around; a magpie with long tail feathers sat like a mute scout on a fence post.

"So we're headed back through Wounded Knee on a road the map has forgotten," I worried out loud to Jay. I imagined peripheral images of a high-powered rifle or shotgun fired from a passing car. We couldn't find the road east, so we went south to Crazy Horse intersection, the only egress I knew for sure. Here, years ago, I first witnessed this field of unburied spirits. Only wanting to surrender, Big Foot died struggling to rise off the frozen ground: "I will stand in peace till my last day comes."

"Danger Ahead," a road sign warned. Then another: "STOP. Intersection." An ambulance rushed toward Wounded Knee, red light flashing, tires whining, pursued madly by a tribal police car. This time I listened to the warning voices of Wounded Knee, braked to a halt, turned east, then accelerated into shadows cast by dying sunlight.

"Why're we leaving so fast?" Jay questioned.

"Don't ask. Move." There wasn't time to powwow. We drove east on Highway 18, the sky troubled red over Wounded Knee.

In Martin, Logan gossiped with a gas pump attendant sporting bushy muttonchops, army boots, and a "Triumph" T-shirt.

"You hear about the shooting at Pine Ridge?"

"Oh, yeah, that." He absently washed the rear windows.

"D'ya ever go over there, to Pine Ridge?"

"Alla time."

"Ever scared?"

"No, you kid'n?" He snapped the washrag against the window pane.

"How do you go over there?"

"We mostly jus' drive through, on the way to Rapid."

"Jus' drive through?"

"Oh, once in a while, mebbe somethin' like five people will be standin' across the road—to block traffic, ya know. No problem." He tossed the washrag in a bucket.

"What do you do?"

"Oh, we stop. The Indians come up to the car. We pull out our guns." He added as an afterthought, "Ain't never no trouble."

"You go with loaded guns?"

"Hey, man, you think we'd go without guns? *Never* no trouble."

·

CHAPTER 18

Winner

Moon in Which the Leaves Come Out (Cree)

It had been a long time before we found Winner, a crossroads Dakota town that braided two parallel streets and the state highway for twenty blocks, all lights out. Main street, which was a motley group of bars and small stores, was squeezed into six blocks north to south under cover of darkness. A red stop signal pulsed sidereal time at the intersection. All five thousand citizens had lowered their shades on Highway 18 to dream the quiet of a vacant prairie night.

A Winner policeman escorted us to the city park campground at midnight. "The Indians sometimes come up here to drink an' raise hell," he drawled in a Gary Cooper monotone, "but I don't think they'll bother you tonight." Kate stifled a horselaugh. "I'll be on duty till five."

At sunrise next morning, a bleary-eyed highway visionary, I walked off the road-ache through the freshly mowed city ballpark. I wanted sage to cense a visit with Lame Deer, whose Indian name, *Tahca Ushte*, was spirited from the ghost of his grandfather, Let-Them-Have-Enough, who during allotment times needed a surname, the story went, and someone shouted "Fire!" Now hailed John Fire in Winner, Lame Deer learned sign-painting in prison, and he had daubed Junior Chamber of Commerce ads on the outfield fence billboards. His work overlooked a field of wild sage. "Medicine man's got to eat," I reasoned.

A thunderstorm building in the west was enough to get the crew up and moving. We washed with cold clear water from a cast iron pump and pondered the odds of finding our medicine man.

"You can't just rev up to the guy's door, park your wagons, and

powwow," Kate shrilled, water running down her neck. "All the Indians I know sleep in Saturday mornings."

For two months we had journeyed across half a continent to talk
with this *wicasa wakan*, literally "man holy"—healer, visionary, teacher,
artist. A medicine man was inspired by his ancestors through dreams,
as Lame Deer received his name, and he spoke with the powers of the
plants and animals and the earth. He could be variously known as a
shaman and priest, holy man and witch doctor, but his tribal role was
to bind the people's spiritual needs with things of the world—to
balance the good red and worldly black roads, sunrise and sunset,
winter and summer. He released the spirits in things to move through
this world, so matter and mind could be one. He doctored and blessed,
counseled and lamented, interpreted signs and kept alive stories,
chants, and visions essential to tribal culture. This made him at once
physician, priest, professor, psychic, poet, singer, and storyteller. He
was respected as a wise man, a man of heart and knowledge, and he
always took a place of honor among his people. Among the Lakota his
single holy investiture was the sacred pipe, first given by Sacred
Buffalo Calf Woman five hundred years ago and still kept at Green
Grass. He moved daily among the best and worst of the tribe; whether
traditional or iconoclast, purist or trickster, he was distinguished as a
man of power, chosen by the gods. In a flash, I remembered that
Jenny Lone Wolf had sent me to find him, a time that seemed long
ago. I had no idea how far or where her advice would finally take me.

We all drove downtown for breakfast at Joe's cafe and boarding
house. The other customers were an elderly Sioux and a few truckers.
After breakfast in the adjacent sitting room, two retired ranchers
cooled their second cups of coffee and lectured us on the protocol for
dealing with local Indians.

In a cordial diatribe, seemingly rehearsed, they warned us not to
waste time mixing socially with "*those* people." It could only get us
and the Indians in trouble. They complained about AIM and their out-
of-state sympathizers.

"Those dang outside agitators hang around and jus' stir things
up," one wheezed. Kate looked at Logan quizzically. "Git a job, that's
what *I* say to 'em."

This retiree, searching for an illustration of Indian shiftlessness,
waggled a bony finger at an arthritic old Sioux named Stone Heart,
eating breakfast at the counter, and denounced him in one word,
"drunkerd." He added, "The old man gets a monthly handout 'cause
he's crippled, but wastes it in a week on liquor." These retired ranchers

still leased land which they didn't use on the Rosebud Reservation. They hoped to buy the pasturage outright, so as to "get it off the hands of them that can't take care of it, and wouldn't do it if they could." I felt as though we'd wandered onto an out-take set from "Gunsmoke."

The older one, with a rosy Spencer Tracy grin, carped that no white man could park his car around Winner anymore without locking up. "Drunk, crooked Indi'ns'll steal the covers off the seats!" he snorted.

"Son, you've not seen nothin' like it," his friend continued. "They'll walk off in the middle of broad daylight, fronta God'n everybody, with your coat or radio, or what have you. An' if you don't see it next day in the pawn shop down on Gordon 'n Main, you bet, it's sold already."

His partner cleared his throat, "N-o-o-o, why you couldn't trust 'em or depend on 'em, surely not when your back's to 'em, not two minutes. They get a job around here, people feelin' sorry for 'em; just work till the landlord's off their back and there's enough food not to starve. Then they're right back to th' bottle again. That's the God's truth. Some'd just as soon burn your money as take a job."

I asked in a roundabout way what they knew about John Fire. The old goats exchanged glances and snickered. "Oh, we all known him for years," Spencer offered. "There's nothin' to him you won't find with any other drunk Indian. Always steps out on his wife, guzzles, and chases little girls like the worst old fool you ever seen." The coffee shop ranchers were eager to proselytize. They hospitably shook hands all around, inviting us to come back and talk again, even if the coffee was boiled a touch bitter.

Out on the street, it was raining buckets. We stepped into a grey little town of five thousand built to accommodate necessity. Quiet, simple, resisting depression because it had known so little of prosperity, Winner looked like any American farm town waiting for a break in the economy, holding on to what little it had.

We got lost looking for Lame Deer's home and stopped at the Enco station for directions. The manager fingered a wad of chewing tobacco. "John Fire's in California, what I hear, at some sort a' trouble-makin' meetin' or t'other—damn his hide—won't get back for ages."

We found Lame Deer's blue Galaxie in the driveway along a street well shaded by elders, cottonwoods, elms, and cedars. An elderly neighbor trimmed his lawn with a noisy power mower, but otherwise the sidestreet was untrafficked. A terrier greeted Logan at the front gate and fawned, while I checked to see if anyone was "t'home," as my great-aunt would say. Lame Deer's granddaughter, a sleepy little girl about nine years old, calmly informed us that "Gran'paw" had been traveling a lot and was sleeping in that morning. We should come back later because he was expecting somebody anyway. Feeling a stare that bore into his neck, Logan glanced across the street to see the neighbor's "Oh-God-what's-John-drug-in-this-time" withering look. Logan deadpanned back.

The students decided to hang out in the Tripp County Library. I met the librarian, poked around the stacks, and was surprised to find *Lame Deer Seeker of Visions* on the shelf. Restless and curious, I strolled down the Winner main street with time to kill, remembering the librarian's good-natured "John's a real character." I wondered what other epithets would crop up.

An Indian in his mid-fifties, dressed in an avocado short-sleeved shirt, lay crumpled on a doorstep near the main street signal. A City of Winner garbage truck paused at the stop light and honked.

"Hey, Nephew, wake up!"

The local black-and-white was making its rounds and pulling away from Joe's coffee shop. North Side Package Liquor squatted a storefront away, and the Church of Nazarene perched across the street. The man slept on in the doorway.

I figured a newspaper office to be the right place to ask questions— not about medicine, but about the man. I crossed the street to the *Todd County Tribune*. The editor, a short-cropped, middle-aged woman named Dolly, strode out of the back room wiping printer's ink on her apron.

"John Fire? Oh, su-u-re, I seen John a lot a times at the court-house," she grinned. "Everybody knows John Fire. Ya know, he used to have his 'movie hair,' he called it, when he went to Hollywood to be in some Indian film."

"*A Man Called Horse?*"

"Mebbe that one, or *Little Big Man*. Those westerns are all the same, jus' like Indians like ol' John."

I didn't know what to say to this. It was like trying to reason with my aunt. She breezed on, "Those *Indian* people, I dunno, got evury advantage, but they *always* go back to the blanket, jus' kinda wild. I don't care—white, black, brown, red, 'r green—peoples no differ'nt! Why can't they live respectable lives?" She seemed honestly to want to know why. My jaw hung dead weight. "With all the AIM trouble, purty soon these farmers around here will lose their farms." Confidential nod. "They lease reservation land, ya know. It's all gonna be jus' barren then, no farming a'tall. America's gonna be just cities and agribusiness, dirty windshield farmers."

I thanked the editor for her opinions and retreated back to the county courthouse library. Muffled voices filtered from the hallway near the sheriff's office, as I passed through a near-deserted reading room and into the hallway to find Jay and Meghan talking with a dark full-blood in jeans. He wore scuffed black boots with rounded heels, a dusty cowboy hat, and a checked green shirt.

"You want to talk to Ind'ns?" the man drawled, his "Ind'ns" sounding like two stones dropped in a well. "Go up there." He pointed toward the upper floor jail of the county courthouse. "You get drunk, get thrown in, talk with fifteen, mebbe twenty Ind'ns. Get to know 'em." He leered and winked at Jay.

Articulate in gestures, a glint of laughter in his eyes, Lame Deer stood there amiably shifting from one boot to another, lighting a Marlboro, placing his hand on a doorknob to make a point. He had materialized like some shamanic stand-up comedian. John (Fire) Lame Deer was dependent on a hearing aid behind his left ear, so like many partially deaf elders he carried on most of the discussion, sidling around to answer a few questions that dovetailed into his thoughts today. He used the students' presence as a way of talking to himself, as Socrates used to carry on in the marketplace or at friends' parties. It was an older kind of common wisdom, one that proved itself in the streets.

"The end of the worl' is coming, you know. Live right, now. We're in hell down here." He looked down, as I thought of Plato's cave, and shook his head. "All that money, those rich men hangin' on to it, tight." Clenched fist. "Rich men all goin' ta hell." His eyes crackled above the cleft in his nose bridge. "The only good Ind'n is a dead Ind'n, I heard say," he winked at me, "but a good white man never was born!" He laughed aloud at this joke, then looked a little sheepish.

"I come from th' earth, *makan*, I am th' earth, red earth man. Ah'm here an' now, right here now," as he rolled his jaw. "Go bare-foot. Take off yore shoes like them hippies. But go last, let the others go first." He looked directly at me and gestured undressing with the wave of a cigarette. "You can live anywhere . . . out in the street . . . don't need money. Give it all away." And then he added quickly, "If people *really* need help, *give* it to 'em."

I scrutinized his face: amber eyes, wrinkled walnut skin, accented laugh lines, bruises and a discoloration under the right eye, short grey-flecked hair. Lame Deer appeared to live for this present heaven or hell, depending on the tilt of his *heyoka* mind. If it grins it's alive; if it laughs, it's in touch with life; and if it makes you laugh, it's smart like a fox. "A holy man can't have money. He'll lose his power. Fifty bucks in my pocket, that's all I need. I can go anywhere, have a good time, be with my friends." Rumor had it this was the man's homely truth, and who would begrudge him? The Moral Majority might take some pointers.

Lame Deer rambled and circled with his thoughts, darting in to count *coup* on the rich, chuckling through straight white teeth like an old horse, then retreating. His stories were told in flashes that lit up seventy-three-year-old deep brown eyes.

"You can be called brother," he said turning to Meghan seriously, " 'cause some of yer father's in you," letting the point register.

"An' you can be sister," to Jay, " 'cause yer mother's in you. We're all the same," as if resolving all odds. "Girls are jus' like you an' me," he swore quietly, letting us in on a private insight. "They got brains. They're smart." He grinned at Meghan.

"You wan'ta know about Ind'ns? Go in there," quizzically nodding toward the library stacks, "an' read alla that. I educated eighteen medicine men; fourteen now are dead. But you find the right holy man now, if you want to be healed or taught—keep lookin' till you find the right one. Sure, there's lots a fakes, but some real too. It's got to be the power a' the Great Spirit, right here, now, between you 'n me." Was this some continued text of Jenny Lone Wolf's counsel or Thomas Banyacya's warning? I listened and sorted things, and listened some more. Lame Deer was no romantic image of a "holy" man.

Indians and non-Indians walked by the courthouse hallway. The Indians nodded, as John took them, his audience, and his storytelling in. His *heyoka* vision scanned all sides of the moment, alert, open, and many-minded as the gods. The man was a wise healer, clearly, but he could be mistaken for another streetcorner character or even a drifter.

"The farm, a few animals, the land out there in the country . . . don't need anything else. That's heaven, right here—don't have to get scooped up into the clouds." He shifted his weight to the side. "There's bad things coming, though. We'll see then how the rich man does. He's in hell now, all that stinginess. What's he doin' with his money but squeezin' it tighter? Don' tell a man yer broke when yer not; give him a dime, say you gotta keep the rest to help yore own, send him on. He'll get to heaven his own way.

"But it's *gonna* fall apart. Only ones left gonna be people like us Ind'ns . . . get their power from the things around 'em—the trees, stones, grasses, animals, spirits." The talk seemed to rest on this note. I remembered Thomas Banyacya warning me in Arizona, "Mebbe it all come crashes." Were we preparing to enter another layer of reality or another "world," as the old myths prophesied? Where did that leave this world?

"What you guys gonna do?" John looked up the courthouse stair-well. "I got a lot a' chores ta take care of."

"Could we talk with you later? This afternoon?" He nodded in my direction. "Maybe at your place, say, three o'clock?"

"Sure, three o'clock." Then this bow-legged, grizzled, Indi'n holy man in a cowboy hat ambled up the stairs.

"Don't call me a stupid Ind'n." He grinned over his shoulder. "Call me a stupid snake or a stupid dog, if you got to. You can be a devil, or a stupid Ind'n or a white man. The spirits'll find us ever'where."

CHAPTER 19

"They're Tellin' You Somethin' Up There"

Moon When the Tribe Plants (Omaha)

Mrs. Evers, head librarian at Tripp County Memorial, opened the seminar room as she swapped information about experimental teaching programs on reservations. On the Rosebud Reservation, Spotted Tail Community College or *Sinte Gleska* was gathering data about Lakota healing and history from seventeen local elders involved in a "college of medicine men." Mrs. Evers noted that many older people, such as Lame Deer, knew enough to revive some of the religions; and as the young people got more interested, part of the old knowledge might come back into use.

Mrs. Evers asked if we would like to meet one of the authorities on local history, "Mr. Luther Clearwater, a nice, clean-cut, well-mannered man, with a good family." He'd had some years at college and was writing the story of the Rosebud Nation. Here was a contemporary tribal historian. She phoned him and set up a meeting for early afternoon.

It was still raining at lunchtime. I planned to wait in the seminar room to meet Mr. Clearwater, and Logan set up the tape recorder, then ran out to get supplies, while the rest of the group ate "fried steak" at the local diner. Using the courthouse rear exit, Logan paused to hold the door for a grave but friendly Lakota man who looked in his early fifties—white-haired, bronzed, tall, and large-framed. He turned toward Logan with a lantern jaw. His broad forehead seemed massively flat, like a ledge, over gunmetal-blue eyes.

I thanked him for coming, and we talked about crops for a few minutes, the usual exchanges in farm country. When Logan returned, Mr. Clearwater, grinning, turned to shake hands, but his expression abruptly changed upon eye contact. The thought crossed Logan's mind that he had done something offensive, but all Clearwater did was alter the handshake, offering his palm conventionally, then quickly gripping across Logan's hand, his right arm cocked as in arm wrestling, and his left hand locking Logan's wrist. Logan felt a little bewildered and smiled nervously.

"Pleased to m-meet you," he stammered like a neophyte nephew before a distant uncle.

Luther was not fifty, but seventy-two and amazingly hale, the grandson of a Brule Sioux *heyoka*, who had taught him much local history and ceremonial lore. Logan glanced at the tape recorder to make sure it was running smoothly. I volunteered a few comments about recent talks with tribal historians and visits to sacred centers such as Bear Butte and Harney Peak.

"Yeah," said Luther, "we got a lot of places like that. Got some you don't know about, you kin bet."

Logan remained tongue-tied. I offered that some of his family were "granny doctors" in the North Carolina mountains and that Logan had spent the last weeks collecting certain Dakota roots, flowers, and leaves for a friend who used them in foods and tonics. Luther glanced at Logan several times during this commentary, as if expecting him to say something, but Logan only withdrew more, like a child shy in school.

After a pause Luther asked Logan what he had done in the Black Hills. Logan said diffidently that he'd gone to the top of a hill for a couple of days and nights, that he'd seen something one morning before waking up, and that he had come down after that.

"There was more up there." Luther looked at him severely. "It's not all there is to it, just go up for a little bit until things get good and come down. What'd you *see?*" Logan recounted waking the last morning, after a long dream, and glimpsing a translucent bird wing, when somebody asked who he was. It had shocked him wide awake.

Luther nodded, ruminating. He inhaled sharply, leaned toward Logan, and said, "Then you should have stayed. You can't go off with just a picture. You got to go back more times, 'cause they're *tellin'* you something' up there. Spirits didn't get through talkin'. It's just a start, doin' like you did.

"Lot of people go up on fasts; but it's tough, that goin' on *hanble-chia*, like nothin' else. Spirits test you up there. *You,*" he drilled into Logan, "*you're* gonna end up at Twin Peaks. You remember that. You got to do that. We got a place here called Twin Buttes. Twin Buttes is our *Sicanju* medicine man's place. Gets real crowded with spirits. I always heard there's fires on them peaks at certain times, weird lights. It glows like rainbows." There was an impish glint in his eyes.

"Did you ever see that?" I asked, straight man in the seminar room.

"*I* don't know if I looked for it," Luther said in a self-effacing way. "All I can say is that's a place you got to go," turning to Logan, setting his jaw hard. "Yeah, the mountain still lights up if it's got to."

Luther was explosively direct, dramatic in his silences and pauses, with a manner of stately courtesy. He could divert an entire line of conversation with a word or gesture.

"A medicine man has to give everything he has to his people, all he can," he said. He kept his house open to everyone on the reservation and in the tradition of his grandfather would not refuse what people asked. He had tried to give his family a chance at white education, to see that people who wanted to work got jobs somehow, and to feed those at his table if they couldn't work. He had regularly held an eight-to-five job and was no great hater of the time card, but he had not let the clock rule him. He wanted an economic base on the reservation so his people could "make it on their own."

"Gover'ment still don't like Indian medicine much, but there's not really more'n a few of the real medicine men left. Don't have to worry much about Indians practicing medicine," he added with a rueful grin, "if they can't even do it right anyway.

"Most don't live right *now*, see? You're havin' to fake if you don't live right. You got to clean out inside, or you get killed trying to do medicine, if you're really tryin'."

"Where does your medicine come from?" I asked. Luther seemed to hedge at first, suggesting that maybe all the shamanic traditions of the West originated in North America and were dispersed from there. Then he shifted his tone abruptly and spoke more plainly. "But you want to know where the Power come from—*ever*'body wants to find that out. We got a name for all them powers. *Tunkáshila*, Grandfather, *Ate*, Father—all like that. But th' powers are mysterious; they don't like you to tell all about things. You don't tell ever'thing you see in a vision; it loses power."

He breathed in deeply, allowed a sober moment for reflection, and said very deliberately, "So much of what we had here is gone now, all tore up, burnt up. We had those bundles that had the power, gifts from medicine men, women too." He smiled and went on more cheerfully, "Different ones held onto what they could, though—it's not *all* gone. Nobody knows how much is still here with the songs and prayers and stuff."

"Could the old knowledge still be salvaged?" I asked, a ghosted image of Jenny Lone Wolf in my mind's eye.

"I can teach people, like what my *Tunkáshila* told me when I was little. He'd take me out to the fields, him with all that paint on, and show me where to dig an' what to get.

"I'm tryin' to write down somethin' about that now. It's hard, nobody to learn, or else nobody to teach at the right time. A medicine man, anyway, can't tell all he knows—just show somebody how he got where he is, mostly, can't teach his vision." He shook his head rapidly. "No, he can't have nobody see what the spirits showed him. Mostly what he knows goes to the grave, like with my granddad, 'cause you forget and can't get it back no more. It's there, you just can't get to where it is.

"Centuries and centuries, they were buildin'," Luther said, indicating a stepwise progression, "and got up, *that* high, white man come, and he pulled it all down on 'em. They were just gettin' where they could fight those white man diseases, too. Smallpox, measles, whoopin' cough, cholera 'd kill 'em easier than any white men, 'cause those Indi'n people never seen it before. They couldn't fight things they couldn't see.

"Medicine men worked on these things, when the army and the missionaries come in here burnin' an' huntin' for what *they* could see. If they'd been left alone!" His hand fell at a heavy slant to his knee. "Said we were superstitious an' didn' know any better," he rasped.

He suddenly became almost dogmatic. "It's hard to be Indi'n, see, but it's almost impossible to be a medicine man. You got to sacrifice." He grabbed at his shirt and pulled at it like lifting flesh. "You got to risk ever'thing, and then you don't get any pay back on nothin' that comes out of you. People might give you things, appreciatin' what you go through, but *you* give *all* the time. It's the way medicine man's got to live with it." His voice fell. He paused.

"Nothin's free, you keep on findin' out. You're takin' a lot of risk, with your family and ever'thing you care about." His voice was firm, but quiet. "You got to be ready, give it all away, or have it taken away. If you're healin' people, you're givin' up a piece of yourself ever' time, like in a Sun Dance when you cut off flesh. You're puttin' up your own family as c'llat'ral lots a times," he said, fading into a slight pause, then added with a note of sad humor and resignation: "An' if you don't think *that's* rough! It's a long hard road, Indi'n doctorin'. You're tryin' to do just right, an' a little thing goes wrong, an' you could lose your sister like I did, or your wife, your whole family. Wipe out ever'thing. No wonder so many medicine men lived by their self by the time they got old. Nobody left!" There was great sadness in his face, ill-disguised in a drooping smile.

"I keep hopin' one of my own kids would do somethin' with it, but they won't learn from me. Don't care nothin' about being *Indian*. Right now I'm doin' all I can with writing my books, so my power goes into that," he said with finality. "I'm tellin' the story of the birth of the Rosebud Nation. Brule, Sicanju, all them people—after Wounded Knee. I got boxes full of things on it, pictures and things a lot of the old people give me. I hope I live to do it," he ended with a slight grin. "Most don't care nothin' about old ways now. All goin' ahead to be white men, even my own kids. Won't be no Indi'ns left if that goes on." Logan was staring into the floor.

"An' the Indi'n militants keep wantin' to put things way back a hundred years ago. We're gettin' pushed back enough without help! Get ever'body killed off or dyin' off, runnin' around crazy and shootin'—*that's* white man. So many of these nationalists get militant and go away and say they talk for their people." He seemed ready to dismiss the issue. "They stay out too long, away from home. They don't know how to *be* Indi'n, so busy *actin'* Indi'n."

Luther swallowed hard and shook his head. "I'm teachin' a little boy how to dance Indi'n, like we used to do, and got him fixed up with the right clothes for it, feathers and songs. He's goin' to learn all about that when he's four—not ever lived in a city or anything, and knows what it's like the old way, an' he'll never forget that. He'll always *be* Indi'n, be rememberin' that when he's old even. This other stuff, talkin' and fightin' people do, gets way off base. What's *left* for the people after that?" He appeared frustrated, almost bitter. "We had *ever*'thing taken from us so many times, so what's left? How many *more* times they take it away? The Little Big Horn and Custer was *one* time." He glanced at Logan briefly, then away. "We got to live; that's what it's all for now, Indi'ns or not."

He looked over at Logan and snickered. "You been talkin' about this *hanblechia* business. Look at these anthropologists out here, thinkin' they'll learn somethin' like on survival courses. They don't see there's sacrifice in it. You ain't comin' down the same, once you gone up," he said gravely. "White man religion ruins people for that *hanblechia*. They go up and think if they'll sit there hungry and see pretty pictures, and it storms when there's nothin' up there . . . What do they have to *get* them through the hard parts? Not a damn thing. Some of these

Indi'n men around here's like it, too—think they'll jus' go up there and be brave. You can't get ready for *that*, puttin' up fights with a lot of other drunks in a bar, kickin' their hind end, 'cause you can't *fight* what's up there that way. Thunder spirits! You go up there an' you find out what's pitiful. All this power is somethin' people want to get at, but it's got to come *its* way.

"One of you guys told me about your grandmother that knew about herbs?" He looked around as if he couldn't remember who and gave up. "We *still* got our herbs. I don't go around and do medicine, except to gather the plants in places hardly anybody knows of. I get 'em in big bags, an' say the right prayers when I gather 'em, and give 'em to the old people around here. They know how the plants're to be used, and they'll trust *them* before they'll go to the health service," he said emphatically. "I just leave the medicines by their door in a paper bag. They'll take 'em for when they get sickness in the winter, then to clean 'em out in the spring. You can't go to no white doctors for it.

"There's plants for about whatever you have wrong. I know a plant, a little vine-gourd, that's for helping *all* parts of your body, and you take the part of it you want to use. You got to pray for that," he said, and he proceeded to pantomime a gathering procedure, including the brief prayer in Lakota he said his grandfather taught him. "That plant is growing in a little wet place about eighty miles to the east of here on the Missouri. I can show it to you, all about it. There will *have* to be young people comin' up to do the medicine again."

Out of the green and white cardboard box he'd brought with him Luther pulled some photographs. He showed us one of Chief Milk, one of Spotted Tail, and another of Rain-in-the-Face. There was a group shot of a ceremony at Rosebud. Perhaps eighty years old, it showed the preliminaries to a dog feast and included a portrait of his grandfather as a *heyoka*, painted with black and white streaked lightning and spots. He was grimacing fiercely, brandishing a small object over his head, and he seemed to be caught in the act of charging the camera.

"*There* was a real medicine man," Luther said, pointing at his grandfather. "He knew it right. They were in the right time for what they were doin'. In my time I'm gettin' it all down, what they done. Sometimes it comes all at once, just a stack of it, and sometimes I get out only *this* much," he said, indicating the length of a paragraph with his thumb and finger. "It's like my medicine. You go out, you sit down someplace, you try and remember what you heard from the old people. They talk to you then. You got to follow out what *they* say. I type it all down."

He fished around and drew out a picture of another *heyoka* hunkering at the base of a big black kettle, coaxing a flame with a few twigs and blowing at the smoke. "That one's heating the water to boil a puppy for a ceremony. You get a blessing from eating puppy meat."

There was a small print of a standing woman in a gingham shift, stocky with big hands, holding what appeared to be a roll of cloth. "That was a badger medicine woman. She was one of the strongest ones. Dead a long time. There was these people called *winktes*, too, like you heard about. Morphodykes. Last one died about three years ago."

He drew out photographs of funeral ceremonies, detailing a series of procedures that could take several years. "I want a burial like that," Luther said. "We would put the dead up on a little platform, or in a tree someplace, for about a year, and sometimes we would keep a soul of one of them, like a name, with the family. The body would be up like that, close to the sky where no animals would bother it, and we would honor it that way. Then take it down like this picture shows, with a little shelter over it. Then cover it with rocks where the body could go on back into the ground. Sometimes we'd want to keep that soul a long time, but missionaries never liked it. Said it was nasty." Luther wrinkled up his face and made twiddling motions with his fingers, mocking prissy squeamishness. "The gover'ment cut nearly all that out. The way we had was holier than the way they acted to us, you kin be sure." His jaw jutted forward.

"We have that sweat lodge ritual still. I do the prayers in the bathtub ever' mornin'. It's somethin' people could do even without a sweat lodge, and it don't need to be all that fancy. I got me some sage to put in the water. The water is so hot hardly nobody could stand it. Then I go in, about five o'clock ever' mornin', and pray for family and friends and people I know are in trouble.

"Look at me here, seventy-two years old, nearly seventy-three. I been made a grandfather over forty times. Not a pain, none of that rheumatism or stuff. I do drink, but not all the time. I clear it out." He seemed to be searching for a definitive stance about personal power. "There was some of our men that could ride all day at nearly a hundred years old. They didn't lose their minds, either. Look at Red Cloud. I want to go on like that. I may live like my grandfather; I may get to be a hundred years old before I slow down." He gave a demonstration of his sinewy strength, swinging his arms around.

"It's not easy to stay with the powers, not a thing you pass on like a name. The power to do that comes out of preparation and visions. I got to live by that. That's how it is. You take a risk to get it, you take a risk to live by it, and you get in trouble if you forget."

Luther grew pensive. "You know, there's wars been fought over Indi'n medicine. One time, if a medicine man goofed up, made a mistake, or did harm, some of the family of the hurt one would go after him, starve, torture him to death. *That* one was supposed to be keepin' the people *alive*. And here he goes—the same as killin'. They'd not know what was on his mind, spite or jealousy. Whatever reason he had, he'd betrayed the people, and they'd be afraid not to get him out of there. A lotta times, he'd just run off or kill hisself, so they couldn't do it first.

"The evil always balances off the good. Maybe not quite always, but some of us still feel like there's goin' to be justice for our people, *some*time. The U.S.A. has done some rotten medicine by us." It appeared suddenly that he might be running out of steam, or out of hope.

"But you can see it, how come *I* don't do the medicine like I used too. I got all these people leanin' on me. I got this new wife an' this young son. What I do is all I can. You got to be open to the spirits in your heart at all hours if you do medicine, just like a medicine man leaves that door open for people needin' 'im."

I had been looking at some of Luther's more than two hundred photographs as he talked. Logan picked up a print made from a glass negative showing an eerily fragile old man with shoulder-length white hair and some kind of light cloth tunic over his shoulders, leaning for support on the arms of two young men in loincloths. Luther poked Logan to let him see and confided, "That was one of the really old time medicine men before he died—didn't live too long after that picture. See his eyes? Like he was lookin' through you. He was blind there." Logan warily returned Luther's stare.

He turned and looked to see what I was viewing and said, "I got somethin' else I been holdin' back on, maybe you would want to look at sometime, since you had that dream about Crazy Horse. I got this plate that's got a picture of him in my office safe." He grew frisky at the thought. "It's in real good condition too. They took it for a newspaper in Gordon just before that traitor stabbed him in the jail. White man never got to look at Crazy Horse in his newspaper! An' Crazy Horse never would let 'em take a picture before—didn' want it. He was afraid for his power.

"One thing, you know how he got that name? His father had it, an' then *he* got it. It was out of a vision where he saw a horse dancin' on its hind legs an' actin' up. So he was Crazy Horse." This image delighted him.

"You don't just go out and take a name. They had special people to do it. *Winktes* would give lucky names. Or, like you gettin' a name in a ceremony where they brought you in like one of the family. I got a name, *Mini Waci*. It means 'Dancing Waters,' or 'Ocean.' That's a name for power, to me. I could go by that with you." This offer of his spiritual name signaled his trust and good will.

I remembered we had to keep an appointment with Lame Deer, so we made apologies, promised to come back, and prepared to go. Mrs. Evers got out her camera and took pictures of everyone with Luther. It was a comical interlude—the flash attachment failed and there was a lot of fuss. Meanwhile, Luther seemed to recall something suddenly and said, "Hey, where's that one that's workin' on makin' a medicine man?" He wheeled around, glared at Logan, and grabbed his hand, playfully challenging him to Indian wrestle.

"You see if you can be back here on this comin' Sunday. There's ceremonies going to be held in Mission." He grew more serious and said, "I got some things to say to you that won't wait. You can come back some more then if you want to, even stay all summer, so I could show you about plants." He grinned, poked Logan in the stomach, and added, "But you better be careful. People like you been away a long time. If you come back here and then go up on Twin Peaks, you might come down bald-headed after them spirits get done!"

CHAPTER 20

Breath in the Pipe

Moon When the Buffalo Bulls Hunt the Cows (Omaha)

Lame Deer's backyard was a place of seemingly casual use. A cottonwood, small apple tree, modest elderberry, and seasoned ash shaded the premises where garbage and weeds bunched freely. An old mattress stood porter to the back shed.

Two young men superintended by Lame Deer were coaxing a tan and white power mower into service. Jay fought with the starter and finally got it going, only to get elected to run the thing. Having nothing else to do, Logan started picking up limbs and debris, while the Sioux helpers cleaned out the garage. Lame Deer seemed delighted at the bustle, not to mention the relief effort; the meeting had already assumed a neighborly tone all its own. He hadn't been home all summer and faced a long afternoon sorting out a season's weeds, stray garments, and nests of new puppies. The communal garbage heap in the nearby alley had made steady progress onto the property with the boost of the wind, children, and dogs, so it was like old home week for the trash.

The rain had stopped and the sun was out now, offering balmy heat. The big shade trees dripped on everything as we boxed up the mess for disposal. After checking his helpers, Lame Deer stopped everyone for a minute to point out a spot in the backyard where he wanted us to camp, if we had time to spend.

Lame Deer joked around with Meghan and Kate, to make them feel at home. He detached himself for a moment and cornered Logan near a white owl house modeled after his own. Pointing at an ash-strewn spot near the fence, he explained, "This is where I build a sweat lodge when I'm at home, right where you see them ashes." He lifted a small square piece of plywood on the center of the circle, and there clustered a nest of fire-bleached, charred stones. "You see all them rocks? They came up to me from Ecuador. I got some friends down there. Sacred stones for the fire—use 'em to make steam for the sweat lodge." He carefully lowered the trapdoor. "You ought to do somethin', find out about it while you're around here."

He looked at Logan sideways, then at the others in his yard musingly, and said slowly, "It's really somethin'. You guys here—you come all the way from California where I just been to talk to a poor old stupid Indi'n." Lame Deer repeated in a distant tone, "Yeah, just a stupid old Indi'n." Logan was silent. Lame Deer continued to look far off for a long moment, then added abruptly, "Just you be sure an' don' forget why you're here."

The wind suddenly picked up as we sorted ratty old quilts, cans, books, tools, bones, broken babydolls, and other relics of grandchildren and heaped them onto the promising fire hazard behind the garage. The hulk of a grey Chevy station wagon with all sorts of old parts, spark plugs, and frayed wires lay in the way. Caught in the rest of the debris was a paperback edition of Cash and Hoover's *To Be an Indian*, encrusted with mud and mold, nearly ruined, with a large photograph of Lame Deer on the cover. Logan decided to save it from the flames and tossed it into the Volvo.

Passing by the station wagon, Logan found a litter of pups on the backseat. In the middle of the squirming pile lay the dam, the most squint-eyed, low-slung, short-faced, suck-egg looking little bitch he'd ever seen. At that moment, practically on top of his feet, two of her boy-friends got into a fight and, distracted by the growls and squeals, Lame Deer asked if he was taking bets. I had a moment's vision of *heyoka* stew for supper. Logan did some last minute policing and saved a puppy skull discarded after a feast, a spotted owl feather, and an old playing card, a one-eyed jack, from the mower blades.

The rain took over again, so we all huddled under a low-limbed ash to wait out the squall. Winds whipped at our jeans, and a chill was settling in. After the granddaughter brought us pineapple juice in a yellow plastic jug, I asked Lame Deer to bless my pipe.

He had often blessed such a pipe. It gradually became clear that the ceremony was more a blessing of the pipe's owner, a consecrating of the smokers to the whole earth's care. It was a rite of investiture. All who held the pipe became connected to the ancestor's blood from which it was carved, the sacred stone "catlinite" or pipestone. Lame

Deer tested the bowl with careful fingers. As lightning and winds began to beat the fields around us, he offered suggestions for right living.

"To live right with *Tunkáshila*, yourself and all men, you don't try to hold onto things. Things is always goin' to move an' be on their way, if it's people, or money, or life itself. Don't be stingy. Don't go holdin' onto life or any *thing* you got now. Just to let you be here, the Earth has been good to you—*Makan, Unchi, Ina*—your mother and grandmother and aunt. She's been good to us all. We should not forget how little time we got. We're all very small. We ain't never comin' back. So do it now."

Lame Deer counseled us to sing with the spirits—and to hear the holy silence of the soul's rest, the life-stirring sounds of pulsing and breathing, gratitude and reverence, the return gifts to *Wakan Tanka*. Humility, sacrifice, respect, kindliness—right listening and feeling to find others' needs—these were proper qualities and graces of a human life. He repeated his words in four different ways as a litany, tightening a circular path to a core of suffering and communion. Then he told us to consider how wide the bowl reached, to embrace all creation in a sacred hoop, offering the pipestem to ancient spirits in all directions.

"When you pray to *Tunkáshila*, don't say, 'Grandfather, I'm beggin' you.' You don't go beg your own Grandfather! Look what you are to him, or why would you think He'd be listenin' anyways? You ain't *wishin'* He's there an' *hopin'* He'll do *any*thing, like a damn fool. You pray, all right; but then get ready to jump!

"You heard it's tough to be an Indi'n, but the whole world is a tough thing for ever'body. People act like the spirits was evil in 'em. At Pine Ridge, an' here off the reservation, Indi'ns even killin' Indi'ns, their own relations. People lose theirself, choke up on sounds of their own talk.

"But you think on this. There's another sound to life you got to remember. The world makes a sound that's not in any words. It's like lovers drawin' together, like relatives huggin' each other close—'haunnhh'—it's like that." A bearlike voice intoned from deep inside the old man, who opened his arms in a wide embrace. "The wind makes it, your lungs 'll make it, a bear and a buffalo make it. So we remember that song when we pray—it's the breath in the pipe.

"Turn the pipe two ways behind, east and north, and two in front, south and west. Then we remember power as it comes and goes, when it is giving life to us every way. Remember Father Sky, Mother

Earth." Then he offered the pipe and passed it, using a twig for a tamper. It circled our small congregation of seven—Logan and Jay, Meghan and Kate, Rachel and myself, and the old holy man.

In a surprise gesture Lame Deer reached across the circle under the ash and took back the pipe, plucking the stem from the bowl, as a broken branch falls out of the sky. We all huddled under the ash as a cloudburst drenched the earth. After an hour talking, wandering, repeating the lessons, impressing on us the holiness and humor of our lives, the medicine man suddenly completed our pipe blessing. As with everything around Lame Deer, the blessing seemed a little unnerving and yet absolutely natural.

This lightning-empowered *heyoka* healer, seventy-three years old, taught that nothing was excluded, everything holy. Many journeys raveled together: from Luther Clearwater's purism, skepticism, and elusive openness to Lame Deer's backyard humor, play and power. These were the lessons of Fire and Dancing Water.

Lame Deer trotted out his battery of cameras and got pictures of us all; then he showed us his collections of photographs and pipes. One pipe he had kept for thirty-five years. It had a heavy bowl and five eagle feathers, which he said must be moved to the bowl end for most purposes and to the stem end for healing.

"I guess you know I wasn't supposed to be here today," Lame Deer said. "I feel really strong about the way all this has happened. It's a good thing we did this, 'cause things like it don't just happen by theirself, you know? An' I can tell you'll be back here. Mebbe right away, mebbe not, but you'll be back. So when you can do that, make sure you come back here, 'cause I got room." It felt like leaving an old homestead.

We had half a night's drive ahead to Alliance. Not long before the sun went down, a big squall covered the sky with lightning, and all of nature was quickened with the earth shaking. Winds smashed down on the cars and flicked them around on the road like nutshells in a thimblerig. Meghan thumbed through the book Logan had found, by the light of all the pyrotechnics, and discovered it was a presentation copy to Lame Deer. It contained weeds, mud, many interviews and photos, and a school picture of one of Luther's relations taken at the age of eight. The interview Luther had given to Jerome Cash had been ripped out.

We continued through eerie prairies, with peach and plum lights flickering all along the horizon, eaten at the edges by night. Cottonwood fluff whirled in violent eddies like swarms of luminous bats.

Things scurried in the road. Riddled forms appeared and were gone. Rats and prairie dogs, scared witless, sprinted in abject terror or froze in the lights of the cars. Bolts of lightning cracked off the roadway, and we saw fused ropes of sand where lightning had connected the sandhills with stormy vaults of clouds. I drove on remembering the words of Sitting Bull's *inipi* song:

> Grandfathers, from above look down upon us.
> You are between earth and sky.
> Water and fire, these are powerful.
> Grandfathers, pity us all!

CHAPTER 21

"A Drowning Epidemic"

Moon of Hoeing Corn (Oto)

After breakfast and a pass through the St. Francis Indian Museum, Jay, Logan, and Meghan stopped at the alcoholic rehabilitation center near Sinte Gleska Community College. The director, Benjamin Crow, sat in his office looking out on a parking lot paved with mud. He was in his late forties; his round face emitted the exhausted air of someone convalescing from a long illness. Like so many Indian alcoholics, Benjamin was diabetic, his heart permanently damaged by what "res" drinkers called "the drug that comes in a pop-top can." If he had continued to drink, Crow confessed bluntly, he would have died long ago, if not from drinking itself, then probably from some accident, in a car or otherwise.

Meghan, still screening her lonely stay on the mountain, asked him about the Native American Church and traditional religion, whether he thought they provided any ways to conquer the problem. Benjamin had some qualms.

"Alcoholism, the way I know it, is not cured," Crow stated flatly. He leaned back and looked out on the mud. "There has to be some other way than non-Indian programs like AA, or church groups, or gover'ment studies. Those are just holding patterns, at best. Got to be tribal an' Indi'n-run. We don't treat people like we got some sort of leper's club runnin' here, draggin' the dead and dyin' into the hospital. We go out to that whole family, not just the ones we get comin' in here." Meghan nodded her understanding, and he continued: "But I'd say, too, that Mr. Indian is not always going to make some better way with traditional religion or peyot'. It depends on who he is an' where he lives. Always ask yourself, 'Does he do better with it?' We're askin' to find out what works, not just what people think is old-time Indi'n."

Meghan had a personal interest in solutions to alcoholism; her own Irish-American father was one of millions with a "drinking problem."

"Myself and all my co-workers, we're all alcoholics, what you call 'rehabilitated,' " Crow continued. "We got a certain method of operation to help other alcoholics get some control back over their lives. So we monitor everyone who comes under our care. Meet with each one, every month at his house, to see how he's coming along. The center keeps up a detox clinic, but we only have space for two patients at a time; we got to service twenty settlements with seven counselors."

"Aren't there state facilities for Indian alcoholics?" Jay asked. He was furiously scribbling notes in the grey-lighted office.

"They treat us as being out of their jurisdiction since we're Indians. Veterans can use the non-Bureau hospitals for vets, but where does that leave Joe Indian or his wife who're not vets? You know, a lot of these people come in here needing other kinds of medical attention than just a place to dry out. They're real sick with tuberculosis or diabetes or kidney failure. If they got no hospital space for them over at the Pine Ridge Public Health Service hospital, an' that's a long way to go, we can only get the doctor here to give librium and put the guy in bed for a while, or else in the drunk tank. Don't cure nothin'. He's back on the streets drinking again in a few hours."

Jay stopped writing and stared at him.

"I would say that even for Indians living off the reservation you need Indian counselors and staff. They understand because they're Indian themselves. They know all the weaknesses and fears, and all the tricks Indians will pull to stay alcoholic. Any alcoholic makes excuses. You got a better chance of cutting through the smokescreen if you know what his people are like, how they live, and all that. Indians know Indians. This work takes an awful lot of energy, an' Indians are damn smart about hidin' their habits."

Logan scribbled something, then asked, "How serious is alcoholism on your reservation?"

"Rosebud alcoholics, beyond just winos like you'd see anyplace, I'll tell you—it's like a drowning epidemic. Seventy-seven percent of all the adults here, and I am *not* talking to you about occasional drinkers or social drinkers. It's about sixty-five percent *under* the age of eighteen.

"I have been through those twelve steps of Alcoholics Anonymous," he said, patting his still swollen right side. "For the most part, that is not going to do for Indians, because they're not behaving as Protestant individuals under 'one God,' and they're nowhere near the 'middle' class. The 'steps' just don't speak to them—they need Indian concepts, Lakota, even warrior codes to fight their disease. If one family member goes down with it, there's a good chance all the rest do the same. You see a whole family—and you know with Indians that *tiospaye* or 'family' is stretching pretty wide—uncles, aunts, cousins, kids—*every*body's going to be sick, right down to the dogs and cats that suck the corks."

"What keeps everyone so down and out?" Jay frowned. "Don't they *see* what's happening to them?"

Benjamin clenched and unclenched his fist. He wanted them to know. "The Indian has got no jobs that are steady, no security, no confidence," he said in a monotone. "About all these people got left is being close to each other, however they can. Misery gets to be a bond. They depend on each other for everything, so they get drunk together and *stay* drunk too—help each other to live, some with sharing food, booze, even protection—but *not* letting each other feel the pain of being Indian. Booze washes that down your gut."

He unbent his arm and opened a clenched hand. "It's better in their mind not to feel the pain. So booze is like bad medicine, a sort of general anesthesia that's slow suicide." He got up and leaned on his desk, seeming very tired against the rain and mud visible through the window.

"It would mean a lot if doctors could come together in this thing, with all they've got—cure the basic problem of what alcoholism is for every American, not just Mr. Indian. Then after that maybe we can boil it down to an individual problem. Right now, it's the disease of the whole people that the white man—and being around the white man—brought to the Indian. And the Indian's dyin' as a nation from it. Probably ninety percent of all deaths here are alcohol-related."

He began to unbend a paperclip with one hand. "The state and the government fight over him, the whites want what little claims he's got left, land an' minerals an' water an' game, even his holy lands an' cemeteries. Mr. Indian's afraid to make anything of himself, afraid somebody will come and take it again, and he's right! That's the worst thing about talking him out of drinking a painkiller to forget—he's right!

"The vanishing American. Damn! He keeps getting told he's goin' to die out; so what incentive has he got to quit drinking, if it's all lost with the next termination act?"

He stopped, grinned a little. "So that's the big challenge to the Indian alcoholism counselor—why that counselor should be Indi'n himself. We got to think up things, try to pull in all we can, all kinds of possibilities, to get to that *one* Indian, then his family, then on out. I think we got a chance of making it snowball the *other* way, if we play it right. If being a group can pull us down, why can't we use that to pull us up?" He threw his paperclip, dartlike, out the window into the mud.

Meg had observed AA meetings and attended ALANON, and she asked if it helped here at all. Benjamin knew how AA didn't work for Indians. "AA wants to get people right with God and fittin' AA's idea of a good person and send 'em home to their communities, you know, to that big white mainstream 'under God' beyond the gate." Crow didn't disguise his reservations. The small-town application of Protestant abstinence just didn't fit. "I'm sayin' no, we got to figure out a way to deal with the problem, besides gettin' Mr. Indian back in the mainstream with God and ever'body decent white. You see, good as everyone's intentions may be, it don't work—it hasn't worked. Look around you. The Indi'n tryin' to go into the white mainstream is either impossible when he's a drunk, or it makes matters worse where he is with other Indi'ns. So naturally the mainstream he thinks about is back home, the *back*water of America, really, of his people's sufferin'. If he goes back to that one, he'll be right back to the bottle. It's a damn drinkin' circle!"

He waved his hands vaguely. "Look what happens when he dries out. He goes straight home—where else can he go? Someplace where he's goin' to starve because he's an 'alky' with no skills? Goes home to stay, or goes home to figure things out, and he gets lonely and guilty and depressed; people get on his back, everybody's hungry, some drinkin'. It's stupid to expect he'll put things any other way than right back where they were, crawlin' inside a bottle. So it's bigger than just wantin' a drink; it's a symptom of somethin' deeper, a pain all around."

"What if a guy can't help craving alcohol?" Jay posed. "Could there be a genetic weakness—?"

"I don't think anybody seriously buys the excuse that Indians have a hereditary weakness for alcohol. So what? It's just one more excuse, just like all the other excuses we've heard for the Indian to give up." He clasped his chest. "Say maybe it is so—we got no history of using alcohol, no genetic tolerance, no way to control it socially, and we guzzle that stuff like kids in alleys. *That* is not the answer to the Indian's problem with drinkin'. The real problem is convincing Mr. Indian that *drinkin'* don't answer anything. Period." He paused and looked down.

"The other night I was talking with this one man in the detox cell, asking him why he was always either drunk or hung over. He told me his whole damn family were dying off from cirrhosis, so he felt like giving up. Parents, uncles, cousins, they were all gone. I said, 'You're not gonna get the past back that way man, just lose out on your whole present. You got to help yourself. There's people, your own tribe, that will help—but all this self-pity is not gettin' you anyplace.' But what's he got to live for? Think about it.

"In the big picture we're tryin' to start things out from scratch," Crow said. "Got to get a program educating all the people about alcohol, starting at the grade school. Little kids watch Mom and Pop and brothers and sisters get drunk and the cats lickin' the empties, so they say, 'That's life.'

"It's got to be a cure-*all*. That's a big word to show how big the problem is. You got to get them free. No new habits, no substitute drugs—Anabuse or librium or even tobacco. We tell people here, 'Clean up!' " His face brightened.

"What it's coming down to is this. You *got* to recondition the whole of the people in the way they look at things, especially alcohol, but not just that. In 1954, Eisenhower days, they started letting liquor on the reservations legally to keep Mr. Indian from being a second-class citizen. You'll notice sometimes that when Congress wants to screw Mr. Indian, they'll say they don't want him to be no second-class citizen. They'll take away his land and his rights or give him some new 'rights' that'll fix him so he's like the rest. Mr. Indian is gettin' wise to that," he noted briskly.

"Now, some tribes, Hopis and people like that, they never let alcohol in. Rosebud did. So you got to tell people that don't remember—drinkin' is *not* part of bein' Indian. He can still be an Indian without it. They'll sit around and pass the bottle, share every scrap of food they got, like the old days so nobody starves. But that just makes it worse. They all die drunk together.

"You *got* to get at the excuses. You got to step on some government people's feet. You got to keep all the bootleggers, including the respectable ones, from peddling on the reservation. Get to the kids in schools. Catch this disease at its earliest stages, before the person loses his job or whatever life he's making." He lapsed into what appeared to be a personal revery: "It's really typical that you'll have some guy, starts out staying under the table on weekends until work on Monday, back in shape Tuesday, jittery Thursday, holds on just barely till Friday, them boom!—drunk as a skunk by six-thirty that night. So get him a job while he's on the wagon, help him change his habits and pay more attention to his kids and wife, and help her. Try to stop him just getting some menial job till he gets paid and then trying to kill himself and his friends on liquor he can buy with that."

He tossed a paper coffee cup into the trashcan. "Still, we're all in this together, red man and white. Its the same disease with different symptoms. There's no Indian mumps and no alcoholism that only kills Indians."

CHAPTER 22

"He's Gonna Be Indi'n"

Buffalo Calf Moon (Assiniboin)

With a few days of rest in Alliance, we drove back to gather herbs on the Rosebud. After a week of bright, hot days, the little grey columns of clouds lurking in the east had filled the sky. Logan and Jay were driving my father's work car, whose shocks had gone bad, and they had to compensate for some quirk in the steering mechanism. The highway had the texture of petrified oatmeal. A cloudburst began in the sandhills, so we pulled off the road as floodwater filled the lanes.

Fortified by a dinner of buffalo burgers, Rocky Mountain oysters, and brown trout in Valentine, Nebraska, we drove on through a light rain and misty sunset; the spring wheat fields were brushed with featherings of rainbows. Drops of rain on the windshield looked like stars come to earth.

It was still raining by morning—no likelihood of herb gathering—so six stragglers went to "Pop's In," a Main Street dive, for breakfast. We had never seen such an establishment—there were septic aquariums, mounted animal heads, a series of velvet tapestries depicting the entire life of Jesus, Christmas cards and two jukeboxes, a menagerie of plaster lawn animals and trolls, life-size flamingos pacing through wilting philodendron, ornamental bears and bats and clowns, and live baby quail and hens, not to mention a proprietor who reeked of alcohol. We settled for scrambled eggs. It wasn't so bad.

The grizzled old would-be sailor (safely land-locked), versatile as owner, waiter, and cook, shuffled along the deck with his zipper partway down and a toothless grin. He wore a green sleeveless T-shirt, blue navy cap, and faded grey washpants. Two melancholy deer heads stared down from the doorway over a plastic canoe that glided spell-bound under pink geraniums.

"Daddy, can I *please* have one of the guinea pigs in the back?" Rachel begged.

"No."

A lone tinsel star reminisced of Christmas past. Lawrence Welk waltzed across a faded poster with the champagne lady frilly on his arm. A plastic American flag poked out of the fake fruit display on a cigarette machine. The doorway was crowned with an oval-framed Statue of Liberty superimposed on Old Glory.

"Only four like it in the country," the proprietor assured us.

A little later we were back at Luther's door. His daughter, Charlene, a Sioux woman in her late thirties, showed us through the enclosed back porch. We filed past the kitchen to Luther's room. The kitchen housed the aftermath of an all-night party still winding down in town, and several people were passing a bottle around the breakfast table. The room was in shadow, but it glowed with a warmth like melon flesh. The shade cooled at Luther's bedroom door, opening on a com-pletely blue room. We could distinguish its furnishings only by con-tours, edges, and streaks—a turquoise dresser set, a watery green bedspread. The blinds were open, admitting a stream of nacreous light. Luther was sitting on the bed dressed in a bright white summer shirt and grey pants, leaning on a stack of pillows and holding his wiggly infant son.

Charlene and Nikki, Luther's young wife, arranged chairs around the room, which people generally ignored, preferring to stand or sit on the bed. Plenty of them could crowd in, and they did occasionally all morning, between sleeping and partying and cleaning up.

Luther sat up when we came in and made a grandfatherly fuss over Rachel. He peered with sleep-bleary eyes at each of us in the dim light. He got Logan to sit on a white wooden chair kept around, he said, for forty years, then spent several minutes showing off his seven-month-old son from his second marriage. Kate's eyebrows were inch-ing up her forehead. Luther asked for an account of last week, details of the field work, and how we had fared. We filled him in, up to the story of the sandhill storms. He continued to wake up, occasionally slurring a phrase, then suddenly slipped into focus.

Luther insisted on a pause, then leaned to Logan from the edge of the bed, poked him in the knee, and said, "You come here, and you see me now right at home. I'm welcomin' you. You're here to learn about what I can tell you." He shut his eyes briefly. "But the first thing: I said it before—you can't go back now. You can't go back to the old days. That time is gone for all of us."

He seemed sadly courageous, insistent that we understand, and I heard what he was saying about my own homecoming. I could go home again, but I couldn't "go back"; it was a subtle but crucial point, one that Indians and whites alike had to understand. Logan appeared to be Luther's selected audience among us. My thoughts scanned back to Lame Deer, Jenny Wolf, Lulu and George Lone Wolf, my brother Mark, and Thomas Banyacya in the beginning. Indian people were trying to tell us something. There wasn't much time left.

"I teach that little Sioux boy to dance," Luther said with his eyes half-closed. "Nobody can take it away 'at he's Indi'n. But nobody can take him *back* there the way it was." He reared up and stared at us grouped around him, as if in appeal. "There's not no place left for bein' Indi'n that way. You can't go out real peaceful and live off 'n the woods or on the fields no more—all in the hands of white man. It spoilt it. All done. Go try to live out under a tree, somebody come haul your ass out or shoot it! You go back to the earth *then*, all right. Things worse than snakes out in the land, now."

Kate and Meghan were talking quietly with the other women. Logan asked the old man about the medicine, sure he didn't mean that the spirit of the old religion was gone too. Luther looked down, picked at lint on his pant leg, and growled, "Unh-uh. They just tried to kill it, that's all. It's still here. It was here before and will be when we're all out in the rocks."

His expression shifted. "Well, I done told you about them healin' plants, that there was three—one cures chest and head, one's for the whole body, and one works on your bowels. There's them different kind of medicine men does different things. They're all over, that white man don't know 'bout. An' there's times we're doin' stuff nobody don't know 'bout.

"There's my brother Elgin's gangrene in his arm, just scummy green-black, till you could see bone. You'd still see a scar there in that arm. He got over it completely. I was prayin' for that. Like I was sayin' to you, there's lots to be learned, can't learn it all at onest, but *some*body got to, *some*time. You go around," he traced points in a circle before Logan, "an' you go here'n here to learn it. There's ones that *knows*, like I do. Got it from spirits.

"You go over to Dalton No Dog's ceremonies like I send you, an' then come back here tomorrow night—I want to show you things here the way we do 'em. You got to get to differen' things. I'll not go to Dalton's 'cause it won't go right—should be just one medicine man to run his meeting at a time, or too much conflictin'."

Others had begun to listen to Luther again. Charlene wrinkled her brow in consternation and seemed about to say something, then looked away with resignation. When he had finished, she said, "Dad, maybe you better not do *that*, you don' know what it's goin' to be. You shouldn't send him out alone to that. Not . . . " She seemed to get lost in her train of thought and sank back in her chair, staring past Logan with trouble in her eyes.

Luther made some fussy grunting noises. "A-i-i-h, it's all right, I know what I'm doin'. He ain't gonna get kilt 'r nothin'." He waved his hand at her limply, dismissing her anxiety with averted eyes. "*You* fuss alla time, fuss-fuss." She tried to hide a grin and punched the other side of the bed baitingly.

Some of the relations in the house peeked in to see what was going on. A little girl came toddling in among them whimpering softly between her teeth. She looked startled when she noticed Rachel, a child a little older than herself, and almost forgot to whimper, then recollected herself and looked around for somebody to implore. The little girl approached Charlene, who looked impassively back at her, and then the other women standing in the doorway. They offered expressions of complete innocence. The child's moan built up to an insistent dull keening. Charlene got tired of trying to bluff the other women into action—after all, said their faces, the baby was staring at *her*. Charlene stood, smacked her lips resignedly, looked down, and edged her way out the door. The whimper stopped.

Luther watched this dumb show attentively, never losing a beat in talking about *hanblechias*. He asked me to describe the Crazy Horse apparition on Harney Peak and bluntly said to turn away from "dreams like that," that Indian militant nationalism died with the martyrs. I'd do better going back to the mountain, as if it were a matter of pulling the right hand at cards, until I picked up a vision of a peacemaker.

"Go up there again, wait for a Red Cloud, or John Grass, or a Gall, or a Rift-in-the-Clouds, before you act on a vision. You try an' follow somebody like Crazy Horse will only get you to trouble." Jenny Lone Wolf must have thought this, too, and sent me asking questions, climbing more mountains. The road had been across a horizon of questions, dreams, and conversations, not at all what I had expected.

Charlene quietly brushed past the crowd in the doorway, who edged backward into the kitchen. She handed me a large bottle of

Coke and an empty baby bottle. I felt sick filling it for the whimpering little girl so she would settle down, but I was there to listen, not to correct, and I kept my mouth shut. My opinion hadn't been asked.

"Look around here, you're seeing some of my relations. There's my wife," Luther said, indicating a gentle-faced and bright-eyed young woman in the doorway who smiled slightly. "Here's Morley, that's my brother-in-law," he continued, nodding vaguely sideways at the young man lounging on the foot of the bed. Morley was slender and would have looked very tired and wan any morning. He observed everything with semiconscious awe. His occasional bursts of enthusiasm proved that he *was* listening and mulling over the conversations around him. Morley sometimes tried to answer a question or to offer a comment pertinent to the wrong conversation. This, of course, necessitated someone routing him to the right cluster of speakers; but we all got the hang of it after one or two glazed stares.

Luther continued to discuss his household and extended family. "Look at them all," he said archly. "Is that Indians? How're they livin'?" It was not clear whether he still intended his comments for visitors or for relatives. He seemed bewildered by his own thoughts and looked around, as if for help, if only for someone to break the silence.

"Who wants to be Indian *now*?" remarked one of the women leaning in the doorway, her arms loosely folded, to no one in particular. "What's the good of that? I can't make no livin' offa that. If he wants to be Indian, that guy, let him go live off somewheres. Let *him* try!" She turned to the other women in the doorway, and they puffed up in support of her position.

Charlene added, "What's the good of Indian, if you can find out some way to be white? I'm gonna go out and be white, I won't be no Indian no more. *My* kids don't have to be Indian these days." She glared at Kate, who sat stone-faced.

Luther received these comments with slow nods, his slack face showing no expression. "Yeah," he mumbled, "they're all sayin' it right now."

He glanced at Jay and asked entreatingly, "Where you gonna *go*? I hain't nobody to come after me! My *gran'*father had me to tell things to when he got older even than I've got. Who've I got now?" Jay took this in, thinking of his own thinning Jewish background.

Luther shifted his gaze toward me. "Look at it! How they all goin' over to white man livin', an' the fine cars an' all that, if they can get it. They don' know what they got to give up, or what their ancestors give up, so they could try to go their own way! Too late! No damn wonder it all slid down the hole, with just a few spots left where ever'thaing ain't all rotted out. Look at 'em!" Luther swept his eyes across the spectacle of his family with despair. They returned his gaze complacently.

"You askin' me what happened to old religion, just look at it! They get job, education, money if they can get it, an' split outta here!" A soft wet wail caught in his throat and he said, "Yeah, all gone to a missionary's Christian church, just like the rest, all my kinfolks. Marry in white down the line, forget their ass. Forget how to pray to their *Tunkáshila.*"

Charlene looked mildly annoyed, and asked, "So what do you want to say to these people, Gran'pa? What you tryin' t' tell 'em? You teachin' 'em to be Indi'n, give 'em names an' pray with 'em?"

She looked at Logan and added, "You know, he don't talk like this, it bein' just to us. He ain' teachin' me nothin' about bein' an Indi'n! He can do all that stuff—acts like he give up on us. What're we supposed to do with it, Gran'pa?" She ended looking at Luther's sleeve, addressing him with the last question.

"It's like I told you guys here, the other day when we were at the library," Luther said, obliquely answering. "You go with a little child, boy about four years; he'll learn what it was bein' Indian and he won't forget that."

He looked at the women, who had been talking quietly to Rachel as she sat at the edge of the bed. What would she not forget?

"But that old way is like it was wiped off the world, an' the Ghost Dance prophets got it *all* ass-backwards." He giggled over the last remark as if it were a huge sad joke, and said, "Yeah, I've thought maybe if Wovoka had went up sixty days, he'd 'a done all right. So if *you* go up, better go for seventy!" he told Logan. He looked back at Charlene slyly and said, "You can listen to this now if you want to."

Charlene wasn't satisfied. "Well, all you doin' is talkin'." She looked at the guests. "Hey—if you guys come here to find out somethin' from Dad and he ain't answerin' *us*, his own people, how come *you* ain't askin' him no questions, or askin' him to show ya somethin' or do stuff?" Meghan looked embarrassed and lit a cigarette. A family debate was heating up around our presence.

"You can stay, like I said," he told her tauntingly and held up his son, who had already made the rounds of the assembled group and was just visiting Dad at the moment. "I said, 'I ain't had nobody to teach,' but now I got *that* one. I got married again for him and to have him to tell things to. He ain't gonna be like them. He ain't gonna have to go to the White cities. I'm gonna teach him what I know, an' he'll have it when I'm dead for the people. I tried teachin' a lot of the rest, but none of 'em wanted to learn, or just were curious an' then went to somethin' else."

Luther admired his son, made silly animal noises at him, and tossed him in the air. The baby burbled and crowed with zany baby answers, and Luther laughed at him. "Look! See them feet? His name's Luther Clearwater, too. Gonna be a big Indi'n. He's gonna go anywhere he wants to, an' he'll be free, and he'll be an Indian, and he's gonna be a medicine man, like his grandfathers." The mother's avocado green blouse rustled at the doorway, but she said nothing. Luther seemed to remember something. "Yeah, if I live to, I'll tell him all that medicine. He can do anything if he's got that."

He looked at Charlene and began to brag on her, rattling off the list of her children and their many accomplishments, their successes in business and general dealings in the non-Indian world. "She put 'em through college, ever' one!" He had hit her point of greatest pride, and Charlene gravely nodded. "But I got *this* one," he said, "an' he's gonna be Indi'n."

"I can tell you things too that you have to know," he said, turning to Logan. "*I* know what you're doin' here for," he said, "an' before I get done, you'll be wonderin' where it's hittin' ya. Once this starts, you gotta keep on goin' with it. I know what to tell ya, where to put ya, even if you're *not* like them, same tribe." He appeared to be referring to his relations in the room. "It's 'cause like ever'body else, you ain't got no big choice once Thunder Spirits start tellin' you what to do. It looks at first like you'll be havin' to give up ever'thing for it, but it's not all like that. Somehow you got the choice—once." He considered that notion for a moment, then nodded decisively, and corrected himself, "No—you always got it, live or die!—that's the choice!"

I asked Luther how the Powers came to tell him things. "It's all gotta be vision, you know, it's gotta go with a vision. I lived my whole life that way since I got to learn how. Them spirits—sometimes they're like people's voices, sometimes it's like mine, an' then like my gran'fathers' voices. Oh! If I was to get drunk, like that, my gran'mother's gonna come aroun' later, she's gonna talk to me. She'll come around here to th' bed with all them other spirits—" He made his listeners endure an awesome pause during which he twisted his face into a grimace of fear—"an' I'll say, 'Gran'ma, whadd'ya want?' "

His voice faded to a silly whine. He held off again, as if waiting for her answer. Then he rolled his eyebrows up fiercely, assumed a booming matronly voice and shouted, "You *cut* that out!" He and his family howled with merriment, and he repeated his Granny's order over and over for them until he was weak. "Yeah, she's that way," he muttered, "don't let nothin' get past 'er."

Luther grew more thoughtful again. Morley was giggling and repeating, "That's real *good*, Bro'!" Luther ignored the effusion and continued, "Aayeah, they still come aroun' me once in a while like that. I don' have to go up the hills, just in the tub of water or sweat lodge, an' they're in it; or I sit with a pipe, an' here they come. When I write, too, sometimes they'll come in and take up with me, an' I'll be able to write real good then; or they won't, an' then I can't do much. So I write, or I think an' pray. I go off like that, in with them spirits, an' I'm back a hundred an' fifty 'r two hundred years ago. It's all different then. Buffalo standin' off outta the groun', an' ya see the big grass an' flowers like that, an' all them people." His eyes followed the light to the window.

"An' then, it may be days after that, I come back. An' when I do, my wife an' them, they'll get on me about doin' it. My mind will still be a long way off. I go down to my office and write with my mind in that other time, maybe all day. That's work, hard, like pick an' shovel work! Come back here, I can' make it, 't wears me out. An' when my folks here get onto me like they do, I gotta get cleaned out, y'see? I call in some friends for a big celebration so I can get back an' start over, keep goin'. Sometimes, I do that. Aw, not all the time, maybe once—" he reflected for a moment, "ever' two or three months, maybe, I do it. Yeah, an' anyway, them spirits all aroun' this bed—I can hear 'em there." He waved his hand all around the room, settling at last on his pillows. I remembered Felix Lone Wolf in the back bedroom at George and Lulu's in Alliance. The spirits got around.

Charlene said with a shrug, "Yeah, that's right, he does that all the time." Turning to her father she asked, "Ain't you gonna tell about prayers an' stuff, an' about givin' names t' people? Why'nt you do somma that stuff, like you're doin' alla time?" Again Meghan flushed and cleared her throat. She looked to Kate helplessly.

Luther sat up for a moment, ruminating and mumbling to himself. His tone was dry and abstracted, and he seemed to get irritable. He muttered about repeating prayers at the wrong time, and half-heartedly sang a few notes of some old chant. Abruptly, his face froze; he held his back in discomfort, and rocked slowly, silently. For a few moments, he seemed to be resting as if he were in pain and then he waved his fingers to get his daughter's attention. "You, Charlene, you go get it, that pipe. You know where I put it?"

Charlene looked at him with a fogbound expression, but then said quickly, "No, why'd I know where you keep all that stuff? I ain't got it. You got stuff scattered all over th' place. How'm I supposed to know where t' find it?"

Luther hesitated, then he looked at his other relatives and asked, "Any uh you know where it's at? We had it here before, before I put it away."

Morley stared at Luther and suddenly got a look of inspiration. "I remember it was on the wall," he said. "Maybe it's still in that front cabinet."

Charlene glared at Morley and said in a deliberate, flat tone, "I don't know where it is, an' I ain' gonna go lookin' for it. I never touched it." She rumbled like distant thunder before a cloudburst.

Luther began to move around on the bed as if thinking about getting up. Charlene persisted, "I don't trust that thing—it'll hurt people. It makes all kindsa trouble ever'time it's out. Ever'thing goes bad with that thing!"

Luther raised his chin at her and said reprovingly, "Naw, that's wrong, now. It ain' like that. That pipe always tol' when somethin' was *already* wrong, like somethin' about to happen to the family, th' way it did. It ain' never hurt nobody if they use it right. It's a thing for prayers."

Charlene snarled, "I don' care what you said, it killed your sister. That stinkin' thing is evil, bad stuff. When you gone, I'm goin' t' take it out an' bust it. Just take me a hole an' bury th' thing where it belongs, down in the ground."

CHAPTER 23

"One of the Last Great Ol' Pipes"

Hot Moon (Assiniboin)

Luther spoke as Charlene turned her face away. "It, that pipe, is a great holy pipe of the people, one of the last great ol' pipes. Medicine men always had it an' was usin' it. Real sacred, just about the only one like it left around.

"They," he said, indicating his relatives, "they don't give nuts about it, but that pipe is what our ancestors believed in. Milk had that one pipe, an' Spotted Tail—hell, that thing's going' back to when Sioux people started *makin'* pipes up here! That stem on it's over a hundred an' fifty years old, nearly old as when Red Cloud . . ."

"One medicine man after another, council fires an' healin' ceremonies, down to me. We used to keep it in there on the wall till aroun' when my sister died, then they made me take it down. They didn't believe it—SSSSHT—! What they made me take it down for? They're scared of it! Ever' time there's gonna be trouble, it would tell, give us a warnin'. Just a little pipe, not all fancy, but it's had the power like no other pipe left. I keep it. It came to me. There's people wanted to buy it, I said, 'Not for sale! Not that pipe.' It would turn over on the wall where it was layin', all by itself."

Morley spoke up excitedly, "We seen it! We tried all differn' kinds of ways to make it do that without movin' it. Jus' laid there! You could beat on the walls an' jump up an' down on the floor, make all kindsa shakin' an' racket, just sit there. Boy, man, but if there was gonna somethin' come, it'd turn over," he said, slowly making an arc above his head with his arms and kneeling over on the bed in demonstration. "Jus' like it knew. Wouldn't anybody dare touch it, excep' Bro'."

During the latter comment, Luther began to make little punching motions at Morley, finally nudged him with his palm, and pointed past Jay by the doorway. "Hey, go in there t' that cabinet in the livin' room. See if it's in that cabinet still, if *she* won't go." Morley squirmed off the bed eagerly. He was nearly to the door, when it seemed to dawn on him what he was doing. He stopped and peered back at Luther and said sheepishly, "Hey Bro'—what'm I gonna do if it's not in there?"

"We gotta *look* for it, then," Luther said smiling, assuring him there was no way out.

Morley vaguely murmured, "Oh, okay," and trudged off toward the living room.

"They all got tired of seein' it do things," Luther turned back. "It would glow in the dark sometimes, could move around itself, show up another place. The Powers would do all kindsa things with it. So that day they said, 'Put it away. We're scared. We don' wanna see it.'"

Morley came back looking relieved. "Ain't got it! It ain't there," he fairly sang. "I don' wanna handle it now, anyway." Some of the relations giggled nervously. Luther eyed Morley wearily, "A-a-a-h, chicken—hafta go find it myself, I guess."

He rolled off the bed and made his way to the closet. "I got all sortsa things in here." He dropped a cluster of bags on the floor after quickly checking their contents. He pulled down a shopping bag from the top of the closet and peeked inside. "Oh, hey, here's my eagle feathers!" He held the bag open so we could admire the scores of hard, even, gleaming feathers. He rummaged around, then drew out one about fifteen inches long, white nearly to the middle, with soft down near the end of the shaft, running to black at the other end. The nib was wrapped with a coil of yellow yarn. Luther handed me the feather. "That is a traveling feather. You take it with you on a journey someplace. It brings protection and shows who sent you. A flight feather—come off the tip end of the right wing of a man eagle." He took the feather back and held it in both hands, offered it up and prayed over it silently, and then returned it. The giving seemed so commonplace and low-keyed. I was startled to be holding the most beautiful eagle feather I'd ever seen.

Morley looked at the gift. "Offerin' feather," he said dolefully.

When Luther had sat back on the bed to sort through his bags, Morley turned to Logan. "You know, they got a special way of catchin' them spotted eagles. They get down under a hut an' it's all covered up with grass an' leaves an' stuff, an' they fast an' pray like for a hunt. An' then they gotta put out a little piece uh that offerin' meat, an' eagle come down on it, so you real quick reach up an' grab ahold with your fists"—he and Luther simultaneously pantomimed this action—"and yank it down in there with you. Don't kill it, though. You just get some feathers, us'ally."

Luther poked Morley and asked him, "You know how t' catch that eagle?" Morley's eyes bulged attentively. "You gotta be smarter'n that eagle!" he whooped with delight and hilarity.

By this time Luther decided to adopt Rachel, putting a feather in her hands. "You keepin' that all your life. That's got power in it— you're gonna understan'. When you're in trouble, or you need for anythin', you say," he paused, holding the feather in both hands in an attitude of prayer before his face, "'*Tunkáshila*, Grandfather, pity me; be merciful, make me good.' He'll give you what you need." He made some joking attempts to persuade her to stay with him, let her father come back for her sometime, and she looked a little fearful at the idea. Luther laughed then, teased her, and made the baby laugh until it cried. By now the baby was getting very tired, so his mother walked over and picked him up, cooing, and took him away to nurse and sleep.

Rachel sat gazing at the little feather, smoothing its barbs together. Meghan pulled her up on her lap. Luther perched at the edge of the bed looking at his hand. He touched his thumbs to his fingers in series, then he leaned his head on the open palm. "I got forty-three children an' gran'children. Now I got forty-four," he said, including Rachel. "I can' do medicine no more, like that. I lost my sister while I was out in the sweat lodge tryin' to heal her. She was real sick for a while, an' tryin' t' do medicine when she died. But the spirits don' stop talkin' to me!"

Suddenly Luther's face lit up. "Oh, I know where . . . " He slid off the bed and excused himself, clambering over people to the chest of drawers behind the door. He riffled through the drawers, finally settling into the front of the second one from the top. He slowly dipped his hands around, moving away layers of clothing and objects, and drew out the pipe. Then he turned, holding it in both hands, and raised it to his chest.

The old man moved into the light in the doorway; in his hands we could see a parchment ash stem with a simple catlinite bowl. The stem was cracked and chipped, incised with many red marks, and split near the mouthpiece. Charlene was standing now, and most of the relations began quietly to scatter through the kitchen and out the back entry. Morley, wearing the chagrined expression of a trapped bobcat, looked wistfully out the doorway his brother-in-law had filled.

Luther held out the pipe, while Charlene waved her hands and rubbed her face, weakly begging her father to stop. "Put it back," she said hoarsely. "Damn thing's gonna kill somebody. Somebody's gonna die in this house if you keep that out." She turned to the guests and said, "Don't you guys touch it; *you*'ll get it too." Luther was preparing to put the pipe into Jay's hands. "Damn thing!" she said in a low, shaking voice. "Damn *thing*! Somebody'll get killed with that thing. You crazy? You wanna die? Get '*atouta*here." She was not just angry; she appeared repulsed and genuinely frightened. "You seen 'em all leave? You know why they done that? They ain't gonna let theirself be caught *near* that thing when it's doin' somethin', is why." She sank on the edge of the bed.

After an uneasy silence, broken by conversation from other parts of the house, I asked Charlene if the stem could be repaired.

"I got news for you fella—it's perfect," she snapped. "It's perfect jus' like it is." She headed resolutely out the door, hissing, "I ain't stayin' with that mess. I didn' know you was gonna do *that*. But's your house." We heard her scratching a chair across the kitchen floor. She slammed something hard and resonant on the table.

Luther peered around the door sill, snickered, and shrugged one shoulder. He whispered conspiratorially, "Lookit that! Mad as hell! Said she didn' believe in it. What Indians! They *don'* forget it. They try it, but it don' work. See that?"

Morley abandoned himself to hungover misery and sank his face abjectly into his hands, watching Luther make the gestures of offering the pipe. The medicine man very formally handed the pipe to each of us, receiving it back each time. He included Rachel in the ceremonial presentations, offered with a prayer. Then he asked Logan, without waiting for any answer, "You know how to use this?" Jay and I were stirring around at this point, somewhat agitated with the mood of the house, no more sure than anyone else what was going on. Jay took his chair by the door. Rachel wanted to go to the bathroom. Luther still handed the pipe around.

Logan offered it back, in his turn, but Luther wouldn't take it. "*You're* gonna hold it now," he said. There was a shuffling sound in the kitchen, and Charlene stuck her head in the door; her face was flushed with concern.

"Hey . . . HEY!" she yelled. "Don' mess wi' that *pipe*!. *You*-gonna-*get*-in-*trouble*! All hell's gonna break out around here now." She squinted with frustration and pity, as if Luther had offered us a drowsy rattlesnake that could warm up any second. Her distress was genuine. We were emotionally entangled in the family dilemma. We felt respect and gratitude to Luther for baring himself so completely, sympathy for his relations and their fears. There was also a growing sense of obligation: friendship with Luther led directly into something few knew much about, even among the Sioux. For Logan it was disturbing, yet somehow like going home to talk with his own feuding relatives. No longer were things being simply presented to him; *he* was being introduced to ceremonial power, and that power was in feeling knowledge, the "Power that Moves-moves" or Taku Skanskan. Here was the meeting place of Logan's recurrent dream, a man's house by the "sea." Luther's Indian name was "Ocean" or "Dancing Water." There was no chance of flight. Logan could only resort to intellectual denial or fearless surrender.

The people left in the room were staring at Logan, who suddenly felt like a pipe rack, with his hands in the air. Kate's face blanched to the color of dry cottonwood. If he moved, Logan thought, Charlene would run right up the wall. He could only look back to Luther, who began to talk about the pipe in Logan's hands.

"You know, that pipe is made out of our people's blood," he almost chanted. "Catlinite. It comes from a place of stone, a vein in the ground, and there's hardly anyplace in the world we can find it, just there in Minnesota. You got to burn an' purify it, an' the black earth cracks off, so you jus' got that left—red outta the fire, like the red man."

Luther continued to Logan directly, "I said I would show you, teach you about the healing. I got some things here, up in that storeroom overhead, and out in the shed. People have given me all kinds of things to save for the people. I've run outta places to put them. This Bicentennial bunch of gover'ment guys come down here, when they found out I had things. If anything happened t' me, it'd all go at once, so they want me to put it all in this museum they're buildin' on. There's some things, though, ain't goin' in there. I gotta make sure I get done before somethin' can happen to me." He turned toward the kitchen and shouted, "HEY! You know that suitcase I got all them things in, where I stuck that stuff?"

Charlene was saying, "No, no, no," before he had even finished his sentence. He waited, and she added, "Not out here—did you try the closet? Maybe in there." Logan handed the pipe to Jay as Luther passed. Steadying himself against the younger man's shoulder as he reached into the closet, Luther felt around and rolled his eyes back meditatively, then found a purchase on something and gave a long pull. He brought down a turquoise suitcase with a battered lid and broken hinges. He opened it and began to unload a series of articles, handing them around.

The first object was a small "number nine" bronze kettledrum with an antelope-leather head. It had belonged to someone who had used it in peyote rituals. *Argosy* magazine had presented an article about it some years ago, he said; it was one of the last original peyote drums still in private hands. The drumhead ties formed a Morning Star design. Luther removed the antelope-horn drumstick incised with a plains teepee, pentacle, cross, and eighteen lines. He handed it to Jay, who took the drum out on the porch and began testing its resonance.

Jay continued making random thumpings until Charlene got up from her kitchen table and told him to "Play somethin' straight" on pain of taking it away. Charlene was standing at the bedroom door as she delivered her ultimatum; she glanced in at Logan, who was holding the pipe again and wondering what to do. She jerked her head slightly and moved back, and Logan followed her out of the room. She sat down, at her table, making him stand in front of her.

"Now," she said, preparing to interrogate him, her eyes shifting focus uneasily, "How come this? What did he get you here for? You ain't even Sioux. Do you expect he'll tell you somethin', or what? You're not here for fun, I know; I don't mean *that*. You could stay here, he could teach you all kinds of stuff—but why?"

Logan apologized for not really knowing where all this was leading, adding that he had to trust her father's judgment. He repeated the story of first meeting with Luther and talked a little about his own family's history of practicing old medicine, one whose particulars were in danger of falling by the wayside with this generation. People like Luther, he suggested, were the only genuine source of understanding of the old medicine traditions—outside the writings and recordings of scholars—and so he was trying to talk to some of the people, maybe to find what was left to help anybody in a practical way. At least people might feel better about their own place in the world and their own ancestors, if they learned to remember and to respect the purposefulness of their traditions.

Charlene asked Logan about dreams, mulling over his answers for a single word to snap things into place. Finally she sighed wearily and looked up. "All right. It was out of my hands a long time ago. Go on back an' talk, see if you *can* learn somethin'. Jus' don't go an' do somethin' stupid t' get yourself killed." She followed him to the door, and dropped a throaty chuckle. "Maybe *I'll* find out somethin' too."

CHAPTER 24

"Somebody Did Medicine"

Moon When Everything Hatches (Tlingit)

Luther was telling Meghan about various methods to connect with spiritual power. At one point he reached down and yanked up his pants leg. "You see any scars there?" He rolled down his sock and roughly brushed the skin. "You know that leg's been in water boilin' durin' some a them ceremonies? *Heyokas*, boilin' dogs. They talk, them tour guides; they tell the tourists about that 'secret stuff' medicine man puts on his skin before the ceremony to keep it from burnin', scarlet mallow an' stuff."

We looked at him innocently. "You know what that heap big medicine is?" We didn't. "COW DOODY!" he exploded, "plain ol' COW DOODY!" Morley got tickled and laughed with him. He settled down and gazed at us. "And it don't burn, all that scaldin' water! Nothin' else. That's *power*." It struck him as a tremendous sacred joke.

Luther paused for a moment, reflecting on his skin, and then abruptly dropped his leg down and perched on his mountain of pillows. He glanced around and gaped at Kate, cutting his eyes back at Logan occasionally, and said, "You know, I can do a lot of funny things with machines. They say I'm good with that." Logan bristled. His stomach felt slack suddenly, and he suspected Luther wasn't referring to tinkering with home-assembly TV kits. "A lot of funny things, not even touchin' 'em or even in the same room. Do it with radios," he continued, glancing at Logan impishly, "tape recorders . . . " He stopped in mid-sentence and bounced up and down on the pillows with a grin of triumph.

Logan began deliberately to tell how tapes of earlier conversations with Luther had come out all haywire. The only recordings we got were faint bird squeals and the sounds of water crashing.

Luther was cackling softly, patting the bed with delight. "Yeah," he said, "that'll bring 'em back alive!"

The old medicine man reached into the suitcase and pulled out a rattle gourd hanging on a tan dowel for use in healing ceremonies and peyote meetings. He took out four sections of wood covered with a glossy red and deep blue leather webbing, which were to be assembled into a staff by screwing brass fittings on each piece. The staff was used in the Sun Dance, *yuwipi*, and other religious occasions. A black deer tail hung at the middle, and a hair roach dangled from the top.

Holding the pipe in the crook of his left arm, Logan assembled the staff, while Luther removed a dusty blue-black bag and a medicine bundle made of an ancient grainbag. It was brightly beaded in red, yellow, white, and black daisy-shaped flowers. Beside these he laid a notched eagle feather fan prominent in peyote meetings, plus a dozen ten-inch feathers that were bound with buffalo hair cord to a wrapped wooden handle. A small bronze medallion, hung from the handle, contained a colored miniature of Christ, dark-skinned under a tiny watchglass. Luther handed it to Meghan, who sat speechless.

By now the relatives were tired of hiding out in the yard and wandered into the living room for a smoke. Luther reached for a russet slide flute of the old-fashioned Sioux make and wondered out loud whether his elk medicine would still work.

"Watch this. I can make th' women crowd all around in a minute. They don' make flutes like this no more, an' hardly *no*body can play 'em anyway." He blew fitfully on it for a few seconds—an odd, lowing melody, just a few bars. Then he stopped and gently began to sing a few words in a minor key, closing his eyes. We sat absorbed until we noticed a rustle and looked up to a cluster of women, grinning, at the door. Luther opened his eyes and started laughing and pointing. "See?" he said gleefully. "I *ain'* lost it!"

I briefly excused myself to retrieve my own pipe, and Charlene took a seat closer to the bed. Jay was still tinkering with the water drum out on the porch. Luther took up his pipe and then slowly handed it back to Logan, repeating his charge, "You know this." He touched the young man's elbows and said, "Hold it up in your hands." Luther riveted his eyes on Logan, who lost contact with Charlene's frightened stare across the bed. The old man's face began to change to intense care. He adjusted Logan's hands, clutching the stem at the bowl with the right hand and the mouthpiece with the left in an overhand position. Logan could see the pulse in Luther's neck, and the elder's chin was shaking as he held Logan's hands under the pipe and then slowly released them.

"You feeling that?" he asked. "You feeling that?" His voice was faltering, fading out. Tears were running down his face. Logan couldn't define the odd quality of weight that lay in the little object. His hands felt dry and hot. "Lift it over your head, on over." Logan did, rapidly. Luther and Charlene were both staring, scarcely breathing. "Follow it," he whispered.

Logan surrendered to an impulse to stand with the pipe. It wouldn't stop pulling. His hands were numb now, and he found himself choking out, "I'm hanging from it! It's got me, up here!"

Luther's lips were moving, and a faint, dry chant came from him. "Yeah," he whispered, "that's It coming down. It's Power coming down in the pipe. If you wanted to, you could swing from it."

Charlene was standing now too. "Here," Luther said to Logan resolutely, "you smoke that pipe."

Charlene started in again: "You two stop messin' with that pipe. DAD! Let him put that away!"

Luther ignored her, got some matches, and handed them to Logan. "It's loaded up. Light and smoke it. We're in the right time now." He looked at his daughter and said comfortingly, "It's all right. He knows how to do this." He turned back to Logan, "Offer it."

Logan turned the pipe rapidly to the four directions, then below and above, just as Charlene was leaving the room. The split in the stem closed between his teeth, and a plume of old burley and willow bark welled into his throat. A pale curl of white smoke hesitated over the end of the pipe, and then it was out. The bowl was still hot.

Luther lifted the pipe out of Logan's hands and pointed to four pink notches in the bowl end of the stem. "That was put there by a medicine man to show the times he offered himself in place of his patients an' lived. Four times. He didn' die. Ever'time you do that for somebody you sacrifice. You got to make sacrifice inside. Be ready to die anytime. Somethin' the people need may mean givin' up your whole life."

Morley scooted over from the other side of the bed and urged Luther to tell what happened to people who misused the pipe, the deaths and accidents. Luther waved him back. "I took it, and I prayed when anybody got sick. My first wife was real sick one time with a fever, looking like she would die at the hospital. I had the pipe out an' took it down the hall to a room an' offered." He mimed the prayer, raising the pipe with both hands level with his forehead, lowering his voice to a whisper, saying the few words in Lakota. "She was at a hundred an' four temperature, then up—I prayed for her to *Tunkásh-ila.* She got better. You goin' never get somethin' for nothin'." He breathed in deeply. "An' she died now, too, see. The same day ever' year that I cured her of that fever since, it comes to me like it did to her, an' I get sick as hell with her fever for days."

Charlene yelled back from the kitchen, "Yeah, that's *right* Gran'pa— sick as hell for days. You oughta remember that!"

Luther turned away and sat back on the bed. "That's why I don' do it no more, this Indi'n doctorin', except in the fall when I get the plants an' take 'em aroun' t' the old people. I got to pass it on. There's hardly nobody. Should go to ever'body.

"So much spirit, so much power," he said turning to look at Logan, "'s unbelievable."

When Luther was settled again, he began talking about his sister. Charlene jumped in with, "That's why, right there. That pipe killed her is why I feel this way. Gran'pa an' her went in a sweat lodge with her sickness. Two went in walkin', one come out under a blanket. That damn thing got 'er down an' *killed* 'er!"

Luther listened, and though one might have anticipated a sharp reply, his manner was surprisingly conciliatory. "No, no—it wasn' quite that way. You shouldn' get all worried about it like that." His voice softened. His manner was conciliatory, but without condescen- sion, as of one finally at peace, laying a matter to rest. "It's all balanced out. Pipe didn' kill her. She went in to get medicine, an' when she got it, somethin' changed for her, that's what it was. Her, me, some medicine men was all in there, an' sang a long time. We smoked, an' all the sudden, spirits was all over in there. They talked— to her mostly. It really wasn' too long they were talkin' an' told her, she said, somebody had to offer up so the people would live, for their life. She seen ever'thin'! What a great peacefulness. Even at that last, she knowed it, what she was there for, what it all meant. She said she was so thankful—to the spirits, to the singers, to the whole world— for all of those chances she'd had all of her life to give of herself. Such peace! She made a decision then, let her time go, let 'em take her out with 'em, them spirits. So she died in less'n a minute. Pipe didn' kill nobody. *No*body killed nobody."

Luther looked at Logan. "Jus' *some*body did Medicine. *Tunkáshila,* the spirits, she done medicine, ever'body prayed for it. All, together, one spirit was in there, that time. We *had* it then, one spirit. And then, she was gone, and it was over. An' I'm afraid I ain' that strong no more. So I don't try to do it no more, not in a long time. See?"

Luther got Rachel to hold the pipe, showing her how, over Charlene's agitation. When that was finished, Logan gently persuaded Rachel to let the pipe go and put it back in the drawer, hoping the daughter would calm down. Luther looked over at Charlene and muttered, "Ain't afraida pipe—afraida *Indi'n*." Charlene calmed down almost immediately, making it clear that as far as she was concerned, the damage was already done. She edged next to Kate, who had kept uncharacteristically quiet through all this. The two of them could have been salt-and-pepper siblings. I unwrapped my own pipe, and we passed it around all the company, as Lame Deer had done with us under the ash some days before. We seemed to be trading medicine, sharing power, to heal our people.

Luther opened the flour-bag medicine bundle beside him. He located a parcel of *kinnickinnick* received through his grandfather, collected and preserved in the late 1700s by a medicine woman. He gave me this medicine, he said, to use in times of extreme need, and only then for the good of nonrelatives. I was stunned. Had Jenny Lone Wolf somehow known about this when she sent me looking for a *wicasa wakan*, a "medicine man"?

Luther turned to the medicine bundle again. He rummaged in the bag and cupped something in his hands as one might hold a small animal. He stared at it in the light from the window, then turned, jerked his chin up slightly, and began moving his lips rapidly over it. Still looking down, he jutted his chin out at Logan, who automatically extended his hands; without a word he dropped a striated, bronzed little root into Logan's outstretched hands. Then Luther sat back, completely relaxed but alert, his eyes wide, scarcely breathing, and watched Logan with rapt attention.

Logan was about to say something, but checked himself, as the pitted root began heating up like a pot handle. He looked for help, but Luther kept the same quizzical expression. The edges of the hot spot spread and the center felt more comfortable, and then the same sensation arose, like a warm finger, on Logan's throat. He clapped his open palm with the root flat against his larynx. Luther turned away, nodding and chuckling dryly.

"For the t'roat," Logan gasped. The words sounded strange. Luther smacked his hands slowly and bounced his head up and down. Then he began punching people around him, making sure they knew what had happened, especially Charlene, who had observed the whole matter sternly. She nodded, sighed "*That* cuts it," and looked out the window. This appeared to have been some sort of test, and Luther was merrily counting *coup*.

"Yeah," he resumed when he was finished, "you can feel all kinds of little things when It's goin'. That pipe tells you. It talks, like you 'n me. That one root there is for doctorin' the t'roat, and for chest sometimes, even heart. Another one is for bowels, and there's one ya cut up for all over. There's lots more of 'em after that—chew it up for toothache, stick it in hot water. You keep that root. It's sacred. It's old, like that tobacco." Logan looked at me across what seemed ages.

"Now, you gotta go to them ceremonies at Mission," he urged. "That's the next thing you gotta take."

Charlene said quietly, "Dad, you better go over there an' show 'm, then."

Luther studiously ignored her: "You go there to my brother Elgin's. He'll know what's what. Take him that traveling feather, say it's from me, an' tell him you're supposed to go to that ceremony No Dog's havin'. You come back then an' we'll see what else you need."

Luther reached for the little black beaded bag and removed a fistful of commemorative minted coins from his Catholic family's baptisms and christenings. Then he shook out a large mahogany-colored peyote button and handed it to each of us as he had the pipe, speaking of it as one of the old "Great Buttons" of the peyote church. In the botton of the suitcase was an oversized buff-colored calendar, thickly marked with tight script in all the date boxes. It had hung in the Wounded Knee church during the occupation, up until the time of the burning. Listening in the kitchen, Charlene said she'd burn that too, if she ever got her hands on it.

Morley got some notion in his head and started tugging impatiently at Luther's shirtsleeve, softly saying, "Bro'—hey, Bro'—Br-*o-o*-o-?" He persisted half-heartedly, as if he were trying to wake Luther to tell him the car wouldn't start, and the latter ignored him, as if he knew already the car had stopped running and didn't care.

"Hey Bro'—did you say a prayer for 'em?" Morley asked. Meghan's eyelids shot up.

"Uhhh, did that already." Luther rattled his head a little and puffed on a cigarette.

"Well, Bro', hey—did you tell about that time you used the pipe as a 'finder' down on the Niobrara, when them people crashed in that little ol' Cub plane?"

"Well, I took the pipe out then, an' prayed with it, an' I saw a coyote run down near the river—that's where the troopers found the wreck." Luther pulled at a tatter of tobacco glued to his lip. "Yeah, unbelievable, that dog-wolf runnin' out like that an' everythin'. It'll happen like that, but you never get used to it, 'specially if it's meetin' death, or like that pipe turnin' on the wall. You can't get away from it." It was all so matter-of-factly unsettling that I double-checked the pipe in my own hands. It wasn't about to move. The eagle feather and tobacco in my lap just waited there.

Luther then prayed again and gave Rachel his benediction, telling her in the strongest terms that if she was ever in trouble, or sick, or in need to get through her schooling, he would take care of her because he was her *Tunkáshila*. He packed his medicine back into the closet.

We had to leave to reach Mission by night. Charlene insisted that Luther pray for our safety. We started gathering our things. While I was taking my pipe to the car and getting Rachel settled in, somehow the conversation in the bedroom turned to fighting and wars and how people could handle themselves in close situations. I came back in to find Morley crowing:

"Oh, Charlene could fight like a man, stand up an' *hit* ya!" He flailed away at the air to indicate punches.

"Yeah, white 'specially!" Luther chortled. "Wipe 'em out, count some *coups*! Me, over seventy, an' I can hold out with anybody!" He joyfully swung a few punches.

Morley suddenly looked offended and said to Luther abashedly, "Hey, Bro'—hey don' talk to 'em like that."

"Hunh?" Luther hummed in mid-swing, confused by the distraction.

"Hey, man, some of these *is* white guys. You don' wanna hurt their feelin's," Morley grumbled in a wounded tone.

"Aw, I'm not hurtin' nobody. I's just tellin' 'em—these are my friends, they're not offended by anything like that no more'n you'd be. They unnerstan' stuff like that." Charlene grimly nodded at Morley. Kate and Meghan exchanged blank looks.

Morley still wasn't sure, and shook hands three different ways with each of us to make certain we knew everyone meant well. Luther watched him, giggled with exasperation, shook his head, and said, "Naw, they unnerstan'!"

Morley's example caught on, and pretty soon everybody was shaking hands, even if they lived in the same house. It started out jokingly, but then it all turned into saying goodbye. Luther was deeply affected by this spectacle, and became very formal and gracious. As Logan started toward the door, Luther grabbed both his hands and stared up. His face darkened, and tears fell easily. His words came in spasms. "You go on to your law school, an' you pray to your *Tunkáshila*. You can be a help to your people. It takes a lot. Remember ever'thing I told. It's hard. I see your family, even th' little kids, horrible sufferin'. You gonna lose a lotta things you wanted—people. There will be things you will pray for, but you can't change them. You'll understand that when you get to that place, Twin Peaks. Be sure of it to come back. We are makin' a medicine man—spirit eagle flies over to protect you. Live for the people!"

Charlene said, "He's comin' back, Gran'pa. He tol' you that's what he's gonna do; he'll come back this week."

He tightened his grasp, pulled Logan down, and said, "You come back, before you go. I wanna see it. I give you Medicine."

We didn't realize our exhaustion and hunger until leaving the house, so we stopped at a nearby cafe for a late lunch. The radio in the lounge was playing a Sobriety Bible service. Jay could barely eat. Logan put the root Luther gave him into a pipebag. Kate and Meghan took turns picking french fries off Rachel's plate. Soon our cars were heading out the west end of Winner through a hard rain.

CHAPTER 25

Mission

Moon When People Know That Everything Is Going to Grow (Sitka)

We drove forty miles from Winner to Mission into the heart of
Rosebud Reservation. Scrawled on a billboard was a welcome of sorts:
"This is God's country. Don't drive like hell through it."

The radio, following grain and cattle prices, warned of Indian
militants harassing anybody in the way. An eighty-three-year-old great-
great-grandmother from Pine Ridge was found dead at home, her
throat slit. Carloads of vigilantes were shooting anything that moved
or didn't move when threatened. Yellow Thunder's "sport" murderers
would soon be paroled, after less than three years in the state
penitentiary.

Near Mission we pulled off the blacktop, and I gave Logan and Jay
the traveling feather. It would serve as their token of entrance to the
Rosebud *olowan* or "sing" with Dalton No Dog. Kate and Meghan in
one car, and Rachel and I in another would drive on to Henry Black
Bear's ceremony at Pine Ridge. If either group didn't get back to
Alliance by the week's end, the other would start looking—a kind of
prairie buddy system. I drove west into a drizzle, followed by Meghan's blue VW. It was late afternoon and slate-grey light framed silo
tanks of "Sioux Grain" ghostly against the bellied rainclouds. We were
headed toward Wounded Knee, father and daughter on the road again;
as in the beginning, the students were on the flank.

"Daddy, does Logan know where he's going?"

"Just as much as we do, Rachel. You take a nap in the backseat
and let me drive for a while. I'll wake you up when we see some
horses."

"Please don't get lost again. Like last time?"

"No, it's not winter anymore. We've got friends waiting for us in Pine Ridge, some of Mark's family where he grew up."

By late afternoon our mud-splattered cars pulled into Pine Ridge Reservation along the Dakota-Nebraska border. A blacktop road cut clean into the horizon like an onyx knife: this was the other road, the worldly black one west to east. I hoped we were on the right road this time.

Golden meadowlarks were chorusing in triads, up and down their spring shortgrass scale, as we turned off on a gravel road and headed south, then doubled back east. Sitting Bull, as I remembered, could understand the songs of these yellow-breasted oracles, or so they say. He was also warned of danger by magpies.

The dirt road ended under an elm and cottonwood canopy that shaded Henry Black Bear's modest clapboard home. Henry was related to Mark's in-laws in some distant cousin way, and we carried an eagle feather as introduction to his ceremony, as well as a baked ham for the feast. Kate said it seemed like a potluck Thanksgiving. Motley dogs ambled up to chase sticks and get their bellies rubbed, and one began to teethe on Rachel's fingers.

"Can we take a puppy home with us, please Daddy?" I winced at those Ojibwa sarcasms about "dog-eating" Sioux. The old *heyoka* or sacred clown ceremonies were still observed in some small communities on Pine Ridge Reservation and included the ceremonial sacrifice of dogs.

We sat beside the car for half an hour, waiting, then wandered down the clay-packed country road, past a large man-made retention dam. No one seemed to mind our hanging around. Henry would "get home" soon, one of the children playing with the dogs told Rachel. We circled the sandhill pothole lake, ringed with reeds and swishing new brome grass, then strolled back to the clapboard house. It felt like a walk around the neighborhood, curious about the neighbors.

About five-thirty Henry rumbled home in an Old Dodge sedan, a big smile on his face out the open window, hair flying in the wind. He waved; we nodded. Henry motioned to the house, scuttled in, and we sat back under a cottonwood and waited some more. Rachel kept up her chatter about taking a puppy home. I kept my mouth shut.

When Henry came back out, he waved us into the barracks building, an eighty-by-twenty-foot plyboard rectangle. I began to wonder if, like Mark's Indian Center in Alliance, most Lakota community buildings were reconstructed from army surplus. The point stuck like sand in a sandwich. We sat down with about sixty Lakota for dinner— a four-vegetable stew, or "four-by-four," beef, frybread, our ham, some fried chicken and barbecued ribs, mint tea, and coffee. The potato salad was gone halfway around the room.

Suddenly, at eight o'clock, everyone filed out the back door. No one explained.

"Where are you going?" Rachel asked plaintively. I wasn't sure, but I didn't want her fussing.

"Sweat lodge, Sweetie. It's a steam bath for grown-ups. You go out in the yard and play with the puppies."

Kate and Meghan had helped to serve dinner and now stood under a grandfatherly cottonwood talking with two Lakota students from Oglala Community College. Kate had grown less outspoken, reflective even, listening and watching the Indian women and powerful elders. Meghan, too, was quieter, as though she knew something I didn't. This "sweat" was traditionally for Lakota men, it was understood, women having separate accesses to power. It was not that one gender was dominant over another; each completed the other differently, from menstrual hut to sweat lodge, or as in the Southwest, from matrilineal clan to male kiva.

Ten men in denim walked across the backyard, up a gentle rise past four junked cars, clockwise around the firing *inipi* or "sweat" stones, and hunkered on a green-flecked outdoor carpet. Several wore rubber irrigation boots. There was the customary smoke and some Lakota jokes. At best, I thought, I was regarded as a white "glooglooka," some strange clown or long-haired professor from Los Angeles. I never asked Mark how to spell it.

A genial, but imposing storm cloud was gathering in the western sky, as the sun fell in plaits across the prairie. Henry pointed to a profile in the tumbling cumulus that somehow resembled his silhouette—long broken nose, sunken chin, craggy brow, whiskery strands of hair that fell around his face like a shaggy skullcap. He got a good laugh out of this wink from the sky and muttered how weird it was to study under Thunder.

We disrobed and crawled clockwise, as is customary with sundance cultures, into a willow mound draped with old canvas. Henry placed me in the middle of the naked line, farthest from the flap. Four Lakota sat to my left, and Henry sat by the doorflap. Three men sat to my right. I took a deep breath and started to sweat.

The fireman brought seven pitchforks of heated sandstones and nudged them into the fire pit, dug two feet into the center of the *inipi* lodge. We sat cross-legged on a kind of clay ledge that encircled the pit. Henry sprinkled each *Tunkáshila* or "grandfather" stone with sage and closed the flap. He then poured water on the rocks, so they produced bursts of steam, and tossed in some cedar chips that popped like small sparklers.

Henry addressed *Tunkáshila* and asked for the breath of the grandfather stones to pass through each of us. It seemed a pipe ceremony without the pipe. He prayed to the spirits to hear our petitions, to heal us, to join us. The lead singer, hunkering to the right of the doorflap, broke into a Lakota song as the light faded into night. We sat on the earth in absolute darkness.

I followed the songs along in soft vocables. I wanted to sing with the others, but not smudge the prayers with mistakes. I felt like a child in church for the first time.

The lead singer called to *Wakan Tanka* or the "Great Mystery" for several minutes, and we sang together again. The second man prayed in Lakota, and we sang some more. Words like *woohitika* or "courage" started to come clear to me, and *wawakintanka* or "fortitude," and eventually *wacantognaka* or "generosity." They built toward the fourth virtue, *woksape* or "wisdom." We were all praying for these, and I felt myself easing into the *inipi*. I began to anticipate the rising and falling vowels, the long slow call of voices singing through darkness. It took me back some years to a family ceremony in Alliance when Mark's relatives and elder medicine people from Pine Ridge sang of us as brothers. It still seemed a language of mystery, of strange power— what the Lakota used to say of the bear singing "with a heart that is different," *cante' mato' ke^{c}a^{c}a*.

The rocks' steam smelled pungent with prairie sage. Sweet breath filled my lungs. The sweat started to pour and open my body, the songs drew us all together. Our differences for the moment seemed to disappear in this darkness, the singing our common home.

Suddenly the third man was praying in English. "The white man wants our land again. He wants the *Paha Sapa*, our sacred Black Hills. He dug up the gold and carved Great White Fathers over the faces of our grandfathers, our *Tunkáshila* mountains. He took everything, our language, our clothing, our religion, our old ways. Now he would take the sacred hills of our ancestors. He would rob our graves.

"I want this person to my left, this white man, to know that you don't play with Lakota ways. You don't play with our medicine man.

No, no more. This white man must go to the east and west, all around
the country, and tell other whites, his brothers, not to fool with us or
steal our land."

I was on the hot box. This was Vine Deloria's "cultural leave-us-
alone policy," another field lesson from *Custer Died For Your Sins*.
Where should I go at a time like this? I wasn't even dressed. The fire
pit of stones gaped between my body and the doorflap. Time to speak
up or get out.

"*Tunkáshila, onshimala ye, wani kte*." I prayed to get it right. "Grandfathers, pity me. I want to live." The old people tell me this—*Tahca
Ushte, Mini Waci*, Jenny Lone Wolf, where I was raised. I come as they
asked me, a white man, asking for brotherhood. I come with my own
pipe for blessing and instruction. I ask that our bodies open to the
land as the skies have opened to give us rain. May we be the flowing
streams and lakes again. May we cross the desert between us and
find the courage to heal ourselves. I ask that we help bring this land,
the body of our people, back to life. *Mitak' oyasin*."

Henry punctuated my monologue with "Ho!" and "Ho-ha!" which
I took as encouragement, though I was obviously under fire. What did
they think? It was no time to plead innocent or remain silent. This
challenge had been on the horizon since we left LA.

The fellow next to me came from North Dakota, where we'd just
been, and he had to speak in English too, since he didn't know
Lakota. He saw his poor fool grandfather drunk and wandering all
over. He wanted to bring the old man home, back in harmony with
his grandson and all things, off the bottle, out of a century of grief.
The man cried as he talked and prayed. He asked our help and ended
with a hoarse song.

The last two men prayed ritually in Lakota. I wondered how far
back these words carried into America, how many of these native
prayers still hung on the prairie winds. A half century ago Frances
Densmore heard such songs among the Ojibwa to the north:

> As my eyes
> search over the prairie
> I feel the summer in the spring.

The *inipi* singing grew deeper and stronger. The high pitches keened
downward in dissonant steps toward the ledge we perched on, and
the songs rippled on and on as audible breathing. The simple harmon-
ies were like soughing grass terraces. The steam warmed and com-
forted our bodies while it opened us. My fears gave way to a sense of

acceptance, at least momentarily, of well-being among friends. It was a good day to be alive.

We filed out naked after an hour, dripping under the night sky and laughing, and tried to dry ourselves in a soft rain. The damp night provided a welcome cooling. Lightning bolts popped across the prairie. The stars crackled blue beyond the lowering darkness.

The lodge stood ready as we dressed, walked down the hill, and shuffled back in. People sat on benches all around the perimeter. Rachel came running up with a handful of cottonwood leaves and seedpods.

"Hearts, Daddy, green hearts! Look! And there's stars inside the twigs." These were the natural and open secrets of the sacred Sun Dance cottonwood.

The windows were boarded and draped with black cloth, and we were asked to remove our watches and glasses. The attendants gave each of us a sprig of wild sage to put behind the right ear—so we could hear the spirits better. A red star blanket was spread in the center of the room where Henry would lie tied up. On the room's north side rested his altar. To the east an eagle feather staff poked up through a square hole in the ceiling. To the west medicine pipes and eagle feathers fanned across a red cloth offering.

After everyone assembled, old and young down to breast-feeding infants, a girl gave a traditional flesh offering. Henry nicked her arm with a small razor and the blood welled up. She didn't blink. It was an old, old ritual of blood sacrifice, still observed in the Sun Dance. A seventy-six-year-old grandmother, Mrs. Good Heart, offered her pipe and asked Henry to cut her arm to heal her grandchildren. I had gone through school with Alex Good Heart, her son's son, and she was raising ten grandchildren on her own. Alex's wife had died. She told me later, as we drove into Pine Ridge that night, "Now I'm mother of them all."

Henry was tied up with his hands behind his back in a many-colored blanket that was bound by a leather cord. Two helpers lay him face down on another blanket. Pinches of tobacco tied in red cloth were laid out in a string rectangle around the bound medicine man. The lights were turned out, and we waited, immersed again in total darkness. I could taste the thick night air that seemed to leak ghostlike through the boarded windows.

Henry prayed to *Tunkáshila*. Everyone warmed up by singing Sun Dance songs in chorus, led by three hand drummers. Gourd rattles jumped and stomped around Henry and seemed to answer the medicine man's muffled laughter and questions. A little whistle could have been carrying on a conversation with him. There were many tearful prayers and joyful praying songs, all mixed together. As the ceremony warmed up even more, sparks began to flit around in the darkness. The rattles glowed fluorescent when they skipped across the room, and thin streamers of fire dropped from the ceiling. Through scatterings of songs, prayers, and tears, Henry answered "Ho-ha" and "Ho" and "Hau" from inside his blanket as people one by one around the room made their petitions. I again asked for all to come together and walk in a sacred manner in a good land. It seemed to have become my theme.

I waited after my prayer. It was stone silent. Nothing. No one spoke. What went wrong? The darkness appeared to swallow everybody. Someone nudged me from the right; another whispered from the left, "All my relatives," and Rachel giggled. The white man had forgotten the traditional "amen."

"*Mitak' oyasin*," I mumbled. It was somewhat comic, but nobody seemed to mind much.

As the singing went on through the night for three more hours, Rachel fell asleep, and the rains came and went like frisky squirrels on the tarpaper roof. The ceremonial lights flickered, the rattles shook and clattered on the floor, the songs built to crescendos and died back down. Henry's voice boomed from the center. People were coming together: to pray, to cry, to sing, to think, not to think, to lose themselves to the spirits of one another and the petitioned powers of a nurturing land, old family spirits, the comforting darkness. It felt good not to see anything at all. I seemed to drop down beneath thought, to let my mind focus on nothing, interrupted by the blend of prayer and play, of communal support and the spirits' abandon. My twitches of uneasiness were overcome by Henry's joyous "Ho-ha!" and "Ha-ho!" and "Hau!" He spoke and prayed in Lakota, punctuated by the occasional English joke, erupting in chuckles; the people laughed with him, or cried with each other, and sang over their pains and losses and fears.

In all this I found clarity to sort out my thoughts. I saw each person on this red road distinctly, each thought as a thought, not a worry. Everything that was made sense. I knew Rachel was growing up with added blessings of my people and their heartland. I thought the others on this journey were well and learning well. Kate and Meghan were blessed by this darkness. Jay and Logan were being baptized on the Rosebud. The Lakota still clearly passed on their culture, despite the changes. This evening would carry all of us along the good red road home.

I felt my life's work would go on from here, back to LA and the university, returning to another kind of work in Alliance, my families, Mark, and the Lakota. One by one my deepest concerns surfaced and found their proper place in the play of the spirits. The people prayed with me, I sang with them; we were in accord under this dark Dakota night.

Toward the end of the ceremony, a hand lightly cuffed me on the right side of the head. Then two palms held my head on either side; it was a laying on of hands. I felt seized. After a second or two, the palms released me. I checked to make sure I wasn't dreaming. I was somewhat fearful, but more relieved and joyous that the spirits had touched me. We were a part of the ceremony.

The last songs were peaking in resonance, though the exuberant drummers got a little out of rhythm. It was delightful and somehow sacred, a ceremony of spirits necessary to our common lives. The hardness of things dissolved in this darkness. There was cause to come together—to grieve and to pray, to know our weakness and fear in the comfort of a common night.

"We're gonna make it as we go along," Henry sang out at the end of the ceremony, just before the lights came back on, "addin' on an' addin' on, generation to generation. *Mitak' oyasin!*"

Back in Mission on the Rosebud, Jay and Logan scratched around wondering what to do next. Jay ordered coffee in the 18/89 Hiway Cafe, at the state road intersection, and fretted whether Luther's brother, Elgin, would be home. They weren't even sure of his address, or whether he had a phone, so Logan walked next door to the Antelope Motel to ask directions. The manager got out the local directory on a chart and let him call Elgin. As Logan was dialing, the manager's wife yelled from the living room, "John Chancellor just announced that Russell Means was shot at Standing Rock!"

Elgin was at home, and Logan quickly recited his brother's message, mentioned the eagle feather, and told Elgin they were at the Hiway Cafe. Elgin said to wait and hung up. Logan thought perhaps he would wait a while and call back. The motel manager offered him some coffee, and wanted to know what he was doing there. Just then Jay walked in followed by a tall Indian. It was Elgin. There were quick handshakes, an allusion to the Means shooting, and suddenly Elgin was hustling them out the door to his car.

Elgin seemed bigger and younger than his brother, affable but businesslike. He had a rancher's wardrobe, gait, and drawl. He asked about Logan's origins and family and also about the discussions with Luther that led up to this meeting. He made some cautionary remarks about attending Dalton No Dog's meetings.

Elgin turned off on a muddy road, passing new barns and silos built by lease-holding whites. Sheep blocked the road, and Elgin had to nudge and pester them clear of the wheels. The link fences gave way to red clay pasture land along the crest of a long ridge. Another length of fencing came up, and then a small *tiospaye*, an extended family dwelling site on top of a hill.

In the center perched a small white frame house. A room addition shelled with green gravel paper jutted off the house, and a pine footbridge led to the back porch. Three Sidley tents were stacked out nearby, and several small buildings rattled in the wind. A grey lozenge-shaped shed sat off to the side. Old junkers squatted on cinderblocks in the south yard. A small horde of chickens and dogs tiptoed up, eyeing Elgin's car.

A Lakota man in his forties was waiting for them on the back porch. He seemed a full-blood, a little under medium build, with short hair and a triangular face. He directed them through a warm, dark kitchen strung with garlands of dried peppers, onions, turnips, and assorted roots. The man spoke Lakota in a bantering tone with Elgin, as he showed them into his living room: the walls were the color of sweet corn and were hung with muted pictures of animals and woodlands. They took seats in overstuffed chairs under the south windows.

Elgin gave them a rather peculiar introduction in English, then abandoned the attempt and talked confidentially in Lakota. It dawned on Logan that the full-blood he addressed was Dalton No Dog, who nodded and asked a few questions, glancing at Logan occasionally. He reflected for a moment, then said, "Luther Clearwater sent you here with an eagle feather. Nobody will refuse that introduction. Well, it's been a long week. I wish you'd been here last night. I held meetings four late nights in a row till finally I wore out. I want to ask if you can stay around here until tomorrow at least, or come back then. I'll be back at it tomorrow night.

"Now, you got to understand it may not be what you think. We got to do certain ways with our own rules. We're not vision seekers, and we're not that peyot' church. An' it ain't what you'd call *yuwipi*, either. This goes back. As far as I know, we were doing this when our people were living way down south. You don't just pick this road out on your own—it picks *you*." Dalton nodded gravely, clearing his throat.

"I got to tell you about Power," Dalton continued. "I was a young man that didn't know what was in me doin' things. I learnt how to plug in, but I guess I spent it on little things, like a kid does. I wasn't seein' it clear that power could be used besides just for me. I was a long time that way, rough-housin' around with it, settin' high-school track records an' such. So finally it hit me—the right way to do things was something I had to learn to do for other people. That's when I begun to do these ceremonies almost every night. I get backed up by the tribal council with a fund, so I can do it right." Dalton knew exactly what he had to say, his instruction friendly but stern.

"Some of what I do is seein' things spirits show to me. Some of it's healing. People come in with all kinds of family problems, sickness, drugs, alcohol—tried everything the government has for them, an' they're desperate. They know my medicine's the last thing they got, and they hopin' it's the only thing they need. See, they don't expect it to come outta me, they just know the Power is in the place where we do these ceremonies. I'm only just a way for the Power to get in— healin' that way is just bein' a road." Jay seemed a little restless but was attentive, and when he got used to the one-sided character of this interview, he retreated into listening.

"If you have to be a healer, the Powers take you to it. Nobody does it just because they feel that way or want to do it. Don't work that way, like some movie. You stand open for what the spirits are sticking through you all the time. At any one ceremony the Powers decide who does what. We got our rules to get there, but then the spirits got their own, too. You ain't goin' to stand in their way tellin' them to do this, do that. You got to respect that—they wait inside for you to make the mistake. So you benefit while they takin' care of you, or you ain't havin' nothin'." He was more relaxed and pensive now, and his voice began to crack with weariness.

"I live guided by what I saw up on *hanblechia*, like a vigil for the spirits to tell me what's what. After that, continual sacrificin', not goin' just any way I think up. I got to be an example, the way I live, to give the young people strength and the old people hope. Live right. Not drink, not fight people that hate you, not tell lies, not do anything to hurt anybody." He stressed the last point. "Not use spirit things to hurt nobody."

Dalton leaned forward on the arm of his chair, staring at the floor, and said, "You got to think about this. I have to fast a lot, four times a year. There is four days in the fall, three winter, two spring, one summer, which I do a few days from now. Any other way would not be the right relation between them Powers and me. So look how we live here. There is no town, no running water, no electricity, no cars to drive. It's like the old ways, as best I can get to it. Not a usual job I could do like a white man, but simple, without a lot of things." His eyes closed. "I have to be ready to help in the community, bein' there for healing when they need. So look at my *hanblechia* that way—fast and pray, no food or water. That is the way a healer is havin' to do.

"Now, there is this ceremony tomorrow night. Elgin, here, is goin' to tell you how to get ready. At sundown we always do purification for a ceremony. It's goin' to be a little different, because tomorrow night we'll take a young man up on *hanblechia* the first time. He's one of our local people finding out if he can become a medicine man. It is always tough. So we'll be takin' him up to the sweat lodge, and then into the hills way back someplace for four days and nights. So you come back early. It won't even be dark for a long time."

He seemed to make some final decision to himself about Logan and Jay, visitors from another world. "You guys be here to take that young man up with us, the priests and the singers. You goin' to make up part of our bunch, like that, a travelin' church up on the hill. This has all got to be done just right. We'll find out things. We'll not be sure what you are here for until then. If it goes wrong, the ceremony or the sweat lodge or the *hanblechia*, nobody will be happy." Jay wasn't sure whether he had just presented them with a friendly admonition or a veiled threat.

"It is sunset before we start the healing ceremonies, after we get that man up on the hill. If you never been in a sweat before, you goin' to have a tough time, 'cause we don't do like you maybe heard. We ain't gonna open that tent flap to cool off anytime. We go right through to the end."

CHAPTER 26

Rattler's Friend

Half Way Moon (Creek)

Logan and Jay retrieved their car at the 18/89 Hiway Cafe and
trailed Elgin to his prefab house in a nearby BIA tract. Their host
offered the use of his back bedroom, a pot of meat stew, and fresh
rhubarb pie made by his sister.

Then Elgin set about preparing them for the next night's ceremonies. He rummaged in an old chest and brought out bundles of two
kinds of red offering cloth, red embroidery floss, and a sack of Bull
Durham. There were also little banners, prayer flags, with seven
colors for the spirits of all directions. The yard-lengths of red cotton
cloth had to be ripped into strips, the large flannel squares left intact
as prayer flags. The red strips were torn into tiny squares and made
into pouches to hold tobacco offerings, "papa bags," then secured
with the embroidery floss in strands of twenty; they would be laid on
and around the altar.

"Tobacco's the oldest offering we know," Elgin said, "*pejuta*—old
as the people offerin' themselves."

Jay had picked up some groceries for the next night—several pounds
of granola as a reasonable substitute for *wasna*, traditionally a parched,
ground cornmeal or powdered meat mixed with dried wild fruits.
Elgin showed them how to fix the flannel prayer flag, using one corner
to secure a small pouch for tobacco with floss. With a sudden smile
he tied the traveling feather to the corner of the flannel flag. These
offerings were to be displayed at the ceremony, and then the holy
women would take them to a mountain to be received by the spirits.
Thereafter the eagle feather would follow, wherever they were, guiding
and protecting.

Logan was curious about Dalton's ceremonies. "Well, now I'll just tell you," Elgin said, "if you're not sure you're going to stick it out, through whatever happens over there, don't go. People get scared, you know, with bein' around things they're not used to. So I wouldn't force it on myself, even if Luther sent you.

"Dalton No Dog has got the Rattlesnake Power. I guess you could say he's like an old-time Rattlesnake medicine man." He grinned slowly. "Yeah, he can get real funny about it. He used to be a real bird around here, I guess, and there's something in him sometimes that's still that way. He'll make jokes with it, almost, and look so serious. He can really scare people, but won't let them get hurt.

"I remember this one time some of us were all sittin' over at his house, and this one guy had just met him—" He slowed down, nearly whispering. "Well, here's that Dalton sittin' there, and everybody's talkin' real nice, you know, just had dinner and everything. And all at once, I can hear this scratching and scratching, and I thought maybe it was a cat under the house, and then here comes this rattlesnake up through a hole in the floor!" Elgin laughed and rubbed his hands together, leaning his elbows on his knees, and his voice rose. "This new guy is up on his chair, an' some of 'em that don't know what Dalton's like are afraid even to move, don't know what's happenin', and Dalton—just as cool—he says, 'Oh, that's all right, just a friend of mine.' That ol' snake, he just slid around their chairs sniffin', didn't bother a thing. An' then they held the door for him and he just eases on out in the yard. Friendly as he could be. Ol' snake didn't sing a time. That's the kind of guy Dalton is, real steady." He laughed softly.

Elgin then pointed out that each of the prepared offerings reflected a phase in the ceremonies—the tobacco bags were for the whole ceremony, a dedication. The large felt flags were for asking about personal affairs. The feather offering was for travel, healing, divination, power, that sort of thing. The ribbon bundles were for health problems.

Elgin took all the prepared items and hung them on a clothesline in the enclosed porch out back. He got out a small paper bag full of dried cedar bark and leaves and crumbled them into a firkin. He heated them until they smoked heavily and then censed the house, the offerings, himself and his guests with sweet smoke. The pungent smell of cedar and sage hovered in all the rooms, a delicate opal haze.

CHAPTER 27

Visible Breath

Moon of Making Fat (Lakota)

Logan and Jay pulled into Dalton's yard late in the afternoon. It was windy and cloudy, with low thunderheads pushing across the horizon. Children peeked from the parlor window as they approached. Small dogs tore around the yard and threw themselves in the path to be petted. Jay tried not to look down, muttering, "Leave me alone. For all I know, you're supper."

They knocked at the back and Dalton came out brandishing a garland of scarlet peppers. He greeted them familiarly, motioned toward the squad of busy cooks at their pots of stews, puddings, and teas, and said, "You're a little bit early still. Stomp around for a while. You got some time yet." He blinked hawklike at the wind and indicated a good direction to hike near the creek.

Abruptly changing winds cut at Logan and Jay walking the heath-like land in its fullest green bloom. There were cornflower flashes in the grass waves, thistles and horsemint, and a fire-colored honeysuckle in crouches under the edges of rotting granite boulders. Poison ivy leaflets, garnet in the late afternoon light, fluttered among ropes of fox-grape on a few sheltered banks. Bird calls, cold and attenuated, broke through the currents of air, as the wind turned every sound into a ring.

Turning west along a dirt road, they passed limestone cairns of used *inipi* fire stones, *peta owihankeshni*, charred, grey, and brittle. Below the ridge ran ditches full of thickets. The wind paths grew visible carrying traces of dust, resinous pollen, and bewildered insects in mating swarms. Strange splinters and flints jutted from exposed sandhill clay banks. Logan found the molar of a large grazing animal, very old, stained violet and brown, near a bone-colored chunk of lightning-fused sand like an opaque mirror.

The cattle of neighboring white stockmen advanced to drink at the scant creek waters. Vermillion starfaces, Herefords and longhorns, crowded under a water oak whose limbs held a rattling thicket of crow nests. The birds circled their rookery brushing the leaves, reaching without settling in the dry branches. The cattle raised their heads and stared vaguely in Jay's direction. Some of the nearest backed away from the water, chewing thoughtfully and preparing to bolt.

Skirting the livestock, they found a cleaner part of the creek under a canopy of sumac and ash. The stream was banked with red desiccated clay. The creek had filled with rotting leaves, and over them— limpid, crystalline, and cold—shimmered an inch-deep veneer of water. Gnats hovered over the long glossy bands of algae. Here, a hundred years ago, the Lakota—Spotted Tail, perhaps, or Big Foot—had fled to nurse their injuries or die. Clusters of puffballs grew in this little darkness, thumb-sized medicine bags whose styptic dust could close and heal a wound; under their dusky, parchment skins lay fibers like flesh, white like snow blindness, like centerless eyes.

Across the creek, a large tortoise waddled patiently through a stand of bearberry. The tortoise's back was rough and sage green, patterned like a fully opened flower. Logan and Jay stopped to lift it up and look at its belly for a moment, glossy from rubbing hard grass. Thin white lines defined blocks of crimson, saffron, brown, and black. There were thirteen patterns in sections on its back, the number of lunar months or "moons" in the year, and around that twenty-eight quadrants, the days in a lunar "moon." It was said that in ancient China the first oracular writing came from heating tortoise shells and "reading" the cracks.

Turning to avoid the grazing longhorns, Logan and Jay started up the steep rocky line of hills leading back to the house. They passed a large den, maybe belonging to a fox or badger. No tracks marked the entry. Above the high drone of wind, Logan could barely hear the rustle of their feet gripping and sliding. He caught himself unconsciously leaning down, the better to detect the dry itchy buzz of errant rattlers.

They found themselves in a small box canyon surrounded by a sheerly eroded ridge. Standing quietly, deciding which way to go out, Jay stared at the sky to indicate the silence. "You know, right now I feel like I'm in some sort of horror movie—I'm one of those national guardsmen on duty, sitting down to eat a sandwich at the bottom of the cliff, just before the giant piss ant reaches down to pick him up by the foot. I bet there's a row of bulls waiting for us just over the shoulder of that hill."

The latter fantasy, at least, sounded somewhat plausible, so the two were cautious about getting out. They still ran into the milling herd, just as they crept onto the ridge. The wind was toward the cattle, and they all stuck up their muzzles. An old bull with huge eyes bellowed and started trotting forward in a businesslike way that suggested they had better be a saltlick or bringing one.

In almost no time they were in sight of Dalton's compound. Logan could see daylight now under the clouds in the west. The wind had been so strong that the cloud cover blew over without dropping anything. The sun, approaching the horizon, turned everything the color of hot straw.

Farm trucks and cars of people, arriving after a day's work, began to fill the yard. Logan and Jay sat in the car and watched groups of women carrying food into the grey rectangular outbuilding, which appeared to be the main site for the ceremonies. Children were lining up at the outhouses and then clustering into the grey building. A few stayed in the yard to play with the ever eager dogs. There was a strong scent of cedar smoke in the air. Logan got out his towel and went to see if the sweat lodge fire was sending up the smoke.

The *inipi* lodge was huddled at the edge of the compound near the tents, chest-high, covered with a huge dusty-green tarpaulin. Several men gathered beside the fire pit west of the flap door. Logan asked about Dalton No Dog, and one of the men pointed his chin at the sweat lodge, where through the door he saw Dalton sitting with an apprentice lamenter preparing for *hanblechia*. He would "cry for a vision" in the old ways of religion. Dalton was mincing herbs and loading the lamenter's pipe while he prayed and chanted. This prospective medicine man, maybe thirty years old, held a blue and white star quilt. He was a mixed-blood, slight in build, and at the moment perfectly still. Logan turned away, feeling somewhat awkward. After Dalton emerged, Logan noticed that the young man's pipe was propped against the small wooden altar set up before the *inipi*. There was no other pipe present for use in the ceremony, and none was smoked.

Dalton exchanged a few courtesies with the Sioux helpers, duly observing the peaceful exit of the storm front, and then turned to Logan, asking what he'd found out there in the creek. Logan mentioned the tortoise but not the bulls. Dalton puckered his chin and nodded, was silent for a short time, and then began speaking in Lakota with the others, who mostly had their backs to the fire pit.

Dalton was talking in short spurts now, very clipped, with long pauses in between, and his words began to elicit monosyllabic responses in chorus: "Ho"—"Tôn"—"Anh"—"Hauh"—"Welo." This continued for some time. Logan found himself staring into the pit and watching the stones wax more brilliant through their fluffy coats of ashes, clicking and chirping, some continually ringing as they expanded, emitting steam. Logan heard his name come up in the address several times, and he glanced up responsively, but Dalton was only alluding to him in some roundabout way, eliciting furtive glances.

Eventually Dalton looked around and began to walk a few feet as everyone started undressing. He told Jay, "Remember, the flap won't be opened till it's over." Stacking their clothes on towels, everyone filed in "clock" or sunwise. Dalton made sure Jay and Logan were put in the middle of the line so they would end up at the point farthest from the door. "Billy Jack . . . A Man Called Horse . . . and the gang's all here," he cackled as they stooped to crawl and enter the pit.

Dressed in long-johns treated with bluing, Dalton took his seat on a pile of small pads at the south side of the door. Jay sat to Logan's right, and then followed a helper and a singer. One man stayed out to tend the fire and carry water. With a pitchfork he placed seven broad slabs of cherry-red stone in the center pit. Then he dropped the flap shut. Dalton was holding a bundle of sage and sprinkling the stones with water; they all sat in the stones' glow trembling through a veil of steam. Tiny sparks jumped where the medicine man sprinkled cedar chips on the fire stones.

There was a long time of prayers, invocations, and singing to honor the spirits. Logan felt himself unfolding into the heat and blackness, giving over to the swelling Lakota chants all around him. The songs drew him into the circle gathering in darkness around the fire stones. He could hear Jay panting next to him. All leaned breathing into the steam, which pulsated in song-waves that circled the trembling tent walls. Dalton's tin dipper emptied creek water into the pit many times, until the mist obscured the stones' glow. The only sequence that mattered was the distance between two breaths. No other time existed.

When they left, calling *mitak' oyasin*, or "all my relatives," the sun was still out and the air seemed warmer. The others who had been in the tent felt more inclined to socialize now with the visitors. The youngest, wearing an AIM hat and a turquoise earring, got into a conversation with Jay about basketball at Pine Ridge.

One of the helpers nodded to Logan and began briskly walking back toward the *inipi*. They removed the covering and folded it without a word. Then the helper turned around and walked away toward the yard. Logan impulsively picked up the tarp and ran after him. The helper opened the trunk of his car and Logan laid in the tarp and slammed the lid. Several men piled into that car then and Logan jumped in with the rest. The vision seeker or "lamenter," Dalton, and the singer were getting in the front car. Logan looked behind to see what had happened to Jay and found him starting up his car with six others in it. The head car revved up, all the other engines started and revved responsively, the front car honked its horn, and they were taking the lamenter on *hanblechia* without further ado.

The convoy rolled cheerfully on, with lots of excited banter. When they stopped at the base of a steep conical hill, the lead cars were already unloading. Dalton's first helper opened the trunk for Logan and ran up the hill after the others. Logan grabbed the tarp up and scurried after him, dodging little rocks that the others were scattering back in their flights up the path. Somehow he was sure they were trying to beat the sunset.

As they got to the crest, the lamenter was standing with his pipe, facing west, wrapped in his star blanket amid furious activity. Four poles with unfurled medicine flags were already planted, several strands of tiny red tobacco medicine bags were strung around three sides of the holy ground, and the central hearth was newly lined with fronds of cedar and sage. They put the tarp over the basketlike pole skeleton of the shaking tent and stood back to let the lamenter, the singer, and Dalton enter the center, as Jay continued to lay down strands of "papa bags."

Logan backed off to avoid stepping on the protected tobacco line. He looked back down the hill, and now scores of people, all adults, were standing around their cars, looking up grinning and waving. He waved back and turned to do a head count. The only ones up here were those who had been in the sweat purification. That recognition calmed him down, and the two circumstances of the sweat and preparation for *hanblechia* clicked into symmetry. Seven. The priest, the singer, and the lamenter stood in a row at the west end of the square. Jay was to Logan's right again, and two helpers stood across from them. They were in the same configuration as in the sweat lodge.

The sun hung as a wedge of light between the singer and the priest. The other men were completely frozen in stillness and light, like fingers of a hand open to the sky. The changing wind was a low whistle. A meadowlark was singing just below, and swallows darted through, going south. Stars were out, cold and white in heavens indigo to a dusky purple. The sky lightened to a cloudless copper bow near the sun, which quickly dropped past the horizon, and the singer began the first word of his hymn. A white meteor trailing carnelian flame careened from the south and stopped like a blink in the valley due west.

The song rose clear and limpid as the creek below. Then the lamenter entered his *inipi*, and the helpers bound the last string of "papa bags," the *canli wapahta*, to the poles. Down behind them, people were leaving in a quietly festive mood.

The men on the hill jogged to their cars and were soon back at the *tiospaye*. The lamenter lay suspended in his own time.

Logan and Jay sat in the car and watched little children playing in the twilight. People continued to carry grocery bags and pots of food into the meeting place where they were to have the sing, the *wakan lowanpi*. They were coming to this place with their troubles and hopes of the present. The new medicine man finding his vision on the hill would be retrieved another day.

CHAPTER 28

Lowanpi

Moon When the Tribe Plants (Omaha)

Everyone helped carry chairs into a long chamber with boarded windows, just large enough to hold the fifty or more people crowding in. Two kerosene lanterns lighted the cavelike room. There was no source of heat. Four posts supported the raftered ceiling; the walls of packed clay glowed full saffron in the lamplight. Earthen shelves provided sitting and storage space along the walls, and all the food was stacked at the south end, where singers and musicians gathered with their drums, flutes, eaglebone and deerbone whistles. On the north wall near a covered window hung a tapestry portrait of the Kennedy brothers and Martin Luther King, Jr., on a maroon velvet background. All ages, bloodlines, and physical conditions of reservation people were in attendance, babies, school children, ranchers, businessmen, day laborers, nursing mothers, and old ladies in their eighties. Logan and Jay placed their offerings in the Farmers Brothers coffee cans near a circular altar of white sand. In the center of the room, where the medicine man was to sit, lay a set of skin-covered rattles or *wakmuga* next to fresh sage wreaths. A helper added tobacco-tie garlands to the altar, decorated with a serpentine line; before it stood a leather-covered red and black staff with eagle feathers at the top and a black deer tail attached in the middle. A green canvas bag near the food cache held small dowels to display the flag and bannerlike cloth offerings.

Logan and Jay approached the altar and presented Luther's spotted eagle feather. The offering provoked a long silence, and then a rash of excited murmurs. They took two vacant seats near the altar just as Dalton entered engaged in light conversation with a final cluster of arrivals. He was out of his long-johns and dressed in a white shirt, grey slacks, and black shoes, appropriate garb for a lay priest of any church in America.

A young, rather drawn Lakota woman in indigo entered haltingly and started for a rear seat reserved by her family. Dalton noticed her and told her to sit near the front to be treated. There were no spaces near the altar, so Logan stood and offered his seat. Jay looked a little confused about what might be developing into musical chairs, but nobody needed his seat.

Dalton directed Logan to sit with a certain elderly woman, Mrs. Morgan, on the north corner earthen ledge, suggesting that she knew all about the ceremony and could explain what was going on. She made some room and immediately asked who they were, who'd told them about doing the right things for the ceremonies, and was especially interested in the traveling feather from Luther. In her fifties, Mrs. Morgan wore a long black dress and shawl and continually rolled cherry cough drops under her tongue. Slender, high-cheeked, and fine-boned, she must have been strikingly beautiful as a girl. Her hair was still black, straight, and shining, drawn back tightly under her shawl. She may have been a full-blood, but she spoke with an almost Appalachian accent, as if she had learned English in school from a Southern missionary.

Mrs. Morgan told about her son who had moved to California on relocation and stayed there with his family. She visited them several times in Los Angeles but hated the "brown clouds." Mrs. Morgan said she sang the women's parts in many of the ceremonies and came every night to *lowanpi*. All this interchange went on in whispers, as people settled down and Dalton took his place on the mats.

A helper censed the room, waving a glowing braid of sweetgrass in every corner, then passed out fresh sprigs of sage. Logan thought there might be a *yuwipi*-style binding of the medicine man, but Dalton addressed *Tunkáshila*, the assembled ancestral spirits, under a sheer red cloak. He blessed the pipe and conducted an invocation, reviewing his own history of visions and his sources of power, including his protector rattlesnake. Then people removed their eyeglasses and watches, and the lights were turned out. The darkness settled around them.

The opening consisted of many prayers. They asked for help from the spirits and blessings on the ceremony and paid respect to the creators and the winds at the four directions. The drums began and with his back to the wall Logan could anticipate the beats. A gourd rattle briefly pulsed and faded away. The singer pitched his voice to a shrill falsetto, capable of cutting a Plains wind, and called an opening measure. Then the people began to carry the song. Mrs. Morgan whispered, "Oh, I like this! It is a good song," and they sang.

> Wakan Tanka!
> Onshimala!
> Ye wani kta—
> Cha lecamun we eya he!

"Great Spirit," the song went, "take pity on me. I want to live, thus I do this." Abruptly an elk-pipe moaned low and throaty, like hard wind in spindly pines. The drumming spread a ground for the ceremony. The flute turned suddenly, sharply, to a higher register, quavering like light off a knife.

In the twilight behind the walls, mockingbirds sang high in the bushes, an owl's "To-hooeet" pervaded the dark inside and out. All boundaries dissolved in the dark of ceremonial chanting; in their voices the people came together as one assembled spirit. An eaglebone whistle shrilled until the sounds contracted to what Logan felt as a throb in his eyes, and the voices soared to the six directions with their singing. The egg-shaped gourds chatted like quartz ticking down cliff walls on bright, cold days. On the deep, untroubled bank of the clay benches they rested; in their feet they felt the tremor of the songs. Logan sensed the warm bodies of neighbors, until at last all fell silent, and the shaman told of being with spirits out in the night, riding thundering wind, seeking a polar star, flying there under the red cloth with knowledge and sacrifice.

Beginning at the east and circling the room sunwise four times, Dalton took in questions, encouraging openness with the interjections "Ho!" and "Hauh!" The people found catharsis in their own plain speaking, eliciting from Dalton direct answers and advice. Some moaned as revelations made them wince. Some asked guidance and blessing in their career ventures—cattle deals, crops being tended, new work off the reservation, college or job training. They spoke of personal and family troubles: a sister had gone into hiding—the spirits told where and why; a son was alcoholic—Dalton's voice counseled patience and professional care. They heard stones talking in the rattles, stirring among powers that had razed mountains and survived life and death. Tiny sparks zigzagged across the well-deep darkness, and they could feel objects whirling through the air around them. It was strangely familiar for Logan to share this singing darkness with others and the spirits, and they found a bond to the mystery in the commonplace.

A new song-cycle started up. The drums echoed valleys where

thunder resounded for hours, and lighting joined sky and earth, through rains that never ceased to renew the land and people. The pipe, celebrating an approaching feast of dog meat, danced with them to the altar's limit. They were carried momentarily on the writhing back of the medicine man's power, out onto the flowering torus of *Tunkáshi-la's* many worlds, all mutually reflecting wonder.

Now, when Dalton spoke from a dance with the thunders, his laughter spilled across the singing. "We are dancing here with lightning," he menaced gaily. "If something went wrong, we could be scorched like squaw wood." And then, with a sudden shift of tone, he counseled petitioners, "Reason with your fear, come to terms with your enemies. The world is its own rule." Being light when near death, suspended in the presence of things beyond death's reach, was the spirit of the song; its one demand was for them to join together heartily and sing through all their pain.

They chanted for the well-being of all, and for the spirits themselves. Jokes and unabashed laughter rang out. The old one, Mrs. Morgan, turned to Logan, and laughed in a melodic ripple, her voice transformed and nubile, "I love—*I love* it that the spirits are so funny."

The *lowanpi* lasted more than seven hours, gathering in intensity as the voices moved in unison through darkness. There was second wind on second wind for the singers. The curings began after several hours, and Mrs. Morgan between sings made Logan tell what he would say to *Tunkáshila*. He spoke of the illness among the Monroe family in Alliance. She said curtly, "Well, okay, wait and he will come around this way to hear you in a little bit. See, he's got to one side of the room at a time, starting south, and then go 'round west, like that. You going to have to say in English, all right, but I tell you what they praying as it goes along."

Eventually Dalton came to their row, and Mrs. Morgan said in a sharp hiss, "Okay, here he's coming, now you speak up—you jump right in there with your voice, and say '*Tunkáshila*' and then you pray to the spirits." She shoved Logan in the ribs when his time came up. "Go on—right now."

Logan presented a petition for Jenny Lone Wolf and her family. There were several gasps in the room when he mentioned names they all knew. Mrs. Morgan followed him, reflecting on the illness of her son. Logan could hear the rustle of her sleeve as she wiped her tears.

There was another period of singing, and Dalton began giving the answers of the *Tunkáshila* spirits, telling Logan that things bode well for his healing petitions. "The Spirits acknowledge kindly your long journey here and welcome you in a sacred manner to their house. We all welcome you when you can be with us, in the body where you stand, as we will when you are here in the spirit.

"As you find your way home, the spirits say they are protecting you; for your home is within you, and the Spirits are in it. Your offering and your prayers are being answered, accepted into the holy winds; and the *Wanbli*, the eagle, stands over you to guide, and protect, and take you down a good road to when you come to him forever.

"You both are right with us, and the spirits have put out their hands gently on their little mother Lone Wolf. They are taking her home to her children to do good again for a while more. As for her children and her children's children, the spirits are blessing them too in their sickness and have not turned their eyes from them—this you may answer them. So walk peacefully and in respect, and the spirits, when they come to you, are going to know you."

On the west side of the room, a child began to cry in a drowsy, expressionless way, perhaps in his sleep. The air had grown stale from the many hours of enclosure. Mrs. Morgan grew worried, then annoyed about the child, who was awake now and bawling angrily. The ceremony continued into another cycle, notwithstanding the deafening racket, and the little boy went back to sleep. He yawned very noisily once, and Mrs. Morgan and others started giggling. "Wish I had spirits around to put mine out like that," she whispered.

Lamps came on finally and people began to smoke. The room quickly filled with a soft blue haze. The people near the altar were receiving herbal teas. The lights went out and another song cycle began. This time Mrs. Morgan told Logan to stand up with her, because they would dance now. The rattles near the altar began shaking over the people there for healing, and Logan realized that Jay was seated among them. A soft aqua auroral fire was moving with the sound of the rattles. Logan shut his eyes—he couldn't see the light so he opened them. The fire seemed to leave a trail as it moved, elongating and swirling, occasionally poising in a tight ball and then expanding.

There was one more cycle of songs, and then the *lowanpi* ended and the lamps were turned back on. Everyone stood and began to mill about. Many people clustered around Logan to shake hands and offer advice, asking whether he was interested in becoming a healer. There were many who knew Granny Lone Wolf and her people, and they gave him personal messages to take back to Alliance.

It had been a good sing. Everyone was ravenous. A young girl began to circle the room sunwise with a water bucket, and another followed her with a plastic bucket of strong mint tea. The food was distributed—cinnamon-colored meat-and-berry *wasna*, bearberry pudding, fry bread, and a big potful of stewed dog in a spicy posole broth. There was a lot of joking and stretching. Families were sitting together. Jay passed out the baggies of granola amid much laughter about his "lumpy *wasna*." When he got back to his seat, he found his soup bowl full of meat and sat down to eat. "This is good chicken, but it's got a lot of fat."

Logan looked up at him blandly, as did Dalton's helper seated on the other side. They exchanged glances across Jay, and went back to eating. Logan said off-hand after a while, "It's a good thing you didn't get too friendly with him."

"With who?" Jay asked innocently, his mouth full.

Logan pointed to his bowl just once, and Jay stared bleakly down at the little red bones and veallike flesh. "You mean they gave *me* bowser bouillabaisse?" Dalton's helper offered him some more when he was finished, but one bowl was plenty.

They cleaned the place up and rearranged the furniture, and then stepped into the open air. It was incredibly bright outside under the starlight, like a flood of white sand in a bowl of obsidian. The Spirit Way bowed north to south overhead, its rainbow of stars bits of shattered crystal.

Dalton approached as they stood there looking up and repeated what he had said in the ceremony, encouraging them to keep coming back whenever they could. "Many people come here only at a distance. You don't have to walk and sit in that room to be there. It goes on with you there, if you're even a thousand miles off. Luther does that. People send the cloth offering, and we know their prayers are in that room, and it's all done for them.

"You are going a different way. See all that you can, and tell the story to all the people. It is a hope and a blessing. It is a good time to be knowing these things again."

They thanked Dalton and left in the rear of a new caravan headed toward Mission. Horns honked along the line, headlights swept the night prairie, and a few playful whoops went up as the cars rumbled away from the *tiospaye* to the east.

And in the stillness beyond the noise of engines, Logan imagined a song that rose up from a hill a little to the west.

Anpo ki kolawaye,
Anpo ki kolawaye,
Anpo ki hinajin ye yo.
My friend, Dawn,
My friend, Dawn,
Dawn, come and stand.
Kola miye cha wau welo.
Kola miye cha wau welo.
Mika sitamni ihayeya wau welo.
My friend, I am coming.
My friend, I am coming.
I come all over the Earth with the entire Power.

CHAPTER 29

Backlash

Bark Loose Moon (Salish)

Jay was at the wheel when they broke off from the caravan. The west wind pushed from the rear, and it was nearly dawn. They were going faster than they'd ever driven, on a hilly, bumpy road at that. Jay was clearly annoyed about something he didn't want to discuss. When the car was beyond Mission, Logan began to fuss about speeding, especially since they were bound to encounter a few drunks or sporting cowboys. Logan tried coaxing Jay to talk, though he wasn't particularly anxious to get him started.

Jay was fighting an uphill battle with events of the night. His background left him unprepared for the strangeness of the rituals— the peculiar behavior of the priest and helpers before the *inipi*, the appearance of the meteor just as the singer began his song on the hill, the sustained intensity of the long healing ceremony. Lacking even an interpreter, he found no way to integrate these events. The feast, the people's familiar behavior, Dalton's response to Logan's petition for healing, the fact that Logan had *made* the petition—these things disturbed him, they seemed entirely irrational. The neighborliness was even more threatening than abuse, and it all mounted an impression of the ceremonies he could not accept. To his horror, Jay had found himself being treated as a patient, along with all the sick people at the altar. While it was still happening he had wanted to say this was a mistake, but he couldn't—no one there would have understood him, and he couldn't even leave the room.

Granted, the ceremony had been engaging during the early cycles; but as the intensity had built among the singers, and the strange noises and the lights had appeared, it all had grown too bizarre to be just another church service. He could rationalize that the rattles were being manipulated by a helper even afterward, but when *he*, the healthy one at the altar, was touched by the rattles too, that was the last straw.

"That guy hit me once, and then the light ran up my arm and all over me, and I could see my outline come out in the dark! I went blue-green all over a little at a time, like when you hit sea water at night with a paddle. I can't figure that out!" It hadn't felt like static electricity; it was more as if someone had sprayed him with a dry luminous paint that had soaked into his skin. His voice crackled with indignation.

He turned from the wheel, nearly losing control, and yelled, "What *happened* in there? They're nice people and everything, but what were they trying to do to me?" He didn't wait for Logan's response.

"Meteor falls just as the ceremony starts. All right, that's just a coincidence; probably it happens all the time out here. But the rattle going over me and leaving that trail . . . and I *know* I don't have that much static cling—"

"Well, try to look at it this way," Logan offered. "They were really taking a chance with us. For all they knew, we might have gone in there on acid or something—the distrust can go both ways." Jay nodded irritably to show he was listening. "You can't really think anybody in there was manipulating things to annoy you! Eating dog is sacred, out of respect for an animal their grandparents had to eat when they were starving in the last wars. It's like Passover with the lamb. The ceremonies went on way overtime, and everybody came out feeling great about the whole thing. Would you take that away from them? If Dalton had lost control of the situation, they'd have put bad-mouth on him from Porcupine to Upper Cut Meat. Somebody like that, people just wait to put in a bad light. But a lot of people depend on him and his ceremonies—if *only* for the moral support and self-confidence. It would be pretty bad if his *lowanpi* got messed up."

The car hit a bump in the road and rocked giddily for several seconds. Jay backed off a little, thought for a moment, and continued, "Do you think what went on in there was supernatural?"

"What do you mean?"

"What do you *mean*, 'What do you mean'?" he exploded. "You know damn well what I mean! Don't give me any of that qualifying-your-terms bullshit! I mean *healing* people in those ceremonies—faith healing, Oral Roberts and that funny-looking woman at the Shrine Auditorium, the one with the frizzy hair that looks like Madeline Kahn in *Young Frankenstein*! People going in there because they think they'll get well, or because they get off on it. Or to find out if something creepy's gonna happen to their mother-in-law so they'll get back the guest bedroom, crap like that." He was speeding again.

"You mean they *act* like something will happen at the ceremony, to help them live more comfortably?" Logan was heating up to the insult of invidious comparisons.

"I can't understand it," Jay fumed, but he drove in silence less recklessly. After a few miles, he started in again more reflectively. "I can tell it's supposed to be group therapy, positive thinking, old-time religion. But *why*, for Christsake, the *Wizard of Oz*?"

"Hunh?"

"If that's all it's for, religious therapy, why do they have to get all that other stuff going?" He pushed back in the driver's seat and eased off the accelerator. "Okay, my father's a neurologist, really good at what he does; and I've learned about the morally and socially worthwhile reasons for having a religion and moral code, how it helps with health an' all. But white man's way is all perfectly *rational*, the way a doctor tries to do it. This Indian guy's doing all kinds of things, not just surgery or psychiatry, but every part of their *whole lives!* They actually seem to *believe* in it, too. How *can* anybody in his right mind . . ."

"Do you believe what happened to you?" Silence. "What *do* you believe about what happened to you?"

"Man, *I* don't know! I can't just say 'sparks.' It doesn't go anywhere near explaining the rest." He paused. Logan looked out the window at the plum blush on the horizon. Jay rattled on. "You're calm about this! It unnerves me, dammit! They act like they *know* you! They don't even mind when you drag *me* into it. What am *I* there for? *You're* that way anyway, but I don't belong to that kind of Halloween stuff. It's got no place in my background. I just want to treat everybody fair and the same, not get drawn into what they do on their own time. Faith healing! Sorcery! Witch doctors! What FOR?" he shrilled.

"Wait a minute—you're lumping a lot of things together."

"But that's the whole point! You act like you believe in all that stuff. I can tell you do!"

"Not necessarily. Believe in what?"

"What? Oh, come on! When they said all that about getting scorched if you *don't* believe?"

"If there are spirits out there, or if they're inside people, or if they're part of everybody joining together in something called 'holy' for a lot of eons—what do these spirits care whether somebody says he believes in them?'' Jay gave Logan a blank stare.

Logan watched the road silently. ''They *do* whatever it is they do in there; and sometimes, and for some people, it *works*. Maybe even a lot of times. Medicine people *can* get to things other people haven't been able to reach. People learn to survive through strange things sometimes, even accidents, or losses, or pain. In those ceremonies it's the *feeling* the people show each other that seems crucial, the way they build up a sense of healing in each other.

''I'm mostly concerned about the practical effects of the medicine, like my great-grandmother was, and so are they. They don't hand out demerits for disbelief. If you show a sense of respect, gratitude, affection—treat people like family in there, without fighting and rationalizing yourself out of existence—you don't have to agonize over your own belief problems. Anybody can just believe, that's passive. But to act, and put all you have behind it, with the risk of losing, or being all wrong or looking stupid, and still to keep going, that's faith. Faith *is* action.''

''Hey, but wait a minute,'' Jay came back combatively. ''They say, those medicine men say, you *got* to believe in it or the whole thing goes wrong.'' He tugged at his seatbelt. ''If they didn't feel that whole thing was spooky, and if they didn't feel like they'd get zapped for *not* believing, they wouldn't huddle up on those benches all night.''

''I don't recall anybody made you go in.''

''Yeah, well, I don't understand that part either. Everything ended up at *this*, and now I don't even know what *this* has been. My head just doesn't want to accept Dalton seeing all that stuff, like they said he did afterward. And all that commotion about Granny Lone Wolf. But then,'' he added with chilly emphasis, ''my guts are telling me, '*Hey!* somebody ran sticky green light all over you!' Now *you're* telling me I don't have to believe that!''

''No, I just said it's still your choice to interpret what your guts say.'' Logan sucked in a deep breath and held his ground. ''You're not bound, anymore than those people, to a supernatural explanation, at least in your sense. How do you know what they mean by 'spirits'? You're digging a hole so fast, you're covering yourself up with reasons. *Some*thing went on in there. Okay. You can just say, 'The spirits came and talked to the shaman,' and let it go at that. You got probably a lifetime to figure out what that means, if it needs figuring out.''

Jay wouldn't let it alone. ''That's really dishonest, though. We took in all those cloth flags and stuff, made those little red baggy things, passed out granola, even offered the feather. Then you're not even willing to commit yourself that faith healing was going on?''

"Whose faith would have done the healing?''

"*How* the *hell* do I know?''

Logan was getting tired of making faith reasonable. He decided to try one last-ditch effort at smoothing the waters. "You've been awfully quiet up to now about everything, Jay, taking it in passively. Now all at once you're boiling, because Dalton got on one frayed nerve. You can't *explain* ritual from the outside. Think about it, people on this reservation are in pretty bad shape. Their religion and medicine would dry up if it served no purpose to them. The Rosebud people live with a lot of despair, and they come up with different ways to take care of themselves. What they do is what the people have always done—come together in ceremony—and they continue it today.

"Sometimes, as Luther says, a whole ceremonial complex like *yu-wipi* disappears for maybe half a century. Maybe nobody even hears about it anymore, and it's forgotten. But if it's a vision or ritual embedded in the culture, really old and strong and useful in some way, somebody can go out and bring it back up from the roots. Whether the 'remembering' is due to some childhood memory, or if it's tribal memory of some sort, or if it's visions from *Tunkáshila* spirits, the people still *use* those memories.

"That's the point—the need for bringing them out. Indians don't throw their ceremonies or beliefs away. If the root is still left, the power can grow back. The old tribal medicine is still functional, stronger for them than any BIA agency or public health service or ordinary clergy. The medicine is what happens when people act on the love they have for one another.'' Jay was listening now, so Logan brought the point home. "Take Elgin's gangrene. He got through a medical crisis suddenly. What Dalton's doing now—and the tribal elders who remember the old days can accept it as an authentic continuation—is not evangelical. It's not denying anything either, the way some religions have to have it all their way.''

"Yeah, who knows what he believes, with those rosaries and things hanging around?'' Jay added. "These guys even claim to be Catholics!''

"It's still worthwhile for the spirits to play a little,'' Logan bore down. "Loosen up the fears and the blocks you have, even the hates of the white man and other Indians. Remember that kid in AIM that wouldn't speak to us until after the sweat lodge? Dalton works on a faith the people keep stored away someplace, a faith that there's still some good in living and trying to change things for the better, even if *that's* based on an irrational belief.

"A medicine man talks about a certain kind of order, a traditional, disciplined living most Indians have forgotten or had taken away from them. If you're in pain, and you don't believe in anything after this life, and this life keeps you down, suicide doesn't seem unreasonable. You know damned well that a lot of Indians *do* commit suicide, get in needless accidents, drink themselves to death. They're facing cultural euthanasia." Jay seemed to be just a little calmer. For the moment he declined to argue.

"Dalton uses a technique, just like your alcoholism counseling friends use techniques," Logan went on, "like Benjamin Crow or Mark. It doesn't exclude any other belief system."

Jay was almost driving at the posted speed limit now. The sun was paling the sky, and the morning star blinked magenta. They rode quietly. Jay started humming one of the *lowanpi* melodies in a low register.

"I didn't beat you over the head to believe anything supernatural, did I?" Logan asked.

"Nope." He started humming again.

"All I ever intended to do, the last four months, was show you what I could, what you wanted to see, help you when you were interviewing and looking for things, stay out of the way the rest of the time. My responsibility ended there. You glowed in the dark all by yourself. Now you've got to live with that," Logan added.

"I'm looking for people who remember what the old medicine was, where it came from, what it's for. An anthro at *Sinte Gleska* has his techniques, Benjamin Crow is sandwiched in the middle, and Dalton No Dog has his dancing rattlesnakes on the other side. Theoretically, they're at odds in some ways, but realistically they're all there to help the people. They're carrying on without much help from politicians or anybody else.

"Indian people say about their medicine what they say about their cultures and councils and everything else: 'We're here, too, and we have something to offer, something to be heard.' They're not out there proselytizing."

"But they're getting close," Jay protested, "with that college of medicine men, and what Luther did to you, and No Dog's fireworks."

Logan countered, "Still, they're not setting up some kind of hierarchy or special club. The medicine man is everybody's resource. He says, 'This faith, for all we know and remember, is open to everybody in the land, and we've got it. It's Indian. We've had to fight even for a chance to express it, fight to preserve our culture. There is no one else likely to help us survive as a people. We do this so the people may live. All we're asking is that you let us do these things and live our way in peace. Join with us if you can, but just don't kill it anymore. Let us go where we can.' "

CHAPTER 30

"That the People May Live"

Moon of Humpback Men (Hopi)

The sun was high over the cottonwoods in Winner City Park when Logan woke. Jay was sitting up and appeared to be talking to himself. He looked abstracted for a few seconds and then started rolling up his sleeping bag.

"I dreamed it was daylight and there was the car, parked where it is now, and you were inside. Then it got dark all of a sudden. By the time I made out the clouds over the trees, this voice was coming down from overhead, calling you, not in any way that I could hear, but it was calling. Then you got out of the car and started talking to it for a long time, and it was telling you all kinds of stuff, but I couldn't understand the words." He pulled the strings tight on the bag. "I was worried what it would do to you." Jay was solemn, staring with concern and a touch of fear.

"You're still on that?" Logan muttered. "It was just my answering service."

"It was the Great Spirit!" Jay yelled at Logan's back.

"You mean Yahweh?"

"Don't get snotty."

Logan trudged on to the car, casually dodging a hail of small stones.

They went looking for breakfast and settled for lunch at a cafe just off the main drag, then for insurance had doughnuts and chocolate milk at a bakery down the street. Luther was in his mobile home office, which was crowded with files and manuscripts. The secretary led them in. Luther was very calm this time, reflective. He showed some of his writings in progress and talked about historical research. He listened as they spoke about what they had seen, smiling and nodding often. Jay talked about the helpers' shaking of the sweat lodge and notions he had about the reason the light came from the priest's rattles. Luther was still nodding, except now he was grinning too.

He heard all they said with a certain detachment, but clearly with sympathy. He emphasized this was only a beginning. The ceremonies they had witnessed were part of something very old, running deep in humankind, that had extended to tribes all over the hemisphere, he suspected, before the Aztecs. The nearest thing non-Indians would find to that tradition, long gone underground, were spiritual disciplines from mystery religions. The power all came from the same place. He told them to use what they were going to learn to help people, for this knowledge was for all lives, all times.

Logan hoped to come back to learn more from Luther after a visit to his own Carolina people. Luther nodded encouragement, but that was all. They thanked him for all he had done, wished him Godspeed in his work, and prayed that the medicine lodges would live again. He shook Logan's hand, as he had that first day, with an odd smile, and told them to hurry on back. Still there was unmistaken finality in the parting.

As they were getting into the car, Logan looked up into his face in the window. Luther nodded—not a casual farewell, something else. It had nothing of the easy cheerfulness Logan had seen the first time they parted, or the joyous yet agonized expression when the old man had sent them to the ceremonies. It was a fixed look of resignation. "You *may* be back," the nod said. "Maybe you have to come back, maybe you will see me again . . . "

Logan asked himself why Luther did that—why he had to show that look. Logan wanted just then to think there was more dialogue.

Logan drove away feeling drained. It was strange not to be elated after seeing so much, just from remembering the sheer beauty of the ceremonies. He could still hear the drums, still hear the hymns to the winds, and see the meteor falling and the turtle's back. But what he felt now was a responsibility imposed with the gift of participation. The ceremony was for Logan because it was for Jay and Mark Monroe's family and for Jenny Lone Wolf. Again and again he had been told, "This is not a toy. This is done that the people may live. The human level is where you will know the answers you *can* know." There was no escape from the tie: a healer is not there to lay out easy answers, to dole out ecstasy, to give the masses anodyne for pain. He is there to help the people learn, because pain touches their lives, and they need something to hold onto, like being able to see a star fall just right.

They headed directly for the Black Hills and Bear Butte. The old mountain rose to the northeast beyond the rest of the range, framed in its own plain some thirty miles out of Rapid City. The drive was uncomfortable. None of it really registered for Logan, though he stayed awake even when he wasn't driving. He could tell Jay was going through some mental struggle, or avoiding one and still hearing the questions. At this point, Logan wasn't able to concentrate well enough to read the road map. They ended up lost somewhere between Spear-fish and Rapid City near nightfall, on one dirt road after another, one of them dead-ending at a cave made up to be a tourist attraction. They found the way back to the highway, and in about an hour were shaking off road dust and standing on a little knoll facing the Butte.

The white lessees of the land, who'd been fishing in the creek below, gave the visitors permission to stay as long as they didn't start fires, so the two parked on the knoll and laid out their sleeping bags to face the mountain. Afternoon breezes stirred over them. They could hear cattle lowing far off and a few crickets chirping hesitantly. But here there was no noise at all. Bear Butte seemed to move toward them as the young men lay there waiting for the night, and Logan could see trees rising in the shadow of the blue-black mountain.

All by itself, the world's largest laccolith in an enormous volcanic bubble, Bear Butte was the last magnificent landmark between the Badlands and the Black Hills. It was still largely unmarred by humans. This mountain had not changed, never been made the site of a ranger station. It was too holy to mess up, too isolated, even holier than tourist-pocked Harney Peak. It was the place the northern Plains Indians, particularly the Sioux and Cheyenne, had always insisted on preserving as their central shrine. For nearly five thousand years Indian people had lived around its base. Here an Indian Noah waited out the Flood, hence, it was said, the ancient name "Noavosse." Here the prophet Sweet Medicine received his visions and brought down the sacred arrow bundle, the convenant of Cheyenne traditions. The mountain's temple-cave was the site of ancient mystery, revelation, and power.

As Logan watched, stars broke out in the darkness like tiny facets of diamond light, and he was restored to the mood of the preceding night, when he stood in the faint kerosene glow of the meeting house, breathing new air born out of lightning and water, sacred breath. The times fused—it was the same night, then and now. There, on the pointed knoll, he could stare up and see nothing but space, as if the earth had stretched into a lava cone and was pointing him outward through star-lighted darkness. He automatically steadied himself with his hands and grew self-conscious, reminded of the exhaustion and sky rapture that conspired to make him feel he was moving. It was so still he should have heard Jay breathing, but the sounds all came from inside. Logan kept closing his eyes; just the seeing of night made him dizzy. The Cheyenne always said this summit was where the sky arose.

Little Wolf, the Cheyenne keeper of the sacred medicine arrows brought down from Bear Butte, had camped his people near here on the Cheyenne Autumn trek from Oklahoma back to Montana. He fasted and sang,

> Great Powers, hear me,
> The people are broken and scattered.
> Let the winds bring the few seeds together
> To grow strong again, in a good new place.

What about the length of time Luther had said Logan was supposed to stay on Twin Buttes with its night fires and thunderbolts? Here he was, watching himself as he'd watched groundhogs staring jaundiced-eyed at their shadows in the snow. Doubts and a willingness to entertain them could be his strength; yet the questions he faced now made no more sense than his feelings tapering into the night. He seemed as confused as Jay was in his way. So he left the first peak just reached in his mind, wondering whether he had thrown something beautiful away by not living up to a capacity to be overwhelmed. Had he missed something in failing to envision an Indian renaissance others claimed they could see?

Then the humor of the situation dawned on him. Despite the conflicts and fears, real and imagined dangers, with all this wonder and strangeness, the mountain itself—the power, the whispers of spirits—Logan had finally realized a sacred in the commonplace. He had seen and heard remarkable things each time he came in contact with the common world of spirits and mysteries, in ordinary daylight or dark; and after all that, after finally coming to *this* mountain and being touched by a sacred place, the voices of his own consciousness were saying:

"You were always here, and it does not greatly signify that your body is here now.

"This mountain is not so old—only its spirit is eternal.

"It is a deep well—you can take all now or as little as you like. You are part of its spirit. Like a pine seed detaching, you will drift off this mountain, not yet done, still alive.

"Do not spend your life, all you have to do, on one view; there are other mountains, other stars, other seeds.

"Here the world begins. It is enough."

Logan thought of the groundhog in February. Hoping for the best, anticipating the worst, the groundhog has to go on living. It sees and accepts portentous shadows in the morning light and promises of eternal renewal in cloudy skies. Even in broken light, there is the memory of new stars.

The priests gather here on Bear Butte to celebrate the creation of the world many times over, but the creation they celebrate is the one that begins all cycles. It was simple. Doing what one must do creates the world, again and again, simply in one's own breathing and moving. Perhaps this is ceremony enough. To do less is to embrace a kind of death.

The world is covered with centers: holy places, human bonds, ways of life. It is enough to say, with the spirits, "It is good to be here while *this* is the center of the world. From here everything begins."

IV

Fall Return

I'd heard that this river was the last of an ancient ocean, miles deep, that once had covered the Dakotas and solved all our problems. It was easy to still imagine us beneath them vast unreasonable waves, but the truth is we live on dry land. I got inside. The morning was clear. A good road led on. So there was nothing to do but cross the water, and bring her home.

LOUISE ERDRICH, *Love Medicine*, 1984

War Dancer—*Oscar Howe*

OLD WAYS

They buried Uncle Ted today, tenacious
And tender, whose Bull Durham breath
Scratched my neck with Wild West stories
As he clipped away sunblond cowlicks

And left memories of lone cottonwoods
On the North Platte River, palomino
Herds, cowboys and Indians. Who would
Have known his stories would outlive snow

Banked family gatherings, old pistols,
Backyard gardens, cats on the sill,
And baking bread in a kitchen of carrot-headed
Cousins chattering time to a standstill?

He survived his losses stubbornly. He
Defied pity dank in an earthen cellar
Of preserves. He knew the voices underground
Continue whispering late when the stars

Abandon light, and we've gone back home,
And no one is touched or amazed by his wild
Concoctions. Keep talking, Uncle Ted,
Crack loose our past, make up the real

Without us when we forget to listen.
When the wind stirs these sycamores
Far away in California, I hear
From nowhere, "Now there was this herd of buffaloes . . . "

CHAPTER 31

Homecoming

Moon of Ripe Serviceberries (Mandan)

Jay and Logan crossed the Nebraska state line late at night, skirting sandhill thunderstorms somewhere east of Alliance. The day before, Rachel and I had driven the sidling blacktop that looped in and over slope-shouldered mounds of sand and sage, while Meghan and Kate trailed along in the dusty blue Volkswagen. The hills seemed to heave and roll under a night blanched with sheets of porcelain lightning. We were all together in Alliance, and I wondered if the others felt my gathering sense of completion. We had traveled many roads together, and these passages seemed to be drawing to certain end.

By morning the storm had gusted east. Logan, Jay, and I jogged over four miles of washboard country road on a clear day. The grass was thick, the cottonwoods heavy-leaved and noisy in the wind, flowers up, birds out. We ran straight into a cool east wind and back down through the middle of Alliance. It felt as though I'd never left this town.

We showered at my parents' home, gathered up Kate, Meghan, and Rachel, and headed for Mark's house, annexed to the back of the Indian Center—past Tekawitha Hall, the day-care and Headstart center, past Jenny and Felix Lone Wolf's frame house, to a little gravel driveway that led into a municipal park. Mark had cleared the garbage off the vacant lots so they could be used as a playground and fairground. The white barracks stood off the end of a dirt road that tunneled under the railroad bridge.

Mark's pale rectangular building looked like it wanted to get its ends together. Inside, it was washed in a hazy turquoise, the lights off in the daytime. Brightly patterned weavings called "God's eyes" decorated the length of a wall, and exposed rafters ribbed the plaster-board ceiling. A rusty-black oil stove seemed rooted next to a metal desk and filing cabinet.

Mark came in from the back of the house, shook hands all around, sat down at his desk, and talked while we all ate the institutional serving for "anyone who declares a hunger"—creamed corn, meat loaf, potatoes, bread and butter in a baggie, chocolate milk, peaches, and coffee. Mark seemed proud to have us visit the Indian Center, and I realized that we had congealed as a small tribe—not all loose ends were knitted together, but we were a band sharing a dedication to native ways of America. We brought all this back to Mark, where my roads started. This was not a conclusion, then, but a continuation, an ongoing learning. We'd traveled a long way from Los Angeles.

I gave my adopted family a small green and brown Lakota bowl and an illustrated history of the Rosebud Sioux. In turn they presented me a handbeaded Lakota belt with mountain and butterfly designs, bold red and blue on a white background. Small bands of diners swarmed in and out as we socialized. Later I brought along my pipe. Mark lit and smoked it, admired the carving and beadwork, and passed it to his left.

Mark watched intently as we handed it around. He looked sur-prised, grinned a little, and with some hesitancy said, "You know, it's really something that you guys would smoke that pipe with me, smo-kin' *after* an Indian done like that, without wipin' off the stem first." Jay and Logan stared at each other, appalled, and then laughed.

Mark led us out of an embarrassing silence: "It's not that strange. Well, it *is* strange in Alliance, and it's against the whole meaning of the pipe ceremony for people to do that. I remember hearing about some government agent going to a ceremony one time with chiefs and old-time medicine men. When the pipe came to him, he took out a great white hanky and wiped off the end before he smoked. Then he passed on the pipe. The old Indian guy next in line just looked him deadpan in the face, didn't say anything, took out his knife, and chopped the bit off."

Mark liked to have a sounding board occasionally, and we, upon our arrival, fit the occasion. He was caught in the mood of transi-tions—partly because summer was setting in, partly because his fam-ily was growing up, but also because he was having to work hard keeping track of local and national Indian affairs. Altogether, his mood was restless but optimistic, not unlike that of many reservation-based

Indian leaders, though clearly the case of off-reservation Indians, in his opinion, was different from that of reservation people.

Kate got into the problem of an Indian identity off the reservation. "Do you see any danger of going over to the white man, Mark, settling for a middle-class way of life and losing Indian culture?"

"I'm doin' that right now. I'm living' a white man's way of life," Mark insisted with no apology. "I've known white men all my life, and I've known Indians, some good 'n bad of both; but if you're Indian, you're Indian. It's not just a matter of personal choice or blood. I don't know how Denver is, or LA, but I know Alliance. Whether the American Indian is here, or in an urban setting, or what—he always manages to live in a close community, among Indian people. Together, we keep the Indian language as much as we can, we try to keep up the dances and the sings, we live a life of our own kind. So no matter what, it's ours, and something keeps on filtering down. It ain't really about to die."

Mark then began talking to Meghan about visions. He didn't know quite what to make of such things, but he knew what questions buffaloed him: Why was the red man the way he was, so different, with visions and all? Why couldn't Indians compete? Why couldn't they save money? Why didn't they catch on fast, like everybody else? Why had they stayed in the Stone Age, like they say, when everybody else in the world was getting so advanced? Why did they get bitten so hard by alcohol?

Mark saw that people all of a sudden were really interested in Indians and wanted to know how they lived—just at a time when he and his family were trying to adapt as fast as possible and learn to survive in the white man's world. There was confusing traffic on these two-way cultural streets. He'd never gone on and gotten his education until a few years ago through high-school correspondence courses. He sure wished somebody would tell him, for example, where he came from, really, and why he was the way he was.

Mark fell silent as the kitchen staff began to clean up the place for the dinner crowd. Emma's sister Ruby was sweeping one end of the room, and Logan sat next to the furnace to mull over what Mark had been saying. Ruby struck up a conversation about the things they had been doing, getting back onto the topic of pipes and smoking mixtures. She pointed out the window, toward the greenery near a flood ditch, and suggested that Logan check the area for red willow bark. He went outside to the creek.

The weather was very dry, even for a Nebraska summer. The

streambed was cracked into sections like charred cornbread; it smelled of decaying fish and frogs. Far up the creekbed were a few crimson switches waving on the bank. Logan gathered some and peeled them on his way back to the house.

Meanwhile, Jay was thumping a drum Wallace Black Elk had made for Mark. It consisted of a lard can painted black with a head of fine buffalo hide. Ruby encouraged Jay to take the drum out under the trees, and then stopped her sweeping to examine Logan's willow bark. Meghan and Kate were in the kitchen learning how to make frybread.

Ruby was in her early forties; she had several adolescent children and was just finding herself at the point where she could spend more time at ceremonies. She told about a family pipe her grandfather had given her; she frequented *yuwipi* and *lowanpi* ceremonies and had learned all the old songs from her mother, Jenny Lone Wolf. "You go to *yuwipi* meetings for help, for all kinds of things, sometimes for real simple things. There are spirits there, and people all around, and the spirits talk to us. You wear an herb in your ear so you can hear better."

Ruby was fascinated with the uses of dreams. She and her friend Mabel, the cook, wanted to find out what Logan had seen fasting at Center Lake. Mabel had the look of one eagerly solving a mystery, leaning into words as if she wanted to snare each one. Logan saw they weren't just going to have a conversation. The dream would become their own by the odd osmosis that sometimes happens among close friends and families. Instead of just meeting Ruby and Mabel, Logan might have been talking to his aunts.

"When I was settled on my hill toward nightfall," he began haltingly, "a bird east in the trees started up singing. The bird flew over to the pines near me and sat still, and it began singing again. The song varied slightly. The bird repeated each melody once and then flew away." He glanced at Ruby, who was making little circular cleaning motions with her broom.

"Squirrels sneaked through the leaves all around me, and something very heavy padded by a few yards away. A dragonfly buzzed a few times, and then slid down the wind toward the southwest.

"Sometime that night, I dreamed about being at UCLA. Someone told me there was mail for me. I went to an empty office, glanced at slots along the wall, and found a manila envelope with my name on it. I drew out an official-looking document with spaces for my vital statistics. Only my birthdate was filled in, no name, nothing else.

"When I woke up the sun was out, but the air smelled rainy. The frogs were quiet in the lake, and the wind came easterly. In three hours I was soaked. Little animals began to scamper all around, trying to find someplace to hide from the rain. I didn't feel rushed anymore. I went to sleep." Logan seemed to sink into the memory; the women were committed to hear him out.

"In the dark more dreams came—about fear, beatings, killings, earthquakes, scandals, the Vietnam antiwar riots. I realized I was standing in the Venice area of West Los Angeles, watching people who were going home or to work for the night. It was between Thanksgiving and Christmas. The faces I saw were tired, worried, scared. I could hear some frantic discussion coming from a radio or TV about all these people and the way they were living. Somewhere someone was wailing.

"I had this idea of trying to get people together to do something about all this trouble. I ran along the street all that night long, grabbing people and begging them to meet at a friend's house, somebody everybody knew who lived around the water. If we really were losing something, we had to find a way out. I tried to talk to everybody on the way, and each time was like the first. This was my whole life somehow. This might be my best chance, or even my only chance.

"The last person I met before daylight was someone I thought I knew. I was almost at the end of my allotted time to get the word out; and though I felt like an idiot for trying to arrange this gathering, at least this one friend would go to the meeting. The two of us would be a start. I told her what I had in mind, and she looked bewildered and finally stopped me in mid-sentence. Very slowly and patiently she said, 'I'm sorry, but I don't know who this person is you're talking about, or where he lives, and I can't understand what this is all for. I get the feeling you think you know me; but I'm *sure* I don't know who you are. Who are you?'

"It seemed impossible that she couldn't remember me. It suddenly occurred to me that *I* couldn't remember my name either! I threw my hands in the air." Ruby shook her head, still looking down at the broom. Mabel frowned. Resignation settled over the storytelling.

"That was the last of the dream, because everything stopped suddenly. The sun was up now over a hill, rising in white mist. Directly between my line of vision and the new sun stretched this long translucent triangle. It was edged with shiny ridges, and they fluffed in the wind. It occurred to me finally that I was looking at my own arm, but it was a crystal-clear wing in front of my face."

Ruby and Mabel nodded gravely throughout this telling. Mabel went back inside to start dinner preparations. Instead of offering any direct observations, Ruby looked off and began to talk about her dead son. She had her turn now. It seemed a little odd that she would change the subject so easily, but she had a purpose.

"He was only eleven years old when he died. When he was real little, he always knew things, saw things in a funny way—not *funny* funny, just funny. Everybody noticed it and some people worried about it, but I just figured it would go away. I let him alone, didn't make him feel bad if he did like that—oh, talkin' like he heard things he couldn't of. But then Old Man Chips found out about it. He said, 'Let that boy learn about the old ways.' I had been away from ceremonies for a long time myself. See, Mom taught me a lot when I was young that I mostly forgot by then. I said it would be okay, but I didn't want him mixed up in any of that till he got older."

Ruby shifted a grip on her broom handle and leaned back to rest against the stove. "It's hard to do what you really believe in, like that, with everybody on your back 'cause it's weird; and I didn't want him, just a little boy, to get embarrassed.

"Well, when he was about ten, this heart condition turned up. He got real sick, and the doctors said put in a pacemaker. At his age it would be okay and everything, they said, and he'd have a hard time without gettin' it." She nodded to herself. "But he said to me, 'Mom, I ain't afraid of gettin' cut, but if you send me down there, I'm telling ya, I won't be comin' back.'

"I thought it was only a little scared boy talkin', and I had made up my mind, so I didn't pay him any attention." She was still looking down. Her tone was strangely dry, even matter-of-fact, but her knuckles were pale. "The next thing I knew his body was coming back from Omaha in a pine box.

"I don't care who says otherwise, no matter who it might be, a person feels inside something like that, and you're foolish to ignore it. It's something that tells you when doing a thing is right or not. I don't know what to call it. But it knew in him, and he went down there and died like he said." She leaned the broom handle forward until it touched Logan's shoulder. "I could've at least tried to see what else could be done. Who knows?

"So, I tell you this, and you carry it with you, if it's all you ever get. Don't you ever turn off and ignore what's inside you, your feelings about things like it's your body telling you. If you go on with a vision, say a dream of things that could do your people some good, don't hide out with people that just want to sit on the world till they die.

Ask from the powers. That's where all the help is that you're gettin'. You find out everything you can! You got to ask which one is the bigger fool, you listening to how people criticize and make fun or your other choice, to go on with what you feel inside is right. Man, I learned it the hard way. That there was my comin' up, my baby, losin' him." She brushed the dirt up and walked off to find the dustpan.

Logan was stunned. She had spoken so deliberately and evenly. As she walked away, there was an almost terrible control, a dignity that appears in people who remember their worst calamity and rebuild their lives in its wreckage.

CHAPTER 32

"We Got to Live Together"

Moon When the Grass Is Becoming Green (Southern Cheyenne)

Knowing we had to leave soon for LA, we all went to see Mark in the evening. Mark heard about Jay's plan to hitchhike to Salt Lake City and insisted he take the bus; he even offered his own money for the trip. Logan was amazed that Mark would dig into his own pocket for a kid passing through. Jay's father could probably *buy* the bus to Salt Lake.

Mark had seen too much trouble come out of thumbing rides, and the road was a hard place to be these days, just not safe. They got into a conversation about taking risks, nonviolence, and the fear of death. Mark talked about how Indians lived constantly filled with fear, prone to violence out of their own overreactive defenses. Generations of danger and contact with pain, he thought, kept the people on edge all the time; these days were the worst. He noticed that educated people weren't so inclined to violence, and he admired their attitude, in a way.

"The Indian's learning! I mean he's learned a *lot*!" Mark tamped an unlit cigarette on the table. "I come a long ways since I first got into Alliance, from fightin' in school, then in the alleys, then on with city managers and city council, all that kind of stuff. We got to live together, so we might as well make the best of it, use each other." Two railroad cars thudded together in the nearby switchyard. "Don't have to live in a tepee to be an Indian." He grinned at Meghan perched on a kitchen stool.

"I think the Indian people are wising up. The *true* Indian leaders are working sixteen hours a day, gettin' done what we need. We don't

need leaders locked up in the penitentiary; need 'em in there *working*."
He lit his smoke and snapped the lighter shut.

"Well, it does seem like there's this old war," Logan put in, "of
the Indians against the whites, the old notion that Indian means
renegade." I thought of the Turtle Mountain elementary class discussion with Moses Cedar.

"Damn right! When AIM first come out, the philosophy was Indian
unity—help the fellow Indian, and also help the fellow non-Indian,
no matter what color their skin is." He took a long draw on his
cigarette. "But God-dang, when AIM come here to Alliance, I think
they left off some leaders that didn't believe in *any* unity. They fought
right here in the Center and turned my American flag upside down.
If they attack *Indian* people, I thought, the hell with AIM." Kate
snorted her agreement.

Emma poured everybody some coffee from a two-gallon metal
percolator as Mark continued. "Since 1969, Indian people started
standin' up to do things for themselves. Indians here started stayin'
out of jail." He tapped the ash off his cigarette, then spoke more
reflectively and slowly. "Damn, a lot of people were out there starving
to death and still are. A woman with no money couldn't see a doctor
in the clinic. We had one Indian lady who went to the hospital to have
her baby, then they threw her out and kept the baby, and didn't want
to give it back when she couldn't pay her bill."

"Is your idea just to hold on—to what you've built—as things get
stronger?" Jay asked.

"If I didn't have the American Indian Community Center right
now, I wouldn't have no way of makin' a living. No house, no dinners
for all the people, no nothin'. We *all* depend on this. Matter of my
own survival. An' hell, it's my work! Like an elder who keeps the
house open all the time for everybody." He motioned with his coffee
cup toward the rest of the Center. "It's really important—without this
here you'd have busloads of dead Indians, caravans of the sick that
didn't make it to the hospital in South Dakota, long-term dyin'. There'd
be no other way to get to Pine Ridge.

"An' hell, the only way to fight that Indi'n jealousy is to ignore it.
The best thing when they accuse us of misusing our funds is to stick
the record in front of 'em. Show them the facts, like I've done to white
men."

Kate banged the oil stove with a coffee spoon. "You betcha."

"The Indians up on Pine Ridge have access to government services
and funds. Bein' off reservation is one hundred percent different. No

BIA funds, no nothin'. Probably what we got to hang onto, once we get past the problem of just surviving, is our art, language, dancing, games, and white men want us to forget that. Not many Indian people are singing our songs."

"I think it's the close family ties, on or off reservation, that Indian people really have to stand by. I could go all the way over to a white man's way of living, but it's like to an Indian losing everything he's got." He stared directly at Emma and punctuated his words with a sense of urgency that shadowed his previous optimism. "The American Indian, damn near, is right at the edge. After our generation's over with, if we don't watch it, the American Indian won't have a language, he won't have nothin' Indian. My kids, they're not talking, they don't know how to sing Indian. So, Christ, I don't know what the hell's gonna happen when I die. These kids are like white people, that's all there is to it. It keeps me awake nights, wonderin' where we go from here."

CHAPTER 33

Mitákuye Oyásin

Thumb Moon (Modoc)

As we banded together at intervals, so we departed in pairs. Our migrant tribe had seeded, taken root, sprung up, leafed out, and was now scattering to the four winds again. And in the way families join part by part and branch into the world, we were extended kin from the bole of this trip. And so Dalton No Dog had offered in the *lowanpi*, or Henry Black Bear in his ceremony, "addin' on an' addin' on, generation to generation." The journey home then was not farewell, but a continued passage into Native America. In this sense we carried home with us, moving in continuity with the land and its peoples. And we would return to Luther Clearwater, to Lame Deer, to my brother Mark.

Chipper and seasoned, Kate and Meghan left for LA at sunrise. The journey back still promised adventure, and the two women, as usual, were ready for most anything.

"How 'bout an Indian taco feed when we all get home," Meghan invited, thumping her stomach. She had worked off pounds that were the proceeds of North Dakota ice cream parlors and local bakeries.

"We've got to get home first!" Kate chortled. "Think we'll run into any June blizzards, Doc?"

"With any luck you'll be home by fall." I hugged her.

"How do you think the medicine man got those sparks to fly around?" she asked me deadpan.

"No books written to answer that one yet," I said.

"Get busy," Kate said curtly, and for a split second she looked at me the way Mrs. Good Heart had when she spoke of her family.

"Well, Pardner," Kate drawled and kicked a tire, "see ya at the county fair. Keep your nose clean, Jay, y'hear? And Logan—don't forget any good dirty jokes!" He mimed the deaf-mute asking a bus driver directions to the laundry. "Come out to my place, folks, and we'll have a real shitkicker!"

Meghan's eyes teared as she embraced each of us and talked of regathering in the city. Her beaded earrings, bright reminders of the Black Hills, swirled through terraces of hair dark over her shoulders. She was another promise at the end of my journey, as John Fire said about our passage through the world, a "find-out." There were new roads, new quests. Meghan's Volkswagon receded across a field of ripening wheat and slipped into heat fissures blurring the prairie into the azure horizon.

Jay was leaving for a Salt Lake City conference on Indian alcoholism and drug abuse; after that he would be taking a Seattle job as an Indian youth counselor. Dropping a rod on the last jump into Alliance, his van had to be junked. He'd ride a hundred miles on a coach of the Star Bus Lines, a swayback fifties limousine saddled by a local ranchhand-turned-cabbie, then catch a Greyhound in a Wyoming border town once a pony express way station.

The Alliance bus stop was a corner Conoco gas station with three pumps and an air hose. The grease monkey eyed Jay's backpack, curly beard, and traveler's check from California, then scratched his jowls. "Legal tender, huh? Well whaddaya know. Okay, you can ride, if there's room. Throw yer pack on top with the freight."

Jay handed a fist of tickets to a squinting, bowlegged driver, bear-hugged Logan and me, and climbed in the backseat next to a middle-aged Lakota woman. Indians across the country call these archaic bus lines The Overland Stage.

The bus made the main street green light, negotiated the second of the town's three stoplights, and rolled west into the open-range grassland.

What had we learned by way of the good red road? Something about the simple details and settings of the everyday sacred in "native" America, where each person could be reborn each day, with each sunrise, and the whole was renewed seasonally at each equinox. It had to do with balance. The good red road and its black intersecting road offered a path between the blinkered God-or-Mammon extremes, a "focused wandering," as the Cree said of a good journey. Instead of "going abroad" for self-enrichment, the students—now family and friends in the most meaningful native ways—had gone into the hemispheric center of North America, literally to the continent's heart. They had seen something of the complexity and diversity of America's peoples. Their own inner fieldwork within the American landscape, among its people and animals, would effect deep and longlasting changes, indeed, would begin a process that placed them consciously—with the attendant privileges and responsibilities—*in* native America.

Jay still struggled toward a lifelong quest of awareness: his continual inner debate and discovery was the evolution of a working conscience, and it would lead him professionally to counsel Indian teenagers. Alternately brash and sensitive, Kate would become expert in crosscultural issues of medicine; her own guards, mirrors of internal personal dialogues, came down as she opened to the needs of dispossessed peoples. And Meghan headed for a teaching position on the Navajo reservation, from there to train as a clinical psychologist and counsel the terminally ill. Her journey from a fear of snakes to supportive healer was a case of patient-become-doctor. Logan would go on to law school, finally to teach Indian studies and law at Berkeley, and I would continue as an educator. Rachel was well along her own good red road—only the grandfathers knew to where, but it would certainly be a bright path. Our tribal parting of the Buckskin Curtain, however momentary, brought to my mind a Zuni prayer. It seemed applicable to all tribes at all times:

> Do not despise the breath of your fathers,
> But draw it into your body.
> That our roads may reach to where the
> Life-giving road of our sun father comes out,
> That, clasping one another tight,
> Holding one another fast,
> We may finish our roads together;
> That this may be, I add to your breath now,
> To this end:
> May my father bless you with life;
> May your road reach to Dawn Lake,
> May your road be fulfilled.

Jenny Lone Wolf, leaning on her hickory cane, gave Rachel a star blanket as we left, a grandmother's blessing. She passed me ten red tobacco ties, "the commandments," wrapped around a pungent bundle of sage. "They will guide you home," she said. "*Tunkáshila esa . . . Tunkáshila esa . . .*" she whispered to Logan. Jenny's graveled voice trailed from another age. She had personally cared for hundreds of relatives in her day, doctored many more, and seen many changes, many roads. Rachel and I were only two more of her countless grand-children. She was born as the Lakota were being herded onto reser-vations like cattle; she lived through Wounded Knee in 1890 and many more wars this century. She had endured great pain; she survived with dignity and power. And still this old holy woman prayed for us all. *"Tunkáshila esa . . . "* Her grandmother vision lighted our good red road across America.

"So long, guys," Mark called from the Indian Center entrance. "I won't say goodbye 'cause I'll see you again soon." It was an old agreement. *"To'ksa."*

We drove west into the wind all day, toward the rainshadow of the Rockies. Lunch at the Longhorn Cafe, a truckers' stop in Cheyenne, Wyoming. The wind picked up again, dry and stiff out of the west, where one of my uncles drove freight trains to Green River. Rangy men who spit on curbs wore tooled leather belts, slouched cowboy hats, red checked shirts with snap buttons. They walked with bowed legs and narrowed eyes, as though forever leaning into a nasty dust storm. It wasn't far from the truth. The women appeared homely and subdued, weather-beaten, with ratty hair and hard jawlines. The men stood booted, blue-jeaned, raw-boned, with stomachs hanging over their bucking-horse buckles; they stood not with the urban tidiness of gibbous-bellied businessmen, but belly forward in a determined sen-sual thrust, even an arrogance. A man here held his ground proud of his gut: "worked hard and ate big to earn that gut, an' by Gawd I gotta right to my pleasures."

In the lavatory a white metal box hung bolted over the toilet: "Embark On A New Adventure With SAMOA. Lubricated prophylac-tics 25¢. New Erotic Experiences: Sunset Red, Midnight Black, Dawn Gold, Morning Blue, Siesta Green. Buy several for an exotic experi-ence. New freedom and pleasure." The decal above the metal box warned: "If She's a Moaner, She'll Be a Screamer. If She's a Screamer, You'll Be in Jail."

We kept movin' toward the mountains.

The big-shouldering Rockies heaved skyward with forest mantle and granite escarpments. There would be snow all summer on the higher peaks. The black pine-greens were silhouetted against spark-ling backdrops. Droplets of aspen leaves shimmered among the birches like sheets of rippling green water.

We turned south from Grand Junction on the Western slopes along

Highway 50 through Ute country. A narrow two-lane blacktop climbed through redrock box canyons to Ouray, 7700 feet above sea level, tucked against humpbacked green mountains, in turn overtowered by a sheer, treeless mass of grey peaks, jagged and mottled against the clouds. A glaciered barrier of uncompromising majesty jutted between the Great Basin and Southwest desert. We had the sense of ancient gods living on these heights, as in the San Francisco Mountains, the Turtle Mountains, Bear Butte, and the Black Hills.

Spring was just settling over the high Rockies, and a new greening floss left the trees blue-green and aquamarine. Thickets of aspen quaked and plashed on the slopes like clouds of birds.

The highway scaled straight up from Ouray, past sprays of glacier-fed waterfalls hurtling two hundred feet into the gorge. Don't look down: no guardrail and the drop was forever.

The car brakes failed Logan at ten thousand feet.

"What? No *brakes*?" I gasped. "What the hell is goin' on?"

We couldn't turn around and go back down with no way to stop, so Logan let the car roll to a halt on the road shoulder. The only way was up and over the pass, driving with the gears, pumping the brakes, no certainty of slowing. Logan slid to the passenger's seat clasping a stone in his hands and stared straight ahead. I drove without looking back. Aspen-terraced slopes drifted away from the road; the meadows were flocked with blue lupin, white daisies, red pentstemon, yellow buttercup. Ahead at the pass towered a talus-scarred ocher- and sienna-capped peak, which Rachel dubbed Rainbow Mountain from the back-seat. Seasonal time reversed as we drove forward into the dying sun, backward in time, to Los Angeles. The gears held the curves, thank God, and I steered hesitantly, by instinct, avoiding the rearview mir-rors. I could taste my own fear. Rachel fell asleep, and Logan sat flustered again by the machine. We passed abandoned mine shafts, blackened and caving in, and glacial scoops in the grey mountain rubble. A white spray-painted boulder by a mining road charged, "Keep Out. This Means You."

The car crested Red Mountain Pass and eased into Silverton, ele-vation 9318. The slopes lay thicketed with lodgepole pine beneath tundra-carpeted peaks. A gas station, at last, where seven-hundred-year-old dusty Ute metates were piled on the office floor. "Arctic conditions here," the attendant informed us as he checked the over-heated brakes. "This is the only place in the continental United States with permafrost," he added, rolling his jaw. Then, as something of an afterthought, he said, "The emergency brake was partly engaged and the system got hot, so it gave out. Should be all right now; no damage done.''

Keep movin'. We traveled on into New Mexico, trying to keep our defenses loose with a return to the city. The smell of fresh rain widened my nostrils, opened the back of my throat with pine and sage, brome grass and clover, the rising odors penetrant with minerals. Mountain spirits seemed to vaporize in summer rainstorms. Then the land flattened out.

Pastel desert tints, land of mirages—receding violet, fading blue, arid green. Swirls of dusty grey, sepia, burnt sage, chalk white. Deserted only to a restless eye, the desert layered space, drew quilted edges across the land's sweep. Giant alluvial fans tumbled off mountains. Umber lava beds swept over the valleys and gave an illusion of cloud cover, while the heat smashed life flat and weightless under a tombstone sky: fragments of life so fragile they had no past or future. The muted colors held out against the opaque weight of an intense heat, but lost, fleck by fleck, in the struggle against final incineration.

Sage-grey with an afterimage of green traced the fringes of stones. Roadsigns: ''Troy Lake,'' ''Hector Road,'' ''Deadman Lake,'' ''Baghdad.'' Wind, dust, cactus, and shards of rock searched for water. Hunger and thirst knifed through the desert as it faded.

CHAPTER 34

Day of the Sun

Moon in Which the Young Eagles First Fly (Quee'esh)

> The day of the sun has been my strength.
> The path of the moon shall be my robe.
> A sacred praise I am making.
> A sacred praise I am making.
> BLACK ELK'S HEYOKA SONG

Back in LA, smudges in the city's outlines, no distinct edges, masses of jumbled detail. Rachel and I deposited Logan and his equipment at his parents' home in the Valley: medicine pipe, seeds, herbs, feathers, stones, books, paints, first aid kit, tape recorder, bedroll, backpack, and a random assortment of playing cards. He handed over the one-eyed jack found in Lame Deer's backyard as a kind of *heyoka's* coupon. Logan would continue his pack-rat apprenticeship in the city. At the end of so many thousand miles into America, it seemed a diminished dream. I scratched around for the right words, then gave up.

"Are you ready for the city of angels again?"

"Yeah, ready as I ever was," Logan answered none too certainly. His stubbly beard and tossled black hair gave him an air of wilderness growth that seemed out of place along a surburban curb.

Rachel hummed to herself, "Thank God I'm a country girl," from her perch in the backseat. "Logan!" she called, "Can we go back with the Indian people again—after you learn to drive and Daddy gets the car fixed?"

He grinned. "We'll travel together some more," he said, giving her a hug. "Just take good care of the eagle feather—and Granny Lone Wolf's star blanket."

"It was a good trip, Logan," I called out to him.

I searched for some reassurance that we hadn't reached the end of the road. "Let's keep it going."

"*How*, do you think? Here in the city?" He looked up at the grey-brown sky.

"Keep listening to the voices," I answered back. "Jus' keep in *touch*, call our ragtag tribe together."

Logan glanced at a leafing willow in his front yard. "How about digging a fire pit up on the ridge? Mebbe put up a sweat lodge in the canyon . . . "

"D'you think the fire marshals would leave us alone?"

"Dunno. It's worth a try. Just another barbecue pit in the valley," he said cheerily.

"Someplace to empty out." I warmed to the idea, suppressing my doubts. "There are deer and coyotes up there, a few scavenger raccoons."

"An' get out to the desert, the mountains, the ocean. We've got it all here." Logan's face continued to brighten. "Keep in touch with all the relatives. *Mitak' oyasin!*"

"See you at the Indian Center," I called back.

Behind our parting the grandfather spirits seemed to chant silently:

> Breathe the sacred pipe
> Touch the holy stones
> Chant the rhythmic bones
> Follow the eagle feather
> Walk the path with heart.

Rotten Moon (Wishham)

Two days later the clutch went out on the Volvo as I drove down Sunset Boulevard to UCLA. The old trooper had ferried us through America's heartland and back, literally ten thousand miles in ten weeks, then gave up its ghost. Thomas Banyacya had warned me in March: "Mebbe it all come crashes."

The Indian spirits kept reviving, though I felt the freedom of the Great Plains slipping away among the cars, the streets, the stoplights, the money passing hands, blank faces, checks, accountability to university deans. The academic offices closed their books Monday; it was the fiscal year's end. "Did you keep a record to justify expenditures?" a secretary wanted to know. What records were appropriate? The accountants wanted dates of departure and return, mileage, who went, who spent how much. I felt the openness of the country receding, the people closing off, the city's pace crowding in again—the ten thousand things that invade privacy.

I drove to work, and the UCLA parking attendant, portly and white-fluffed, collected a dollar so I could park the car. The attendant took his time and checked me out, then spoke with an abrasive Bronx accent, "That's a handsome Indian belt you're wearing." He leaned toward the car window.

"Thanks. My Lakota brother gave it to me."

"Oh yeah? You know, I once wrestled an Indian named Big Heart, in my professional days. You ever hear of the Masked Marvel? That was me!" He looked off to a grove of eucalyptus.

"Big Heart taught me the Death Hold. The Indian Death Hold— most powerful grip of them all. Won me a lot of matches, that and the Sleeper—legs around the middle, right here." He clutched his ample belly. " . . . Powerless . . . can't get out." Another driver pulled in line behind me. "Have a nice day, ya hear?"

I knew I was back home in LA.

Moon of the Spiderweb on the Ground at Dawn (Oto)

Dear Ken,

September 1975

Received your letter last June but I have been very busy for the last few months.

I am running for office and have been very busy at that.

Some of yor students attended Dalton No Dog's and he told me they have made the grade in this group.

Tell them to do a research as this ritual came from the days of Aztec and is a old ritual. This type of ritual is used for the docoting the sick, other wiase known in the modernworld as faith healers. The sioux poeple are useing the ritual a lot.

Tell Rachel, hello and keep herself like a member of the sacred White Buffalo lodge some day I will explain to her the sacredness of woman hood.

I am under Doctor care right now and excuse my mistakes will do better next time.

Enclos you will find a booklet which is of this country but it might interest you.

Will hear from later again. Enclose my campaign literature.

Your friend

Mini Waci
or
Luther

"Grant that I may not criticize my neighbor until I have walked a mile in his moccasins."

MINI-WACI

or

LUTHER CLEARWATER

As a candidate for the Tribal Council, I am but one man, but if elected I want to be the voice of my people. Whatever their hearts are, that I will speak.

I lived like a white man, and worked for them for many years and know their thoughts. You might say that I am too old for the job, but remember it was the old Chief that made the many treaties that were made.

It may be very small in your ears, therefore I entreat you to hearken with attention; our forefathers had to use the tomahawk for treaty making. But today you have the pen which is mightier than the sword.

Select your candidate with a lot of thought so that our women would not look around them and turn pale and our children cling close to the necks of their mothers.

My writings are now lodged in your hand, because you are an important person to me. I place myself in your hand, and in closing it, you could crush me.

We Indians love the land that holds the bones of our Grandfathers, Fathers, and Mothers.

I will work to preserve our land and resources which our children and their children after them are to lie down upon.

Ashes Moon (Taos)

Dear Mr. Lincoln:

We would like to thank you for the considerate letter to our father.

Dad became ill in September and after much coaxing finally entered the hospital. We knew he had not been feeling well but did not realize the seriousness of his illness. He passed away from cancer in Rapid City. We only learned that he had cancer the day of his death. We brought him home to be buried in Winner. Many friends and relatives sorrowed with us and we were grateful for their support and prayers.

Because I have undertaken the completion of Dad's second book his correspondence has been given to me to answer. Since working on Dad's book I have begun to realize the caring and wanting to record the history of our people he felt. I believe I have begun to know him at his best. The challenge now is to put the book together in such a way that it will be a tribute to his memory. I am doing my best.

While I have no knowledge of the healing plants, Dad's sister goes to a healer, so if Mr. Slagle does come to South Dakota perhaps I could introduce him to my aunt.

If you should come to South Dakota, we would like to meet you and your family. In remembrance of Dad there will be a feast and giveaway about a year from the date of his death. If you would like to be present, we would be honored to have you as guests. This is our way to say thank you to relatives and friends for supporting us in our grief. If you can attend, could you please let us know. We look forward to meeting you some day. Dad had many friends and it has been a pleasurable experience getting to know them.

Yours, in friendship,
(Mrs.) Felicia Grey Hawk

Rosebud News

Luther Clearwater funeral services Tuesday.

Funeral services for Luther J. Clearwater, Winner, were held Tuesday at 2:00 p.m. at Trinity Episcopal Church in Winner. Wakes were held at the home of his widow, Nicole, at Mission Saturday night; at the Antelope Community Hall, Mission, Sunday night; and at John King Memorial Hall, Winner, Monday night.

Surviving are ten children, over forty grandchildren, and six great-grandchildren.

Luther Clearwater's hands clasped a Lakota pipe as people filed by to pay him homage before his casket was closed the last time.

OLOWAN

Dakota calls the eagle's heart
to sing the tribe alive
in stones and bones and willow bark
to chant the tribe alive—

Calls all the snows and winter geese
to test the tribe alive
floods and winds and lightning nights
to charge the tribe alive—

Prays Sitting Bull and Crazy Horse
to call the tribe alive
chants Crow Flies High and Sweet Grass Girl
to feed the tribe alive—

Cedar bark and red sweet earth
to cense the tribe alive
racing sorrel and bloodred stone
to blush the tribe alive—

Wicasa wakan and *wasicu*
to pray the tribe alive
Tunkáshila in *Paha Sapa*
to touch the tribe alive—

Kinnickinnick and vision quest
to draw the tribe alive
calls all the leggeds, roots, and wings
to sing the tribe alive.

Afterword

Events in *The Good Red Road* occurred between March 24, 1975, and September 23, 1981. We have sometimes altered names, the order of incidents, and the places where they actually occurred. No personalities or characters in this narrative, except those of public figures, should be traced to any particular persons whose consent has not been obtained. Thus, the identities of real individuals, families, and communities have been protected. Nor should the reader look for any revelation of "secret knowledge" or technical explication of Indian rituals not already in the public domain. Parts of the manuscript have been read and reviewed from time to time by a variety of correspondents, including friends and relations who have lent kind support and criticism. Our aim here is to record the effects of real-world events with appropriate literary creativity and humanistic science, to celebrate and reverence the sacred in the commonplace. To lend continuity we have adopted a single narrative voice for both Ken Lincoln's text and mine.

In addition to using our own resources, we conducted our research with the aid of numerous grants, including graduate and undergraduate fellowships for field research from UCLA, from the American Indian Tribal Court Judges' Association, and from the National Institute on Alcoholism and Alcohol Abuse (with Drs. Joan Weibel-Orlando, principal investigator, and Kenneth Lincoln and Logan Slagle, co–principal investigators, grants 2R01AA04817-01,2,3, 1981–1984, "Native Healers in Alcoholism and Substance Abuse"), as well as faculty research grants since 1979, and a Humanities research Fellowship at UC Berkeley, 1984.

As the narrative suggests, following the 1975 fieldwork, I went to law school, passed the California Bar, and have taught Indian law, health, history, and institutions in law-related undergraduate and graduate courses at UC Berkeley since 1979. I have been a business advisor to my own tribe, the United Keetoowah Band of Cherokee Indians in Oklahoma, and a pro-bono legal representative and consultant for a variety of Indian tribes, Indians, and Indian organizations—working on problems of health, education, business, law, cultural affairs, and religion, particularly in the area of Indian religious freedom. Since 1982, I have been active in the Indian Shaker Church of Washington (1910). I am principal researcher and author of several federal status clarification projects for California Indian tribes, and I have participated in the drafting of several tribal constitutions and sets of by-laws.

I would not have done any of these things without the support, the prayers, the encouragement, and guidance of my family, elders, and community, and I have worked as I could with this in mind: my efforts represent my desire to justify and repay their support. My contribution to this book is an attempt to return thanks to them and pay homage to the faith we share.

It is important to offer this postlude, including a personal statement, because I believe the future of Indian tribes and communities will depend, in this era of federal Indian policy called "Self-Determination," on the willingness of Indian professionals and citizens to give back to their communities in kind. For the means, blessings, and emotional support needed to achieve an education, self-reliance, and professional credentials, professionals must return their efforts and skills as community resources. One who burdens a community's resources owes something in return, at least a moral obligation, a tax if not indeed a tithe.

Gone are the days of easy federal spending for anything, for education, social services, or anything except "defense" in the strict military sense. We are allegedly living in the era where "volunteerism" is to replace the federal and state commitment toward equal opportunity, toward providing minimal living standards for the handicapped, aged, and indigent, toward a healthy environment and a warless world. Surely the call for volunteerism rings hollow in tandem with the broad endorsement of unbridled Social Darwinian competition.

As chair of California Indian Legal Services and a board member of the Bay Area Urban Indian Health Centers, Inc., I find that no amount of lobbying or pleading will alter the prevailing attitude of the public, civil administrators, and politicians that the trust responsibility between the federal government and Indians is reducible, indeed, erasable; though surely two hundred years of treaties justify national measures to assure the survival of tribal governments or their constituencies, in keeping with spirit of the Indian Self-Determination Act of 1975. Yet in the past six years the Reagan administration has moved to eliminate or drastically curtail federal support to the National Congress of American Indians, National Tribal Chairmen's Association, American Indian Law Institute, off-reservation (and to a lesser extent, on-reservation) Indian education and health programs, Indian Legal Services, and most other Indian-targeted programs and organizations: this, in the name of Indian "self-determination."

The national deficit cannot be relieved significantly or conscionably at the expense of the trust relationship. House Concurrent Resolution 108, which sounded the gun for the termination of over one hundred federally recognized Indian communities in the 1950s and 1960s, remains on the books; this is notwithstanding pleas for rescission by a succession of presidents from Nixon to Reagan. The truth is that we have lived in the era of termination since the founding of the country, if by termination one means the progressive, if fluctuating and inconsistent, expropriation of tribal resources and sovereignty by the United States and its citizens. Even the Indian Reorganization Act of 1934 (IRA) was undeniably *intended eventually* to "mainstream" Indian America. The Meriam Commission in *The Problems of Indian Administration* (1928), a study on whose recommendations tribes were encouraged to be "self-determining," said that the proper aim of federal relations with Indians is to aid Indians to "merge into the social and economic life of the prevailing civilization as developed by the whites or to live in the presence of that civilization at least in accordance with a minimum standard of health and decency."

American politicians are only human. They follow the lead of their constituents, and some Americans take the gains in land and resources over the dead and rotting bodies of Indians as an acceptable moral cost of doing business. Too many Americans seem to feel that the United States does not owe Indians just compensation, "in kind" or in any other way, for what Indians ceded not only by conquest but by agreement. Only in 1986, after thirty-seven years' delay, has the United States finally signed the International Genocide Treaty because some politicians feared international accountability. Not all, but arguably many of the United States' historical acts and omissions regarding its indigenous peoples have met the treaty's various definitions of genocide.

Some Americans feel these events are all in the past, and that the treaties and agreements with tribes should be forgotten. Justice Rehnquist, dissenting to the Blackmun majority's opinion in *United States v. Sioux Nation of Indians*, 448 U.S. 371, 100 S. Ct. 2716, 65 L. Ed. 2d 844 (1980), wrote:

There were undoubtedly greed, cupidity, and other less-than-admirable tactics employed by the Government during the Black Hills episode in the settlement of the West, but the Indians did not lack their share of villainy either. It seems to me quite unfair to judge by the light of "revisionist" historians or the mores of another era actions that were taken under pressure of time more than a century ago.

The case at hand concerned the United States' legislative usurpation of the Sioux sacred lands of the Black Hills, in direct contradiction of the Fort Laramie Treaty, wherein the United States had promised the Sioux they could keep that part of their original lands forever. Why the betrayal? Expedience and gold—for after the Fort Laramie Treaty gold was discovered in the Black Hills. Rehnquist concluded:

That there was tragedy, deception, barbarity, and virtually every other vice known to man in the 300-year history of the expansion of the original 13 Colonies into a Nation, which now embraces more than three million square miles and 50 states, cannot be denied. But in a court opinion, as a historical and not a legal matter, both settler and Indian are entitled to the benefit of the biblical adjuration: "Judge not, that ye be not judged."

Does this dictum represent a "minimum standard" for health and decency? Would the new Chief Justice be as quick to tell Israeli-Americans and survivors of the Holocaust forty years later to let bygones be bygones, to forget the prosecution of war crimes, let alone to forget claims to Jerusalem and the West Bank?

Having recalled a sorry record, let me hasten to add that we must not waste time on genuinely pointless striving, but deal with what is urgent and achievable. It is idealistic to expect the United States to carry out its treaties and other contractual obligations toward Indians. The purpose of federal Indian policy has always been to address the national interest, as initially a matter of foreign and strategic concern during the Indian Wars, but by 1890 a matter of purely domestic policy. Even as U.S. citizens, Indians are not a significant national constituency for United States Representatives or Senators and have little clout outside their own reservations. Some wags have suggested what students of contemporary fiscal and budgetary policy will appreciate, that the Indian budget might do better if the Bureau of Indian Affairs were put under the Department of Defense, as its predecessor was before the 1840s! The American Indian Citizenship Act (1924) and certain other pieces of legislation have "rewarded" Indians with the protections and entitlements of American citizens, but a tribal individual's primary fealty is still to one of the tribal sovereignties called "dependent domestic Nations" under federal law.

Indians must work even harder than ever to show the United States and the world that we "mean business" in the broadest terms. Politically responsible Indians must resolve Indian problems. The United States' real "Indian Problem" is its failure to address and abide by its commitments to Indian people. The United States has attempted to disavow the policy of active interference with tribal affairs, realizing that without self-determination tribes inevitably became dependent on a government that by its own widely publicized standards of "decency" lacks the moral fiber or means to buy tribes out of the federal-Indian relationship, or to define away the legal significance of Indians, or to retain perpetual and plenary guardianship over so many wards. As persons with not only anthropological identities, but with political, social, and economic responsibilities and rights, Indians today must act as though they expect to succeed or fail on their own, depending on their own retained sovereignty as tribes and individuals, their own heritage, their own arts and skills. The current shifts in federal-Indian policy may afford an opportunity for some tribes, as for some local governments, to find out what they can do without federal help.

The Reagan administration has insisted since January of 1983 that the "volunteerism" of Indian people, the presumably beneficial "involvement of the private sector," with a lessening federal role and diminishing financial support, will assure the success of tribal communities. Herein lies an ultimatum, not a promise. Indians know treaties and agreements can come and go, but federal ultimata are rarely abrogated. Until tribes can make their own way as local governments, which retain the limited advantages of tribal sovereignty, their future is in question. To travel the good red road is to seek a standard of living greater than the welfare state's "minimum standard of health and decency," which the Meriam Commission promoted.

In *The Good Red Road*, "Luther Clearwater," the Sioux elder, challenged us to recall a spirit, not of futile cyclical rebellion and reaction, but a spirit drawing hope and life from our foundations. He gave me a root of calamus, representing to me the root of the Medicine Tree, the source of health and wholeness. In 1981, I left that root at one of my tribe's ceremonial grounds in Oklahoma, next to the shed where members of my clan sit during dances. I have learned since 1975 that many Indian people share the belief that "health" is not only a matter of physical well-being, but a characterization of processes and living organisms. Health is the condition of individuals and communities which live and grow in a harmonious, stable relationship with their environment as it continuously changes. Health is a kind of freedom and (in the original sense) "wholeness" that can only be enjoyed through discipline. A "healer" in the sense that I use it here and elsewhere is not only any "successful" physician or curer, but anyone who promotes or effects such "wholeness." Those who do not work for that condition in themselves and others work against it.

I mention these matters because they are clarifications pertinent to *The Good Red Road*; they also constellate a critical point in the narrative. Look at the Medicine Tree. It represents all the instruments and means of achieving health, or wholeness. It also represents everything we have, everything we have been, and our potential for growing without losing our integrity, our wholeness. Whatever else happens to the "tree," if its roots remain intact, the "tree" can revive, even produce new leaves, flowers, and fruits, indeed all that we need *now*. One must have faith in the root. One must start where one is, with something, a root, a seed. With faith, which is effort exerted in keeping with belief, Indian country can flower again. If we, as Indian people, can live out the quest and mission of this faith in the promise of the good red road, regardless of failures and giving thanks for successes, we will have done our best. We ask no more of an acorn or an onion than it do the best with what it has.

This is something one can do day by day, in fact, only day by day, even if one only has one day left to live. Sophocles said, "Only count that man happy who carries his happiness with him to the grave." Sioux warriors used to say, "It is a good day to die." One who is at peace, living in wholeness, can die happily any day, saying, "So far, so good."

After law school, I began to worry full time about the law and Indian problems. February 9, 1980, I learned something from Raymond Lego, a dying elder from the Pit River Tribe, that reassured me. He had asked me and Ritch Stone, one of my students, to spend the weekend at his rancheria home in Montgomery Creek, California. At one point that evening, we were sitting at the woodstove talking about sacred sites and aboriginal territories his people wanted back from the federal government. I asked why he kept going on, despite all his disappointments. Raymond said:

Yeah, been one step back, two steps forward all the time, and sometimes two steps back. But you know, we have this sacred place out in the river. It's a rock. It's not real big. It has two red streaks down the side. That's really sacred because that's the place where we learned there that we have to keep goin' on like this, not just for our own sakes or our childrens' sakes but for everybody.

Well, one time, long before the whites came, two of our young hunters were down there and seen this little small boy sittin' out on that rock, all naked and cold, and he had white skin and long blond hair to the water, and he was lookin' down in it. They got scared, and instead of followin' the rules and treatin' him right, askin' 'im home for some food and clothes or somethin', they, one of 'em, shot him, right here between the ribs through the back, and the arrow went right out through his heart so he fell in the water. Well, they went out to find him, and there was nothin' there. They got scared, then, and they run home. They didn' say nothin'.

So then there was hunger and a drought for years, and the old people came together to find out what was wrong and did medicine. They found out what happened and called those young men out. Those boys were scared, cause they figured they would be killed to take away the trouble, but the old people said, "No, we're not doin' that. It's too late—we can't take it back. The laws of our own hospitality have been broken. From now on, we will have trouble. Many more like this little white child will come and they will overrun us, and we may be driven down to nothing. But we have to fight for our sakes and their sakes, because that law of hospitality is worth something. It has a meaning for us and for them. We were put here to love one another, to respect one another and care for each other. If there's only one of us left, that one has to hang on and say we belong here. That's all we have left to do. We got to stand up for ourselves and what's right—that's all we got to hold onto."

Implicit in this story is a teaching that the whole universe pulses with life, and we have no right to feel superior to anything or anyone else, nor to arrogate to ourselves the claim of absolute control over life—all living things must share in order to survive. To do violence to these principles is to endanger our own prospects for peace and life on an increasingly crowded earth.

In 1982, my Indian Shaker sister of Crescent City, California, Lena Black Bommelyn, a Karuk Indian, taught me that it does no good to claim the right to hoard for one's own children; in this world, every child is each person's responsibility. Every child "belongs" to all, and an actual parent is simply one who has received the special gift and burden of raising a particular child. A child is not our property, but the realization of our heritage. In a greater sense, we are each other's children. We must learn to see and love the child that is in each of us, or by the next century there may be nothing left but the broken toys and bodies of this generation.

What have we to gain, in honoring commitments to more than perceived or presumed military needs? Perhaps some hope of survival itself. We all must have consideration, patience, and forgiveness to attain "health."

Perhaps health is not so different from decency. In 1981, my friend John Eagleshield assisted in our fieldwork funded by the National Institute on Alcoholism and Alcohol Abuse. While driving through Seba Dalkai in the Joint Use Area of the Navajo and Hopi reservations, he told me about a Native American Church ceremony where an alcoholic Navajo in his forties received treatment. In this story of healing are lessons about atonement, charity, and forgiveness that transcend time, place, society, and species. As I recall, he told me:

He had a bad drinking problem. His marriage broke up; he couldn't talk to his kids. His family didn't know what else to do, nothing had worked. So they went to this Navajo medicine man and hired him to do a sing. He made a kind of gruel, and you had to dip it out of this big bowl with a wooden spoon. I was watchin' all of this, and pretty soon he set up his big quartz crystal in the middle of the tent near the fire. They went around with songs and prayers all night. People prayed for this and that and for the man who was sick. Toward morning, it seemed everybody was getting helped except him! He was down there on the end, seemed sort of out of it. There were these green lights flashing around from the crystal. Then, all at once, this little black dog, some little mongrel, came in through the door. He was all nosey and friendly and went all around the circle. The medicine man and everybody just went on, so he sniffed at people, wagged his little stubby tail, and went lickin' people and pesterin' them for attention, showin' his little rear end like those little dogs will. Everybody just let him go, but when he got to the far end where this Navajo guy could see him, that guy went nuts! I mean, screamin', and with his back tryin' to push up the wall, fannin' around, tryin' to make the dog leave him alone. The little mongrel was barkin' and yelpin' like he knew him and hadn't seen him in a long time. So then, the man just sort of collapsed sittin' up, and that little dog jumped up into the guy's lap and started lickin' his face. The guy was all cryin' and sobbing, and he picked up the little dog, carryin' on, and everybody knew something strange was goin' on. So then, this little dog got down, and he trotted back around the circle the same way, counterclockwise, and went out.

Later, some of us went out to find where the dog went, and the tracks just stopped. We even checked the next day and never did find him. Finally, the medicine man told what he saw and made the Navajo man confirm it. He said the guy had a really bad temper. He'd been drinking too much, and he got so mad that he went out where his kids were playing, his own kids. They had this little black dog; right in front of them he took his whole anger out on that poor little dog—just picked him up and tore him apart—and all the time his kids were screamin' and cryin'. He could never make up, or admit he was wrong, or forgive himself. So he had just gone downhill from there, complaining that he was bein' haunted, that he couldn't sleep, had to drink to get along, couldn't work. He was sick all the time, fought with everybody, acting crazy.

After the sing, the Navajo guy seemed better, more clear-headed, smilin' and talking to people. The medicine man was talking to one of the sponsors when we broke the fast in the daytime. The sponsor was saying how they were grateful for what the medicine man did for their relation, and the medicine man just listened; but then he said that this ceremony wasn't so much for the Navajo, because *he* was responsible for accepting his own healing, and *he* was the one who had to do it. *He* was the one who had to do right. The ceremony was really for that little dog, a chance for that little dog to come back to the man and release himself from that man's guilt by letting that man know he was forgiven. Once unburdened, the little dog was free. Now that man has to decide if he's going to get well and stay that way, and forgive himself.

You have to unburden yourself, forgive, not carry guilt or put it on people, and do your best; and then it's the other guy's place to do the best he can. That way you can be really free. You get on the Creator's side, then you don't have to complain that the Creator should be on your side.

This is a time when we need a world full of healers and healing, where not just the martyred Gandhis, not just the heroic Mother Theresas, but everyday people realize the healing power they carry in their hands. The recent nostalgia for America's "golden age" touts the tradition of hardheaded self-reliance. Let it not be forgotten that our old ones aspired and dreamed, created and struggled, *and that they cared for one another*, at their best. Their greatest legacy is the teaching that everyone has healing gifts to build our common decency and wholeness. Without remorse and recrimination, but with struggle and faith, Native America will walk the Good Red Road, leaving not tracks that mar the earth, but a spiritual legacy that will continue to enrich and restore America. Ours is a nation that forgets its way only when ignoring the best in its path.

There is hope; and it is in hope that we have written *The Good Red Road* for the children, as the Elders who have spoken to us have asked. We have delivered ourselves of a burden writing these things, that the people may be free, *and live*.

Al Logan Slagle (Keetoowah Cherokee)
Native American Studies
University of California at Berkeley